Clean Coding in Borland C++

The complete guide to learning Borland C++

Clean Coding in Borland C++

Robert J. Traister

M&T BOOKS

M&T Books
A Division of M&T Publishing, Inc.
501 Galveston Drive
Redwood City, CA 94063

Printed in the United States of America

Library of Congress Cataloging-in-Publication Data

Traister, Robert J.
Clean Coding in Borland C++ / by Robert J. Traister.
p. cm.
Includes index.
ISBN 1-55851-205-5 (book only) : $26.95. - - ISBN 1-55851-207-1 (book with disk) : $36.95.
1. C++ (computer program language) 2. Turbo C++ (computer program) 3. Microsoft Windows (computer program) I. Title.
QA76.73.C153T73 1991
005.265- -dc20 91-14645
CIP

Project Editor: Christine de Chutkowski

Cover Design: Lauren Smith Design

94 93 92 91 4 3 2 1

Dedication

This book is dedicated to the memory of C. Hugh Williams.

Contents

CHAPTER 3: GOING FROM C TO C++

CHAPTER 8: TURBO DEBUGGER FOR WINDOWS

CHAPTER 9: THE WHITEWATER RESOURCE TOOLKIT

Why This Book Is For You

This book was written for ANSI C programmers who want to make the transition to Borland C++. It was also written for C++ programmers who are using a compiler other than Borland C++ and who want to become knowledgeable about all that Borland C++ has to offer before switching to this new and powerful software developer's environment.

With this wide range of readership in mind, *Clean Coding in Borland C++* will serve as a tutorial for readers who are making the (painful) transition from ANSI C to C++. I believe you will find the teaching method used throughout this text to be straightforward — presenting new ideas in small blocks, each of which can be tested immediately on your own machine and modified by you in order to "see what happens when I do this." It is through such experimentation that rapid proficiency in a new language is acquired.

When learning a new programming language, the experience level of persons who program in another language is sometimes less significant than many would think. However, C++ might be thought of as a superset of the ANSI C. Therefore, readers with high levels of ANSI C experience generally will have an easier transition. However, the object-oriented aspects of C++ may present the same comprehension for programmers of diverse experience levels, assuming they have no previous object-oriented training.

For this reason, all discussions are handled in bits and pieces. This will allow readers of different comprehension levels to absorb the text at his/her most efficient rate. The author, having made the transition from BASIC to C to ANSI C and to Borland C++ (with a smattering of PASCAL, FORTRAN, LISP, and ASSEMBLER thrown in for good measure) fully understands the "pain" of misunderstanding. For this reason, you will not see many long, comprehensive programs used as learning examples in these pages. The intent is to demonstrate a feature with the simplest program examples possible. If you feel this is beneath your experience level, then modify what I have written to suit your own yen for complexity.

Programmers who specialize in Microsoft Windows will certainly want to check out the ease and speed with which Windows applications can be developed without the need for any other software — including the Windows SDK (Software Development Kit). Borland C++ comes packaged to write Windows applications immediately, and an entire chapter is devoted to just this purpose.

In summary, if you are a person who already knows how to program in ANSI C at any level, you will find this book to be friendly in its approach. If you are a professional software developer who is making the transition to C++, the same applies. And, if you are a Windows programmer who is looking for an easier way of accessing the Microsoft Windows environment, you will find the discussions on this subject adequate for starting out on the Borland C++ route.

CHAPTER 1

Borland C++

Borland International has earned a reputation in the software industry, and it's a good reputation. For years, this company has been offering highly efficient and easy-to-use products at a fraction of the cost of similar products already available on the software market.

Turbo Pascal was their first product, and it was an immediate success, particularly among home computer enthusiasts. However, the power of this language quickly brought it into the realm of the software developer, even though its low cost caused many of the "professional" set to be wary.

The old saying, "You don't get something for nothing" certainly applies to the software industry, but Borland proved that professional programming environments don't have to cost an arm and a leg. All axioms aside, Borland, in my opinion, is directly responsible for reducing the overall cost of most professional programming environments offered on the market today.

On the heels of Turbo Pascal came Turbo Prolog. Next was Turbo BASIC. This was followed by other offerings of Turbo-this and Turbo-that. All of Borland's products received high ratings, especially in regard to efficiency. It's one thing to develop a programming environment that is easy to use and inexpensive. It's another thing to wrap these features in a package that offers high execution speed. In the beginning, most of Borland's products were being marketed through mail order companies for less than $100.

Although programming environment prices were dropping in many areas, the C programming language remained an expensive commodity. It was not unusual to pay $400 or more for a C compiler for use with an MS-DOS machine. It has only been in recent years that the C programming language has become an affordable programming environment for anyone who has a yen for tackling this beautiful language with the weird syntax. Prior to 1987, a professional C-compiler package cost a minimum of $350 and could even top the $1000 mark.

In 1987, Borland shocked the C programming world by introducing Borland Turbo C++ at the astounding price of just over $100. Mail-order houses were hawking it for about $85, and Borland received in excess of 30,000 advance orders. Initially, many members of the professional C programming community scoffed at the idea of a C compiler available at such a ridiculously low price. Their criticisms were quickly transformed into begrudging acceptance and then forthright praise.

The fact is that Borland Turbo C, Version 1.0, offered the full C programming language (not a subset), a pleasing user environment, and many high-powered features common only to high-priced compilers. Additionally, compiled programs ran faster than almost any other compiler package on the market.

The competition no longer seemed to be competitive. These other companies, however, quickly geared up to offer low-priced versions of their high-priced offerings. None, however, met with the success of Borland's original Turbo C.

Borland quickly came out with Turbo C, Version 1.5, which offered a full set of graphics functions. Next came Turbo C, Version 2.0, and Turbo C Professional, which included Turbo Debugger and Turbo Assembler. Priced at around $200, the professional package could stand on its own against any C programming environment on the market.

Borland International had certainly carved a niche for itself. This company was thought of as a "champion" of the amateur C programmer as it lowered prices and made C available to hundreds of thousands of programmers who would not otherwise have been able to take advantage of a professional C environment.

Continuing to improve, Borland finally offered Turbo C++ (originally named Borland Turbo C, Version 3.0). However, the niche that Borland had carved for itself may have become somewhat of a liability; the term "turbo" had come to be associated with the amateur programming environment, even though Borland's products could just as easily be used by the professional programmer.

Borland's newest release carries the very understated name of Borland C++. The turbo designation has been dropped—perhaps an intentional move on Borland's part to break with the past in regard to its C programming environments. Borland C++, then, would seem to be aimed directly toward the professional programming market. The "whistles and bells" connotation that the term "turbo" brings to mind is being purposely avoided. Borland has already captured the non-professional C programming market. Now they're after the professional market.

Borland obviously wants it all and is willing to offer a product that has the possibility of capturing every programmer personality, ranging from the high school kid learning C to the seasoned software developer. They may well succeed.

Prior to the release of Borland C++, this company's products appeared in standard and professional versions. The main difference between the two versions were that Turbo Debugger, Turbo Assembler, and Turbo Profiler were included in the professional versions. Borland C++ is a departure from the norm and replaces Turbo C++ Professional as Borland's product for professional developers.

Borland's new offering comes complete with the debugger, assembler, and profiler—in addition to the C++ compiler—in a multitude of memory models. It also offers a number of additional tools for the professional programmer.

Borland C++ offers support for 80286, allowing software to be custom-tailored for the high-level machines, as opposed to producing executable programs for the full range of MS-DOS machines, starting with the 8088 microprocessor. Borland C++ allows for the efficient use of extended memory and even the direct support of large hard disks.

To accommodate all of these professional wants and needs, the Borland C++ package offers advanced features that include protected mode versions of the compiler, linker, and the Integrated Development Environment, now interchangeably referred to as the Programmer's Platform. Also included is the Whitewater Resource Toolkit, a powerful utility that makes development of resources for Microsoft Windows applications far easier.

Borland International has stated that the company had three primary goals in mind when developing Borland C++. The first was to deliver full support for Microsoft Windows, as well as for the standard DOS platform. The second was to offer a high-capacity compiler, coupled with high speed. The third goal was to provide a package that allowed programmers to develop Windows applications in an environment that was easier to use and didn't require the Microsoft software development kit (SDK).

Borland C++ is everything Borland Turbo C++ was and is, but it offers much more to the professional software developer. In direct conversations with Borland, it has been stated again and again that Borland C++ does not represent a trend of moving away from the non-professional programmer. Rather, Borland C++ marks a branch in the road that will widen the company's overall appeal. At this time, the word is that Borland will continue its "turbo" line of products with the intention of continuing to fully support the non-professional programmer in at least the same style (and probably much better) as before. The branch, however, is the beginning of Borland's foray into the realm of pure professional software development. At a price of $495.95 for the Borland C++ package, there is no question that the software professional is being targeted, although, undoubtedly, Borland C++ will sell for considerably less than this suggested retail price when the mail-order outlets have been adequately supplied.

For that matter, any C or C++ programmer who is not a part of the professional software development community and wishes to develop Window applications may be money ahead to purchase the Borland C++ package while foregoing the Windows SDK (Software Development Kit). Many software developers who are not exactly professional programmers (i.e., those who do not make their living authoring software) will undoubtedly be very attracted to Borland C++ for its Windows capabilities alone. Here, in one off-the-shelf package, is a complete programming-and-development environment that is already set up to address the programming of Windows applications in basically the same manner as one would program applications for the DOS platform. Nothing else is needed (except for Microsoft Windows 3.0) to have full development control over Windows applications.

Borland C++ 2.0 is bundled with just about everything the professional C++ programmer needs to develop standard and overlaid DOS programs and Windows applications. The one-package aspect of Borland C++ is pleasing. Professional software development usually entails purchasing a package here and a package there in order to address the environment or environments necessary for the particular application. I think of Borland C++ as a universal programming environment that is complete in itself. If programming general applications on MS-DOS machines as well as venturing into the sometimes mysterious world of Microsoft Windows is your goal, then Borland C++ has everything you need to get started and to keep on going.

The C++ Compiler

Borland states that their C++ compiler is really two compilers in one: a full C++ compiler implementing AT&T's C++ version 2.0 and a C compiler that is 100 percent ANSI-C compatible. To say that it is two compilers in one is a little overstated, since C++ is a superset of the original C programming language. However, the Borland C++ package does blend the two aspects of the language in a rather elegant way, and C programmers who are moving up to C++ will most likely use the compiler in exactly the same manner as they used their old C compilers.

With Borland C++ 2.0, you can program in ANSI C or C++, or you can mix ANSI C and C++ code at will. A built-in assembler allows programmers to include assembly language routines in their C and C++ source code in a very straightforward manner. Of course, there is the full set of C++ class libraries and a wealth of sample programs that will allow the C programmer to make a rapid transition to C++.

As an aside, while Borland is targeting Borland C++ at the professional programmer, the package reflects the fact that many C programmers are just now making the transition to C++. There is definitely a tutorial aspect to Borland C++, as opposed to a development kit that assumes full C++ knowledge by "all" its potential users. I have observed that Borland C++, for all its professional characteristics and capabilities, still retains a large measure of the "take you by the hand and lead you through it" approach of Borland's turbo-mode products.

As the C programming language developed, header files began to multiply at an alarming rate. With early C compilers, the stdio.h and ctype.h header files were often the only ones that were required. Later, we saw mem.h, dos.h, and many other examples of .h this and .h that.

The inclusion of header files when writing programs under these early compilers was to be avoided, and in many cases, programmers simply pulled the necessary definitions and structures and created their own personalized header files. The reason for this lay in the relatively slow compilation speeds of these early compilers and the increased overhead (substantial, in many cases) incurred by header file inclusion.

Borland C++ uses header files extensively, and while this makes for very high compilation speeds, the overhead might still be a concern, especially for programs that are designed to be run under Windows. Borland C++ features pre-compiled headers, which eliminates recompilation time for header files. This can greatly reduce the overall compilation time.

The complaint of long compile times due to header file overhead is particularly applicable to Windows programmers. As a matter of fact, the size of the source code for the windows.h header file is in excess of 120K.

The idea of a completely compiled header file is quite attractive. However, it is impossible to predict just which portions of a header file will be preprocessed. This is dependent upon both how #define directives are interpreted and the specific compiler memory model used. For these and other reasons, it is not possible to use a specific set of precompiled headers that are appropriate for any and all applications.

Borland C++ precompiles header files on a case-by-case basis, with recompilation occurring only if the header files change or if the aggregate of header files used in a module is changed. In simple language, the header files are recompiled only when it is necessary for the proper functioning of the program. The first time a source file is compiled, the compiler reads and compiles all of the included header files. At the same time, it creates a file of symbols that may be read directly during subsequent compilations. This applies as long as the header files listed in the original source code do not change. The very pleasing aspect of this method lies in the fact that Borland C++ makes all of these determinations. If the headers need to be recompiled, they are. If they do not need to be recompiled, they aren't. This alone has a significant impact on the compile times required for all programs, especially those that are written to run under Windows 3.0.

For additional leverage, the programmer may choose to insert a #pragma statement in the source code. This will groups all headers above it in the source code. In other words, all of the headers above #pragma are compiled once and then saved as symbols tables. All remaining files are recompiled along with all source code modules.

The idea here is to place all of your stable header files (and any other code, for that matter) above #pragma. All other header files that may change as the program evolves are placed below #pragma. As the program continues to evolve, additional headers will become stable and they may be moved above #pragma. Again, when moved ahead of #pragma, the headers are no longer recompiled and program compilation proceeds at a more rapid pace. When a new header is placed above #pragma, all of the headers are recompiled. As long as the list of headers above #pragma remains the same, no further compilation takes place.

To the programmer, this means that initial programs compile more slowly than those that evolve. As program evolution takes place, the code compiles increasingly faster. This allows the programmer to interact with C++'s ability to determine what needs to be compiled and what doesn't.

Be aware that selective compiling also has some drawbacks. One drawback is the fact that separate sets of compiled headers are stored for applications having different headers. In these situations, simple tables can become quite large and often consume more storage space than the original header. Disk space is quickly eaten up in cases such as this, and the programmer must weigh this factor against the increased compilation speeds to determine if the increased storage allocation required is indeed worth sacrificing. In general, unnecessary reprocessing of header files can save large amounts of compilation time. Assuming a more-than-adequate hard-disk capacity, this is certainly well worth the storage drawbacks.

It has been necessary to build in some syntax extensions in order to reconcile the C++ language with the requirements for programming Windows applications. These syntax extensions offer programmers the necessary flexibility, which is absolutely mandatory to implement C++ classes in Windows programming.

One of these additions is the _export keyword, which allows for classes to be included in Dynamic Link Libraries (DLLs). When function code must reside in DLLs, the _export keyword is used. When this keyword is used to modify a definition or function declaration, the compiler automatically generates the prolog/epilog code for the function. Additionally, a special record is placed in the object file to show that the particular function is exported from a DLL.

As an alternative to the use of _export, the programmer must place an entry for each exported function in a .def file. This is used by programs to identify the exported functions.

The use of the _export key word relieves the developer of the time-consuming task of searching a class hierarchy to locate exportable members. The programmer must then make individual entries in the .def file used to build a DLL.

The Programmer's Platform

The Integrated Development Environment (IDE) is interchangeably referred to as the Programmer's Platform in Borland C++ terminology. This new package comes with both real and protected-mode versions of the platforms. In protected-mode operations, far greater capacity is achieved without having to swap information to disk or to break large modules down into a series of smaller modules. The latter can significantly increase the time it takes to develop a complex program while adding to the confusion by necessitating the referencing of code that is scattered here and there.

When in protected mode, the Programmer's Platform can be run in a DOS screen under Windows' standard mode. This allows very large applications to be written, compiled, and debugged far more rapidly than would be the case with any of Borland's earlier offerings. The platform offers multiple overlapping windows, mouse support, a multifile editor, an internal debugger, and it is replete with on-line help. The Project Manager offers support for Windows tools. This makes it easy to use the Resource Compiler in the Import Librarian.

One especially nice feature in the editor is the Undo and Redo commands, which can prevent a lot of headaches if the wrong key is inadvertently pressed during an all-night programming binge. Any line that is mistakenly erased or corrupted can quickly be returned to its original state by clicking the Undo panel.

In comparison with previous programmer platforms, the one offered with Borland C++ has been designed to facilitate the programming of Windows applications. This feature also adds to the programming effectiveness of any application. The protected-mode version is a welcome addition that finally allows the high-level MS-DOS machines with up to 15 megabytes of extended memory to be used to their fullest capacity.

As was noted earlier, the protected-mode version can be run in a DOS screen under Windows standard mode. This means that programs may be developed, compiled, debugged, and executed under Windows 3.0 without having to constantly switch between programs. Additionally, hard disk capacity is not sacrificed.

Windows programming tools are completely integrated with the platform, allowing for the creation of Windows applications in a smooth, straightforward manner. The Undo command discussed earlier allows most keystrokes to be canceled. While Undo has legitimate application in direct source-code input, it will be used most often to correct mistakes due to accidental inputs or deletions. Again, most keystrokes can be undone, but actions such as changing the tab-stop size or toggling insert/overwrite mode cannot be undone, because these are not stored in the Undo buffer. The actual number of actions that can be canceled by Undo is controlled internally and depends on the specific actions that have been taken.

The Redo command will probably be under utilized by most programmers, but it can serve a very worthwhile purpose. There is even an option provided by the C++ Programmer's Platform to set up a "group" Undo. This allows for contiguous groups of keystrokes to be undone with a single command, as opposed to undoing individual keystrokes. In general, the Undo and Redo commands available in the platform make for a higher level of control of source-code input.

Using the C++ Programmer's Platform, you can now set MAKE to generate import libraries using either DLL file exports or .DEF file exports. Again, this option addresses Windows programmers and provides a much higher degree of flexibility in this endeavor.

In the past, the linker provided with Turbo C++ was able to link only standard DOS-executable files. With Borland C++, however, you can also set up the linker for the generation of overlaid DOS executables, Windows .EXE, and Windows DLL files. Due to the increased versatility of Borland C++, it is necessary to keep track of several possible combinations of compiler and linker settings. The exact settings will depend on whether the program is to be a standard or overlaid DOS application or a Windows application or DLL. By using the application option available in a dialog box in the platform, the programmer may easily set a combination of default settings that will directly address the specific project under development. This dialog box can be used to determine the type of prolog/epilog code generated, the memory model, and the type of linker output. The Set Application Options dialog box automatically makes all changes. All that is necessary is that the programmer select the specific application desired. This is another timesaver, because the programmer does not need to incorporate a series of environment changes every time a different type of application is tackled. With Borland C++, there is little chance that switching to a new type of application task will create the usual problems associated with such a change.

VROOMM

The 640K memory barrier is broken using the Virtual Runtime Object-Oriented Memory Manager (VROOMM), which is a part of Borland C++ 2.0. This is the overlay manager, and it relieves the programmer of the sometimes difficult task of determining how and when to overlay a module.

Windows

Borland C++ 2.0 completely supports Microsoft Windows applications. The Microsoft SDK is not needed with Borland C++. Windows-compatible code may be written, compiled, and linked in a straightforward, natural manner. Using the Whitewater Resource Toolkit, Windows resources may be developed quickly. Turbo Debugger for Windows runs in a character screen under Windows, permitting debugging of Windows applications. Using this package, you can set breakpoints based on messages received by the application during execution.

The Turbo Debugger package generally has received rave reviews from all sides of the programming community, and Turbo Debugger for Windows should get even more attention. With this utility, Windows programmers can debug programs using a single screen while retaining two-monitor and remote debugging as options. With Turbo Debugger, developers can now debug Windows applications and DLLs and even view global and local heaps. This utility has the capability of automatically detecting and loading the correct DLLs for an application, and breakpoints can be set, depending on Windows messages received. As before, Turbo Debugger offers support for object-oriented debugging, reverse execution, and a host of the other features that have made the product famous.

Applications that run under Microsoft Windows 3.0 may be generated directly with the Programmer's Platform or by means of the standalone command-line compiler and linker and the Make utility. Both of these environments can be set up to generate either pure Windows applications, DLLs, or DOS applications.

The ability of Borland C++ to produce applications for Windows 3.0 is due to the windows.h header file that is licensed from Microsoft Corporation. This is the same file that comes with the Windows Software Development Kit (SDK). However, minor modifications have been made in order to effect an interface with the C++ language. The Microsoft Resource Compiler is also included with Borland C++. This allows developers who already have .rc files (resource files) to reuse them in programs developed under C++.

Turbo Assembler

The familiar Turbo Assembler is a part of Borland C++. However, there is a protected-mode version that runs under enhanced mode, allowing the programmer to take full advantage of extended memory. This allows larger modules to be compiled without breaking them down into smaller modules, and thus the compilation time is faster.

The WINDOWS language modifier generates the proper Windows prolog and epilog code for an assembly language procedure, and CALL instructions can now specify languages and argument lists. This permits routines written in other languages to be called in a manner that is largely language-independent.

Whitewater Resource Toolkit

Developed by the Whitewater Group, the Whitewater Resource Toolkit (WRT) is a powerful utility that aids the development of resources for Windows applications. In a sentence, it "allows users to visually build, modify, and incorporate resources into Windows applications."

WRT edits dialogs, cursors, string tables, menus, icons, and bitmaps. Programmers who are familiar with the Windows Software Development Kit will see an immediate improvement when using WRT, which provides editors for strings, menus, and accelerators. With WRT, menus may be tested immediately instead of first having to process and then add them to applications. Developers will also appreciate such features as alignment and automatic sizing control in the dialog-box editor. There is even a Resource Manager that allows resources to be copied and moved from one file to another.

As an overall description, the Whitewater Resource Toolkit 3.0 allows professional programmers to create graphical user interface elements such as the dialog boxes and cursors, both interactively and on-screen. Also, programmers can quickly create keyboard accelerators and string resources. WRT allows the beginner and the non-programmer alike to customize the look and feel of a Windows application — choices that traditionally have been under the exclusive control of developers. WRT is a visually intuitive and interactive tool for complete Windows customization, while Borland C++ provides the power of object-oriented programming to create sophisticated Windows applications.

The Whitewater Resource Toolkit utility eliminates the need for the Resource Compiler found in the Microsoft SDK. However, it is complementary to SDK and is completely compatible with all Windows 3.0 resource-file formats. In addition to reducing the amount of time required to customize an application's look and feel, WRT 3.0 eliminates the time-consuming edit-compile-link development cycle required when working with traditional resource compilers.

While WRT 3.0 is bundled with Borland C++ and is included in the $495.95 price, it is also available from major resellers and directly from the Whitewater Group for $195.

Although Borland C++ is relatively new (just released in February of 1991), a host of support from other major software developers has been forthcoming. Many add-on packages were announced simultaneously with the release of Borland C++. One such offering comes from Blaise Computing Inc., in Berkeley, California, a leading manufacturer of software development tools. Called Win++, the package is essentially a C++ class library that can be used to develop Windows applications by taking advantage of the object-oriented programming capabilities of Borland C++. Win++ contains nearly 100 classes, the majority of which offer a simplified, high-level C++ interface to Windows. In addition, other classes can be used to represent internal data structures and to integrate data into applications.

A key feature of Win++ is its ability to provide a class for all common types of display objects in Windows that are accessed by handles. Included is a base class, as well as derived classes for the more common forms. Also, Win++ includes ready-made classes to represent dialog boxes, child controls, pens, brushes, maps, bitmaps, cursors, icons, printers, the clipboard, and much more.

Win++ supports construction of dynamic link libraries (DLLs) as well. Here, programmers are able to use Win++'s ready-made DLLs in programs, which will save both time and memory space. Additionally, multiple programs can share DLL code, which eliminates the waste of memory space consumed by duplicated routines. These DLLs can be modified or added to, and programs can even build their own.

Win++ is priced at $249. All source code, a comprehensive manual, and many sample programs are provided. DLLs may be distributed with finished applications without restriction or royalty.

Another product whose release coincides with that of Borland's newest offering is db_VISTA III, which consists of db_VISTA, a database engine; db_QUERY, an SQL-based query and report writer; and db_REVISE, a database restructure program; all from Raima Corporation of Bellevue, Washington. Raima is a developer and marketer of database management systems (DBMS) and complementary software tools.

db_VISTA III provides advanced power and flexibility for the professional database developer. It differs from other DBMS products by offering a unique, combined relational- and network-model database technology, which gives developers the flexibility to create complex database applications. The system includes an SQL-based query and report writer, which can be used for ad-hoc queries and retrievals or can be linked directly into the application. db_VISTA III also provides a third module for restructuring existing databases.

db_VISTA III is available for many C environments: Microsoft Windows, MS-DOS, OS/2, VMS, UNIX System V, Sun/OS, the QNX operating system, and the Macintosh. Prices for db_VISTA, the high-performance DBMS module of the db_VISTA III system, start at $695. As with other products from this company, the system is royalty-free for distributing applications without additional cost. Also, source code is available for porting to any C-language platform.

The company has also announced a special "developer's edition" of the db_VISTA module, available to purchasers of Borland C++ 2.0 for $195. This special edition allows developers to create complete database applications and perform all testing. When distribution is desired, developers are able to upgrade and acquire a royalty-free distribution license from Raima.

Another company, XVT Software Inc. has announced plans to provide compatibility with Borland C++, expanding this company's current support for Borland Turbo C. Based in Boulder, Colorado, XVT Software Inc. offers XVT, a software library that provides a common, or virtual, programming interface for developers writing applications that will run under multiple graphical user interfaces. This library makes it possible to program graphical applications that are portable across a variety of window systems, including both OSF/Motif and OPENLOOK for the X Window System; Macintosh, Microsoft Windows, and Presentation Manager for both OS/2 and CTOS; and XVT's own character-based window manager.

Using XVT, identical-application source code runs on all platforms and looks native to each. Instead of rewriting applications from scratch each time a new windowed environment is entered, developers can use XVT's library to create and maintain a single set of source code to address multiple environments.

Yet another new offering comes from Sturmer Hauss Corporation, of Santa Clara, California. Called TIER, this product offers a complete C++ class library available for Microsoft Windows. When combined with Borland C++, users will have the capability of developing their Windows applications with predefined objects that can be used and reused.

TIER has more than 115 C++ object classes, including WINDOW, an abstraction of a generalized window; DIALOG, an abstraction of the Windows dialog manager; GLOBALMEMORY, an abstraction of the global memory pool; and MOUSE, an abstraction of the mouse as utilized and viewed from within Windows. Other development capabilities include support for single and multiple inheritance and the ability to both add and delete object classes.

By providing developers with abstractions of the Windows operating environment, C++ developers can begin programming in Windows more rapidly. Also, the combination of TIER's and C++'s object-oriented paradigm allows for better program design and code that can be reused within a single application or across multiple applications. TIER also offers enhanced flexibility, because all Windows functionality is built into this product, which means developers can create any type of Windows application.

Sturmer Hauss Corporation has entered into a co-marketing arrangement with Genesis Development Corporation, of Richardson, Texas, a software consulting firm specializing in object-oriented technology. TIER is available from Genesis for $450. In addition, a TIER/Borland C++ 2.0 bundle can be purchased from Programmer's Paradise in New Jersey.

Xian Corporation, in Ridgewood, New Jersey, has announced the introduction of Winpro/3, an easy-to-use application designer, prototype viewer, and C/C++ code generator compatible with both Windows and Borland C++. The application designer allows you to start from an existing resource file or to construct one using Winpro/3. Additionally, resources can be imported from other resource files, and resources can be created, copied, or renamed.

The beauty of Winpro/3 is that non-programmers can design and prototype a Windows application and then hand off the code for further development. Programmers with little or no Windows experience can create top-quality, well-commented code. Changes to the application interface are integrated automatically into existing code.

Experienced Windows developers can modify directly the code-building algorithms to tailor the generation of code to their specific requirements. The Winpro/3 Windows code generation provides unparalleled customization power.

Winpro/3 is priced at $895 and requires both Windows and Borland C++. It is also available for Microsoft C Version 5.1 or higher.

Sequiter Software Inc., of Edmonton, Alberta, Canada, has announced the release of Codebase ++ 1.0, a multiuser, database-management library for C++. Because this product works directly with the data, index, and memo files of dBASE IV, it allows C++ developers to build dBASE IV-compatible applications.

CodeBase++ demonstrates how the object-oriented programming capabilities of C++ can be combined with the database-management capabilities of dBASE IV. C++, with CodeBase++ or a similar class library. CodeBase++ offers high-level database-management capabilities, speed, low memory requirements, portability, flexibility, and the advantages of a low-level programming language. At the time of this writing, the price of CodeBase++ had not been announced.

C++/Views, from CNS Inc., of Minneapolis, Minnesota, is an object-oriented development environment for Windows that is compatible with Borland C++. C++/Views offers more than 75 ready-built C++ classes, as well as a completely integrated C++ Windows development environment.

C++/Views incorporates New Browser features, which provide a more highly integrated developer environment. It also offers a new dialog-box code generator that allows you to automatically generate C++ dialog classes from the Dialog (resource) Editor. This also produces all C++ code for portability to other platforms or uses resources for complete Windows 3.0 compatibility. Source for the code generator is included. Additionally, C++/Views offers numerous extensions and additions to the existing class library to provide a more robust and functionally complete object-oriented framework for Windows 3.0 development. Product price was not available at the time of this writing.

Greenleaf Software Inc., of Dallas, Texas, has announced that all of their C and C++ library products fully support Borland's newest offering. Among the products modified to support C++ are Greenleaf CommLib, Greenleaf DataWindows, Greenleaf Functions, Greenleaf SuperFunctions, Greenleaf Financial MathLib, and Financial MathLib++.

Greenleaf CommLib 3.1 is a new version that features support for intelligent and non-intelligent multiport communication boards, normal COM1-COM8, including modems across networks, 16550 FIFO support, ZMODEM, XMODEM, YMODEM, Kermit, XON/XOFF, RTS/CTS, full configurability of ports including buffers, a special WideTrack Receive mode, and a great many other features.

Greenleaf DataWindows 2.12 is a professional developer's user-interface toolkit that features logical windows, extremely flexible menu systems, and a feature-rich data entry. It is supported by a WYSIWYG (what you see is what you get) screen generator, Greenleaf MakeForm.

Greenleaf Functions and Greenleaf SuperFunctions are non-overlapping "general" C libraries which support developers with a wide variety of tools, including limited windowing, menus, DOS and machine interfaces, string, time, date, and more areas of functionality.

Greenleaf Financial MathLib++ is a class library for C++ that provides very complete financial and business solutions within a new math paradigm that clearly represents precise decimal numbers. Financial MathLib is the C version of the latter. The prices for these new products was not available at the time of the writing.

Once more addressing Borland's headlong advance into the professional software developer marketplace, it should be understood that Borland is not leaving high and dry the programmers who don't require the level of professional support provided by a product like Borland C++. Up to now, Borland languages have appeared in standard and professional versions. What distinguished the two packages was the inclusion of Turbo Debugger, Turbo Profiler, and Turbo Assembler in the professional versions.

Borland C++ represents a departure from this standard/professional approach and replaces Turbo C++ Professional 1.0 as Borland's key product for professional developers. Borland will continue to develop and market Turbo C++ further, thus making the C++ language available also to programmers who don't require as high a level of professional support.

In summary, it appears as though Borland has come out with another winner. Borland C++ is significantly different from Borland Turbo C++, but it incorporates many features that will be of interest primarily to the professional software developer. Many programmers who are currently using Turbo C++ 1.0 will want to upgrade in order to take advantage of the added capabilities and especially the Windows programming/development environment provided by Borland C++. However, many programmers not specifically developing applications for the professional market will probably be content with Turbo C++ 1.0 for the time being. Ongoing development will take place on this package, and more than likely improved versions will be offered in years to come, just as Borland C++ will be improved.

As is the case with all of Borland's products, the introduction of Borland C++ has been met with excitement. The C++ environment is an excellent one for the professional software developer and will probably set a standard for this type of development software, just as Borland Turbo C 1.0 set a standard for a C programming language environment intended for general programming applications.

Borland may have done more to improve software development among the general programming audience, which ranges from the high school amateur to the paid professional, than any other company of its type in the past. Borland now goes further in an attempt to capture the brunt of a more narrow corner of the market, the one that consists solely of professional software developers. Borland probably will succeed.

CHAPTER 2

The Programmer's Platform

What has been known in all of Borland's previous releases as the Integrated Development Environment (IDE) is now interchangeably referred to as the Programmer's Platform in Borland C++. In short, this is a programmer's windowing system that permits direct on-screen authoring, editing, compiling, linking, and debugging of Borland C++ programs. Basically, it is a full-screen text editor from which all of the compiling, linking, and debugging operations may be called.

The Programmer's Platform—or IDE—initially allows the user to establish environment criteria such as mouse support, default libraries, compiler memory models, and linking conventions. Once the desired programming environment has been established around a task-determined set of default values, it's an easy job to proceed with actual programming activities.

Overall, the IDE is highly efficient and easy for first-time users to adapt to. Users quickly become accustomed to the advanced features of the Programmer's Platform and they may find themselves wondering how they got along without it in the past.

Within the framework of the IDE is support for multiple movable and resizeable windows. Cut-and-paste commands allow the quick and efficient manipulation of blocks of source code. With Borland C++, the IDE now contains full-editor Undo and Redo, which will save valuable programming time, especially when a programmer makes a keyboard input mistake and a significant portion of the program appears to be lost or altered. This error can be undone in a keystroke.

For programmers who are being introduced to the Borland IDE for the first time, there is immediate on-line help available at the touch of a key or the click of a mouse. Full mouse support is offered and really should be utilized for the smoothest control of this environment. In addition to the windows, pull-down menus, dialog boxes, and on-line help, the IDE has a built-in assembler and an editor macro language, and it incorporates options that allow for quick transfer to other programs in a direct manner without the user having to permanently leave the IDE. Of course, you can temporarily leave the IDE and reenter the DOS shell for the usual DOS activities while still keeping the IDE in background memory.

Borland C++ is a powerful software developer's tool because of this excellent Programmer's Platform that is coupled with an excellent compiler, assembler, debugger and several other powerful programming utilities. The programmer's Platform is not just an "extra touch." Rather, it is an indispensable and critical component in this C++ programming environment.

Using Borland C++, the IDE may be run in either of two modes—real or protected. Programmers with systems that offer extended memory will most often opt for the protected mode in order to utilize the extended memory. Those users with machines less well equipped still have the full capabilities of the IDE in the real-mode version. From a user standpoint, the IDE works exactly the same in both modes. Protected-mode requires a 286-, 386-, 486-, or 586-machine with a bare minimum of RAM and at least 1 MB of extended or expanded memory. These are absolute minimum requirements, and, in fact, larger amounts of RAM are recommended. The author's own research machine for evaluating Borland C++ is a 25-MHz 80386-machine with 4 MB of on-board memory coupled with an 80-MB hard disk and a VGA card.

It should be understood that whether you choose real or protected mode, the Programmer's Platform, or IDE, runs in exactly the same manner. Also, protected-mode operation of the IDE still results in C++ programs being generated for real-mode operations. Advantages of protected-mode operation of the IDE include speed and memory area; the compiler and any authored applications have far more memory area in which to operate. In protected mode, the linker runs considerably faster.

Real Mode Operation

To run the Programmer's Platform in real mode, type:

```
BC<Enter>
```

at the DOS prompt. This brings up the IDE in standard real mode and the programmer can proceed from there.

You may also elect to include one or more command line options upon invoking BC. The /b option causes Borland C++ to recompile and link all the files in a project, print compiler messages to the monitor screen, and then return immediately to DOS.

The /d option allows the environment to work in dual-monitor mode, where, for instance, a monochrome and a color monitor are incorporated into the same hardware system. Using this option, the environment will automatically detect the appropriate hardware for operation. If only one monitor exists, the command is ignored. However, if there are two discreet monitors, one will be treated as the active unit and the other as an inactive unit. In such conditions, the Programmer's Platform will appear on the inactive monitor while all program output will be displayed on the active monitor. The DOS mode command may be used to determine which monitor is active and which is inactive. Caution: don't switch the active/inactive screen configuration while operating in the DOS shell under the auspices of the Programmer's Platform, because this will create havoc within the system. Also, user programs that write directly to the inactive monitor are not supported and can cause problems if their use is attempted.

The are several other command-line options that may be invoked with BC. These allow display of command line options available, support of LCD screens, palette swapping on EGA video adapters, and the creation of a RAM disk. These command-line options are also fully applicable in protected-mode operation of the Programmer's Platform.

Protected-Mode Operation

Before Borland C++ may be run in protected mode, it is necessary to establish a path for the automatic loading of the protected mode files BCX.EXE, BCX.OVY, and TKERNEL.EXE. Once the path is set up, BCX.EXE will load automatically all appropriate files.

Protected-mode operation is entered by typing:

```
BCX <return>
```

Again, all the command-line options applicable to real-mode operation apply equally to protected-mode operation. When BCX is invoked, it loads TKERNEL.EXE. For those programmers who will be operating BCX under Microsoft Windows 3.0, it should be understood that the protected-mode IDE will run only in Windows standard or real mode (the latter not being particularly advisable). It will not run under Windows enhanced mode.

Leaving Borland C++

There are three basic methods of exiting from the IDE and thus from the on-line version of Borland C++. To leave the environment permanently, press the

```
ALI-X
```

keyboard combination. Also, you may exit permanently by selecting EXIT from the FILE pull-down menu.

Another command yields a temporary exit to the DOS shell. To do this, simply type:

```
ALT-F ALT-D
```

or accomplish the same thing by using the FILE pull-down menu and opting for the DOS Shell option. To reenter the Programmer's Platform, type

```
EXIT<return>
```

on the DOS command line.

The last method of exiting Borland C++ is also temporary. This involves invoking the (≡) option from the main menu, thus bringing up a list of available programs (user-defined) into which the user may be transferred. The IDE is reentered after the selected program has completed its execution.

Moving Around in the Programmer's Platform

When the IDE is first invoked, the basic platform is displayed on the screen. The platform consists of three basic components, arranged from top to bottom on the monitor screen. Figure 2-1 shows the basic platform.

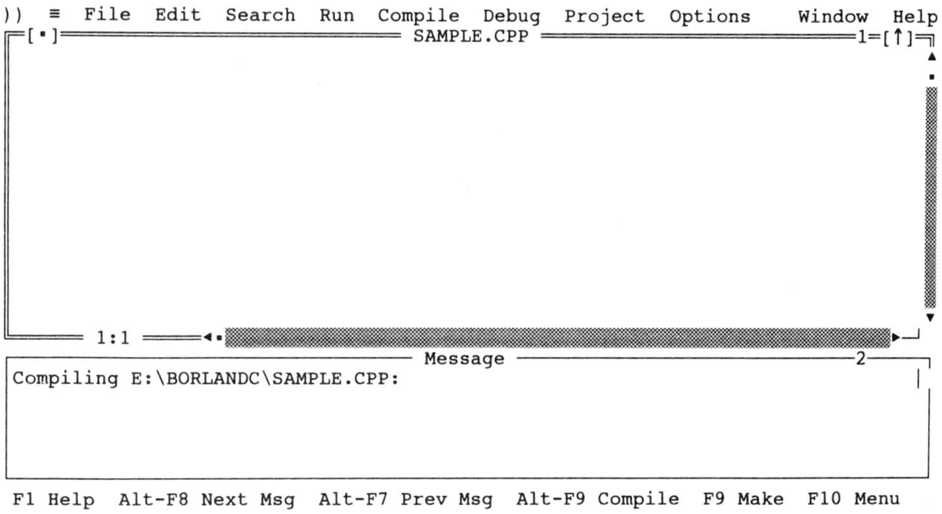

Figure 2-1. The IDE's basic platform.

At the very top is the master menu bar. This is the primary access to all the menu commands. It is visible at all times during the authoring, compiling, linking, and debugging processes. The only time the master menu bar disappears is when a user program is actually executing or when transferring to another program. Whenever a menu option has been chosen or is active, it will be highlighted in the master menu bar.

Below the menu bar is the window area. This is the area of main activity where your program is displayed upon input. Editing takes place in this window, and the great majority of hands-on activity will be viewed from the main window.

Below the main window is the message window. Messages about the operations that are taking place or are about to take place in the main window will appear in this window.

At the bottom of the platform is the status line. The purpose of this portion of the Programmer's Platform is to constantly display the hot-key options available. The options available on this line will change as windows are switched. This line will also change to provide some on-line help as you select options from the main menu bar.

Menu commands may be invoked using only the keyboard. For instance, the F10 key activates the menu bar. Pressing the ALT key while simultaneously pressing any key representing the first letter in the menu option (i.e., ALT-F for the FILE option) will bring up the pulldown bar for that selection. However, the Programmer's Platform is best navigated by a mouse. You may place the mouse pointer on the menu bar command bar and then drag down to the desired selection from that bar. Now all menu commands are available at any given time, depending on what operations are currently taking place. If a menu bar or specific pulldown selection is not highlighted when dragged by the mouse pointer, then that selection is unavailable during the current phase.

Although most programmers will want to use Borland C++ with a mouse, the actual use of the Programmer's Platform will undoubtedly consist of a combination of mouse and keyboard operations. Sometimes its quicker to use a one-touch keyboard selection than it is to click a menu command with a mouse. For other selections, the mouse will be the main access instrument. All this will depend on exactly what is being invoked and also on what the programmer's "internal system" may be. The latter relates directly to how a particular person chooses to interface with the platform and will differ from individual to individual.

Figure 2-2 shows a chart of all of the applicable general hot key, menu hot key and editing hot key availabilities. Again, these may be called to operate within the platform without using a mouse, or they may be used in conjunction with a mouse to suit the preferences of individual programmers.

<table>
<tr><th>Key(s)</th><th>Menu Item</th><th></th><th></th><th></th><th></th></tr>
<tr><td>F1</td><td>Help</td><td>Alt-Spacebar</td><td>≡ menu</td><td>Ctrl-Del</td><td>Edit | Clear</td></tr>
<tr><td>F2</td><td>File | Save</td><td>Alt-C</td><td>Compile menu</td><td>Ctrl-Ins</td><td>Edit | Copy</td></tr>
<tr><td>F3</td><td>File | Open</td><td>Alt-D</td><td>Debug menu</td><td>Shift-Del</td><td>Edit | Cut</td></tr>
<tr><td>F4</td><td>Run | Go to Cursor</td><td>Alt-E</td><td>Edit menu</td><td>Shift-Ins</td><td>Edit | Paste</td></tr>
<tr><td>F5</td><td>Window | Zoom</td><td>Alt-F</td><td>File menu</td><td>Alt-Bkspc</td><td>Edit | Undo</td></tr>
<tr><td>F6</td><td>Window | Next</td><td>Alt-H</td><td>Help menu</td><td>Ctrl-L</td><td>Search | Search Again</td></tr>
<tr><td>F7</td><td>Run | Trace Into</td><td>Alt-O</td><td>Options menu</td><td>F2</td><td>File | Save</td></tr>
<tr><td>F8</td><td>Run | Step Over</td><td>Alt-P</td><td>Project menu</td><td>F3</td><td>File | Open</td></tr>
<tr><td>F9</td><td>Compile | Make EXE File</td><td>Alt-R</td><td>Run menu</td><td></td><td></td></tr>
<tr><td></td><td></td><td>Alt-S</td><td>Search menu</td><td></td><td></td></tr>
<tr><td></td><td></td><td>Alt-W</td><td>Window menu</td><td></td><td></td></tr>
<tr><td></td><td></td><td>Alt-X</td><td>File | Quit</td><td></td><td></td></tr>
</table>

Figure 2-2. All general, menu, and editing hot keys available with the Programmer Platform.

Another table outlining the window management hot keys, on-line help hot keys, and the debug/execute hot keys is provided in Figure 2-3.

<table>
<tr><th></th><th></th></tr>
<tr><td>Alt-#</td><td>Display window #</td></tr>
<tr><td>Alt-0</td><td>Window | List</td></tr>
<tr><td>Alt-F3</td><td>Window | Close</td></tr>
<tr><td>Alt-F4</td><td>Debug | Inspect</td></tr>
<tr><td>F5</td><td>Window | Zoom</td></tr>
<tr><td>Alt-F5</td><td>Window | User Screen</td></tr>
<tr><td>Ctrl-F5</td><td>Change size/position of active window</td></tr>
<tr><td>F6</td><td>Window | Next</td></tr>
</table>

Figure 2-3. Windows management, on-line help, and debug/execute hot keys.

Figure 2-4 shows the FILE pull-down menu from the main menu bar. This may be invoked by placing the mouse pointer on FILE and dragging downward, or by using the ALT-F hot key combination and then the up/down arrow keys on the numeric keypad to highlight the available choices.

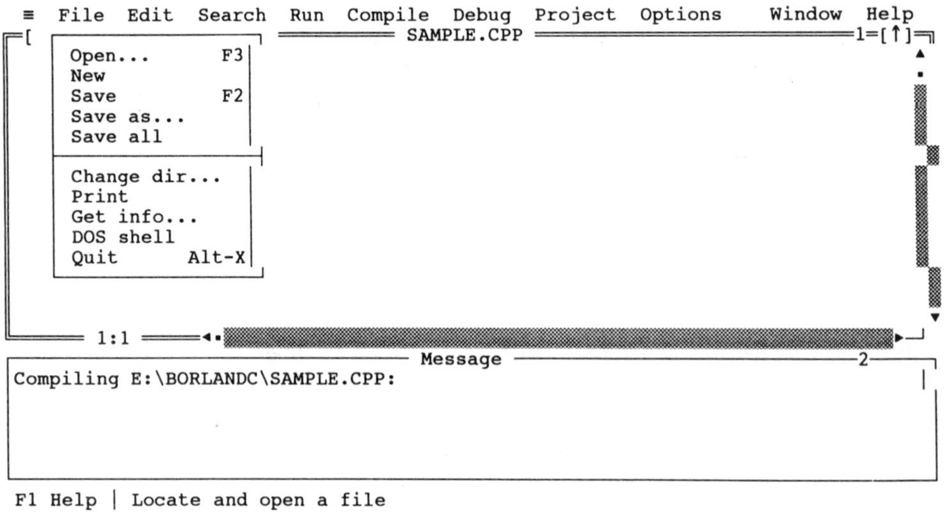

Figure 2-4. The Programmer Platform's FILE pull-down menu.

IDE Windows

There are several different types of windows present in the Borland C++ environment. Two or more may be open at any one time; however, only one window may be active at any one time. The active window is always the one with the multiline border, as shown in Figure 2-5.

In this example, the window named sample.cpp is active even though it does not currently contain any script. We know this because of the twin-line border on the left and at the top. The Message window below the main window is not active; it is exhibiting the single-line border. We could easily make the Message window active by placing the mouse pointer within the desired inactive window and clicking once. This was done within the Message window from the previous figure. Figure 2-6 now shows that the message window is active while the main window is inactive. Again, look for the twin-line border to determine which window is active.

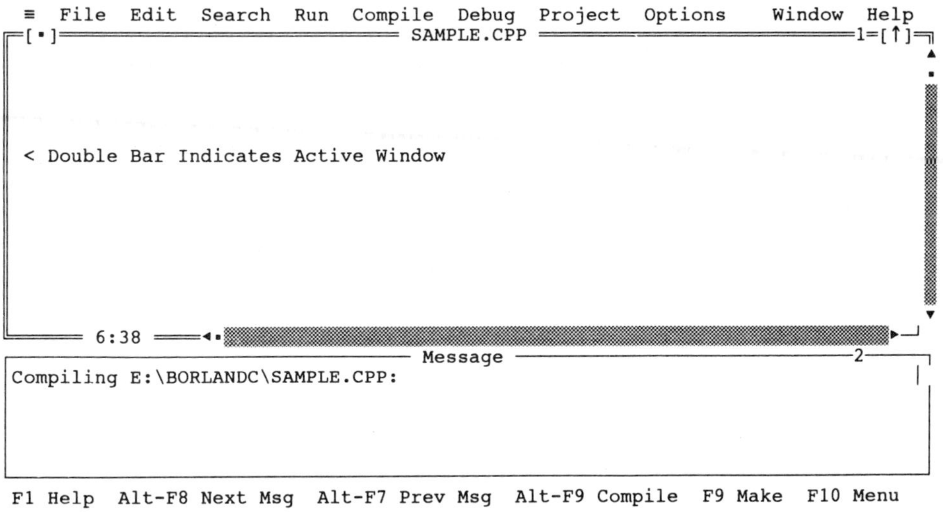

Figure 2-5. The outline border shows that sample.cpp is the currently active window.

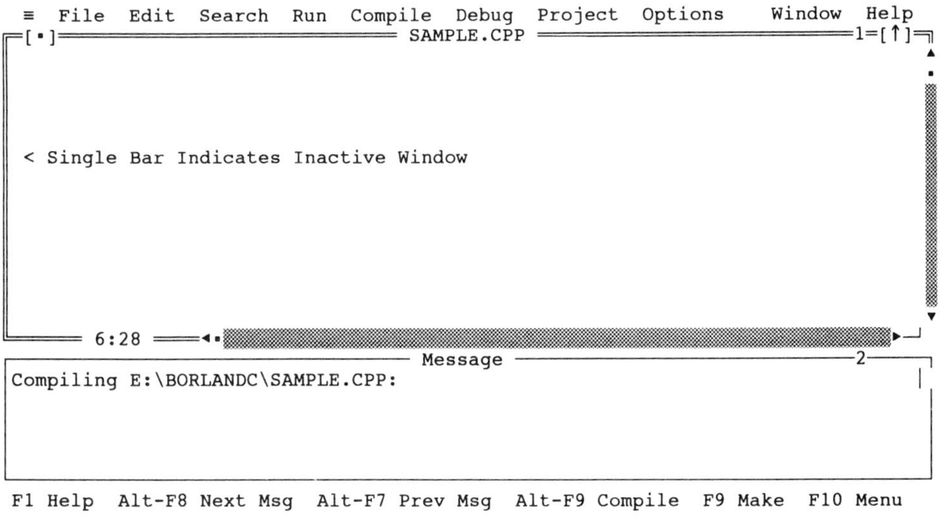

Figure 2-6. Clicking once on the Message window makes it the active window.

Although there are different windows for different purposes and applications, they all have several things in common, as Figure 2-7 illustrates. The active window is the editing window, the largest one that covers the center of the screen. At the left top of this window is the Close box. Place the mouse pointer on this box and click to quickly close the window. If you are closing out of a window containing unsaved or un-updated source code, a dialog box will appear asking if you wish to save the window code before closing the window. This can prevent an accidental loss of source code.

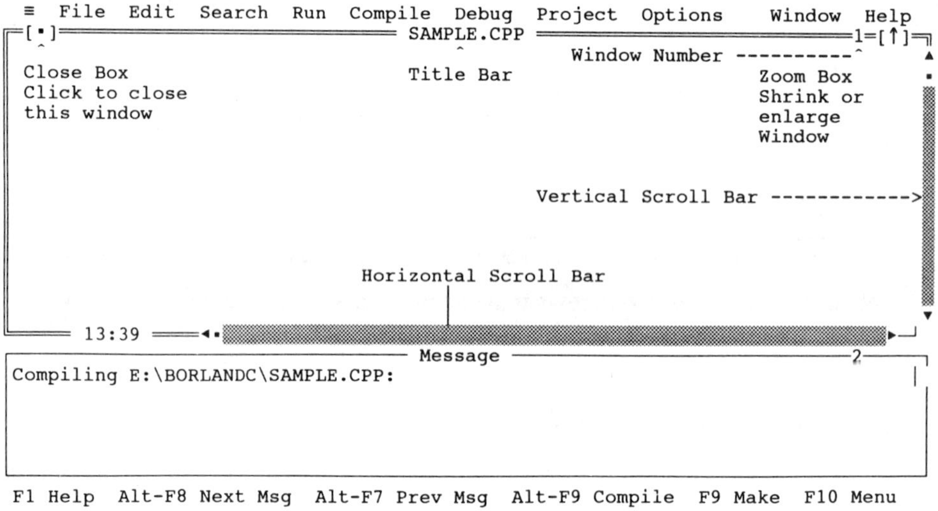

Figure 2-7. The Active window, with other options open.

At the center top of the screen is the Title bar. This is the title of the program contained in the window. If other modules are overlaid on the primary screen, their Title bars will indicate the module name. At the top right of the screen is the Window Number. This indicates how many windows are currently in place on the platform and the number of the active window. The first nine opened windows are given numbers in this manner. Pressing the ALT key followed by the window number will make the specified window active.

To the right of the window number is the Zoom box. Clicking on this box will either enlarge the window to full screen size or shrink it back to the size shown in the figure, depending upon the window's configuration when the click occurs. The size of the window in Figure 2-7 is the default size. However, the window can be enlarged or shrunk linearly by placing the mouse pointer on either one of the bottom corners and dragging down to enlarge or up to shrink. When the Zoom box is clicked to reduce the window from full-screen size, it will reduce the window to the default value or to the size set by the programmer using the drag method just described.

At the right edge of the screen is the vertical scroll bar, which is used to scroll the window text vertically. There is an arrow pointer at the top and the bottom of the scroll bar. Either pointer may be clicked to scroll the text up or down a step at a time. Alternately, you may click at any point on the bar to immediately send the text to that relative position. Clicking on the bar's center scrolls the screen to the center of the text column.

The horizontal scroll bar lies at the bottom of the window. This bar works in an identical manner to the vertical scroll bar, but controls horizontal window adjustment.

Dialog Boxes

Figure 2-8 shows some of the selections available from the FILE pull-down menu. Note that some of the selections are followed by an ellipsis (. . .). This means that invoking this selection will result in a dialog box. This is a special window that takes precedence on the platform. Its purpose is to allow the programmer to view and set multiple options. Figure 2-9 shows the dialog box that appears when the LOAD option is selected from the FILE menu.

This dialog box allows the programmer to specify a single file to load or, alternately, to use a wild-card directory listing. The latter would be used to list all files in a specified directory that exhibit a .cpp extension, for instance. Directing the mouse pointer to a particular entry and double-clicking on it will load the entry into the editing window.

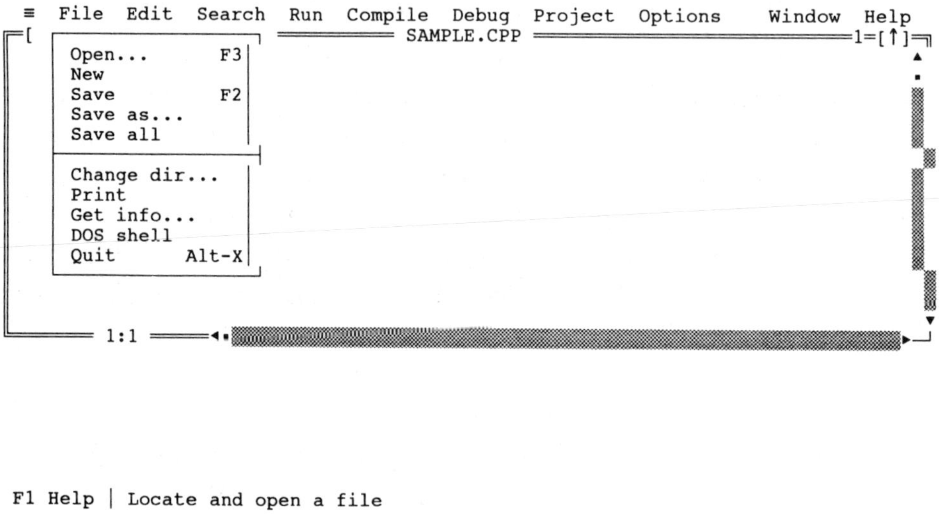

Figure 2-8. File pull-down menu options.

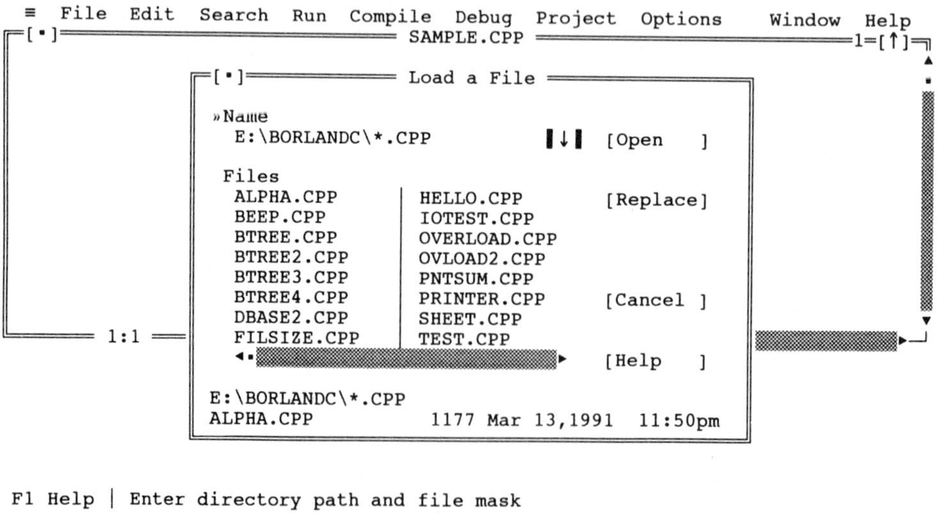

Figure 2-9. Standard screen with Load dialog box.

Each dialog box exhibits several other attributes. You will find radio buttons and check boxes. When you point to a blank check box with the mouse and click, an 'X' will appear in the box, as shown in Figure 2-10. If an 'X' already appears in the box, it will disappear and the option will be unselected.

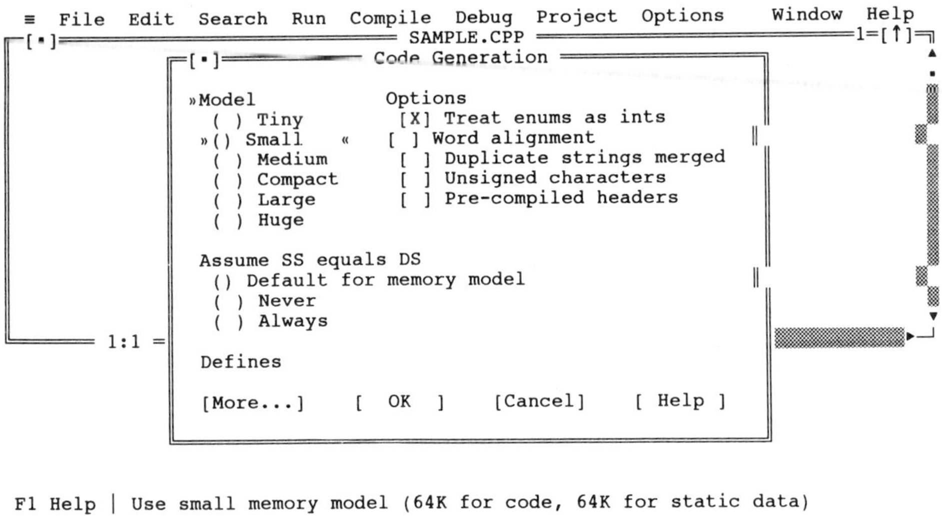

Figure 2-10. Selected items are designated by an X.

Radio buttons are used to represent exclusive choices (i.e., to choose one out of the group), whereas check boxes allow for multiple selections, if desired, by the programmer. To choose a specific radio button, simply point to it with the mouse pointer and click. The use of radio buttons is shown in Figure 2-11.

Another entity that appears in some dialog boxes is an input box. This is a specialized window that allows a programmer to input data. Figure 2-12 shows an example of an input box that allows a new line number to be entered in order to create a branch. While this is not a hard-and-fast rule with all input boxes, in most instances the standard text-editing keys will work in the same manner as they do in the editing window. With these you can scroll to the end of the text and generally input and edit information in a familiar manner.

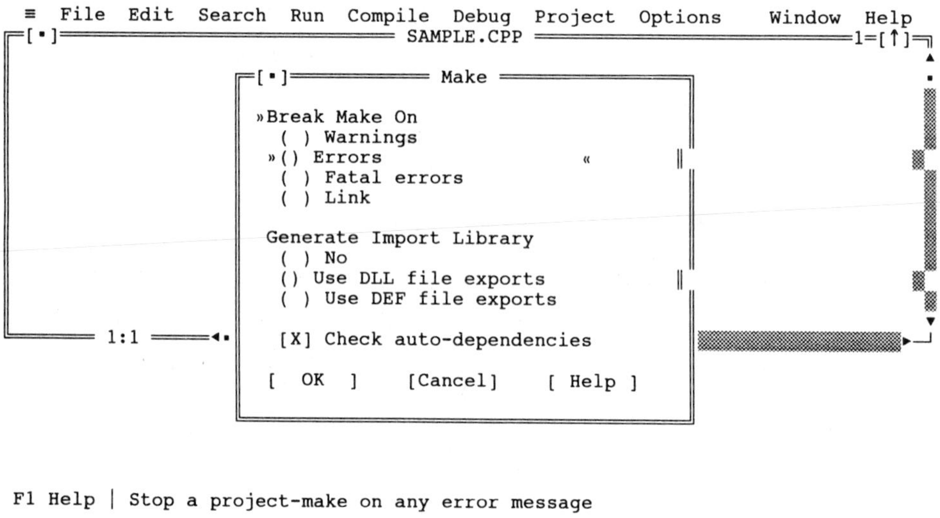

Figure 2-11. Screen showing use of Radio buttons.

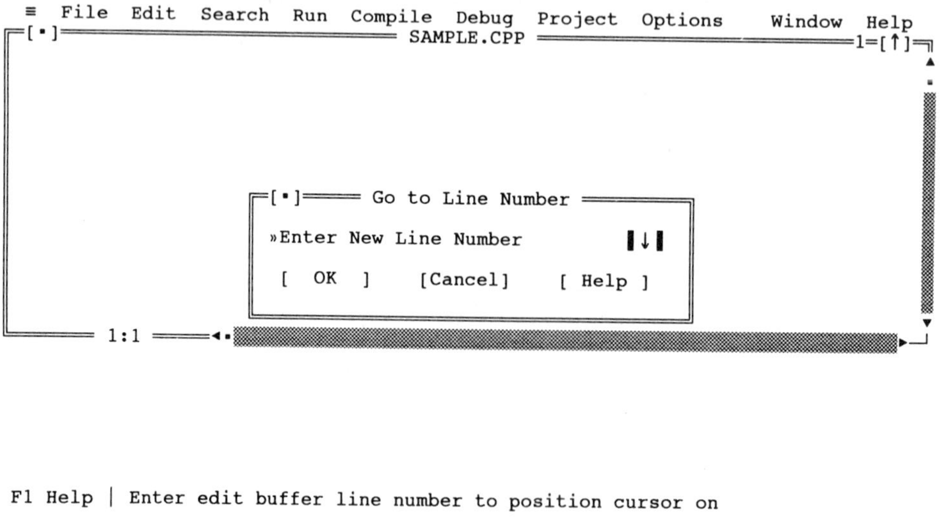

Figure 2-12. Example of an Input box.

The Borland C++ Editor

If you have used other Borland products, the Borland C++ Editor will seem like an old friend sporting some substantial improvements. The multiwindow capability is standard and allows many files to be opened at one time, each occupying its own window. By pointing and clicking the mouse in any window, that window and its file become active in the editor. Naturally, the windows may be shrunk or enlarged and positioned at convenient locations on the screen.

The Borland C++ Editor now offers support for files greater than 64K in size, with a limit of 8 MB for all edit windows open at any given time. The Undo and Redo features add a significant degree of versatility. A clipboard is provided, allowing the user to cut, paste, and copy text between windows. A transfer function even allows other programs—such as word processors, spreadsheets, and databases—to be accessed directly from the Programmer's Platform. Upon exiting these external DOS programs, the IDE will return to the screen.

Files

There are several different types of files associated with the Programmer's Platform. These are files that are generated during the editing process or just prior to beginning a new editing session. Users of Turbo C should be warned that the IDE treats configuration files in a different manner. In earlier Borland offerings (prior to Turbo C++), the IDE worked on a configuration-based format, whereas with Borland C++, the format is project-based. Where a Turbo C user would load a configuration file with a .TC extension defining the project, a Borland C++ user will load a project file that contains a list of all files needed to produce a program.

The Programmer's Platform collects all the information needed to build a C++ program and stores it as a binary project file. The information in the project file includes a list of compiler and linker options, directory paths, and other general information about the job. Once set up, all of the criteria for compiling and linking a job is in place. New modules can be added at any time, so the project file will increase in size as the job size increases—very convenient when large programs are being built from many different modules. A quick change in the project file can allow different modes of compilation and linking to take place immediately and over the entire range of modules that make up the job.

A project file is created by selecting the Project option from the Main menu. After selecting Open Project from this pull-down menu, the user is asked to input a project name. The name should have a .PRJ extension, which signifies that it is a project file, as in:

```
SAMPLE.PRJ
```

If there is only one project file in the default or current directory, the Programmer's Platform automatically loads this file. Naturally, if no project exists, nothing is loaded automatically. Also, if more than one project exists, no project is loaded. When it's necessary to load a new project file (one that already exists on disk), again, the Project pull-down menu is chosen and the same Open Project selection is made. All that is necessary at this point is to type the name of the project to be loaded. When the project exists, it is automatically loaded. If it doesn't exist, it is created.

Because each project has its own desktop in the IDE, loading a new project will cause the desktop for that project to be displayed on the screen. Each of the project files has its own desktop file, which bears the same name as the project, with a .DSK extension appended. When no project file is loaded, the Programmer's Platform resorts to the use of two default files that set standard parameters for compilation and linking.

Menus

In this part of the discussion, we will go through the Main menu of the Borland C++ IDE and view available options. It is from this menu that all activities are accessed. In most cases, it is not necessary to permanently exit the Programmer's Platform, because all activities—from program authoring to compilation and linking to execution and debugging—may be accomplished from within this environment. Figure 2-13 shows the Main menu bar. It is from this bar that options are selected which, in turn, display submenus. Even these submenus may have nested menus.

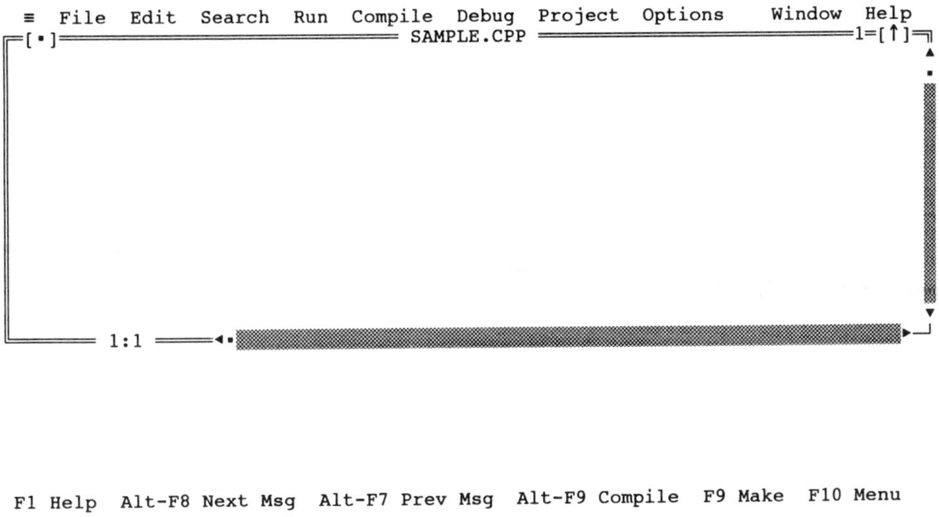

Figure 2-13. Screen showing the Main menu bar.

System Menu

The first option on the Main menu bar is the System menu. This is referenced by the icon formed by three horizontal lines (≡). If you don't have mouse capability, ALT-SPACEBAR will access the options on this menu. Figure 2-14 shows the pull-down menu and the available options. With the exception of the transfer items, these all are fairly straightforward. These programs may be called up from the Programmer's Platform. Any executable program may be placed in this menu by choosing the Transfer selection from the Options menu, a process which will be discussed later in this chapter. Other options on the System menu allow the user to clear the desktop, redraw the screen, and access minor copyright information.

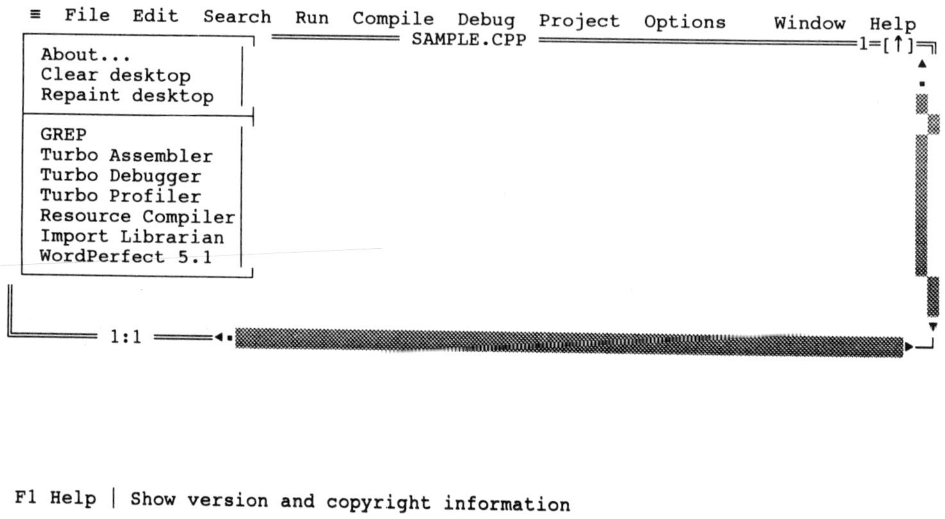

Figure 2-14. Screen showing the Pull-down menu with available options.

File Menu

The File menu from the Main menu bar is shown in Figure 2-15. This menu offers selections to open and close program files, save files, print files, and go to the DOS shell for extracurricular activities.

When the Open option is chosen from the File menu, a dialog box will appear on the screen that allows the user to select a program. This box is shown in Figure 2-16. The top portion of this box allows you to type in a complete filename for loading, or you may specify a wildcard combination that will list files of the specified extensions in the file window below. Pressing the down-arrow key or clicking the horizontal scroll bar with the mouse will scroll the files in this window. Again, the input box allows you to enter a filename without scrolling through files. If a file is to be chosen from the Scroll window, double-clicking its name with the mouse will cause it to load. Alternately, it can be highlighted with the arrow keys and then loaded by pressing Return. The File List box contains a list of all of the files in the current directory that match the wildcard criteria.

```
≡  File  Edit  Search  Run  Compile  Debug  Project  Options    Window  Help
[                         SAMPLE.CPP                                1=[↑]
   Open...        F3
   New
   Save           F2
   Save as...
   Save all
   ─────────────────
   Change dir...
   Print
   Get info...
   DOS shell
   Quit        Alt-X

          1:1

F1 Help | Locate and open a file
```

Figure 2-15. Screen showing the File menu from the Main menu bar.

```
≡  File  Edit  Search  Run  Compile  Debug  Project  Options    Window  Help
[•]                       SAMPLE.CPP                                1=[↑]
             [•]            Load a File
             »Name
               E:\BORLANDC\*.CPP              ↓   [Open    ]

              Files
               ALPHA.CPP        HELLO.CPP         [Replace]
               BEEP.CPP         IOTEST.CPP
               BTREE.CPP        OVERLOAD.CPP
               BTREE2.CPP       OVLOAD2.CPP
               BTREE3.CPP       PNTSUM.CPP
               BTREE4.CPP       PRINTER.CPP       [Cancel ]
               DBASE2.CPP       SHEET.CPP
          1:1  FILSIZE.CPP      TEST.CPP
                                                  [Help   ]

             E:\BORLANDC\*.CPP
             ALPHA.CPP           1177 Mar 13,1991   11:50pm

F1 Help | Enter directory path and file mask
```

Figure 2-16. The File menu with the Open option selected.

At the bottom of this dialog box is the File Information panel, which displays the pathname, filename, date, time, and size of the file selected in the File List box. The Open option is chosen to load previously written C++ programs and often to bring a new source-code module into an ongoing project on a temporary basis. (Later, the module may be made a permanent part of the job by placing its name in the project.)

The second option in the File menu is New. As its name implies, this option allows you to open a new editing window in which to write a new program. Whenever this option is chosen, the newly opened window will have a default name of NONAME00.CPP. If a file by this same name already exists in the default directory, the name will be NONAME01.CPP. Should this name also exist, a 02 extension will be substituted. This number-stepping process will continue until a new filename is found. Selecting New from this menu always assures that a new file window is opened and a new file is created.

The Save option saves the file in the active IDE window to disk. It is saved under the name in which it was first opened. This option probably won't be chosen from the pull-down menu, because an easier and more immediate method of saving is to press the F2 function key. All that is necessary to save the contents of a multiwindow desktop is to make each window active and then press F2.

Whenever a new program is opened using the New option, it is given a temporary name, such as NONAME00.CPP. When this new program has been written, it is prudent to rename it in order to free up the New option's list of available names. Failure to do so results in a mess of files beginning with NONAME00.CPP. This is a poor operational practice that is bound to lead to confusion. When users select New from the pull-down menu, they should always rename this file before saving it.

The Save As option displays a dialog box on the screen and allows the user to type in a new filename for the program in the active editing window. The name may be entered with drive and path specifications, or the filename by itself may be entered if it is to be saved to the current directory.

Another file-saving option on the File menu is Save All. This is very handy for large and complex projects that may involve many different modules in different windows on the Platform. This option works just like Save, except that all modified files are saved under the names under which they were loaded, as opposed to saving only a single file in the active window.

Other options under the File menu allow the disk directory to be changed, the contents of the active window to be printed, entry to the DOS shell, and permanent exit from the Programmer's Platform. The Get Info option displays a dialog box that contains information about the file in the active window. This box is shown in Figure 2-17.

While using a mouse with Borland C++ is most convenient, the entire Platform can be accessed with the keyboard alone. This keyboard control feature was initially built into the Borland IDE in order to preclude the mandatory use of a mouse. However, having the ability to control this desktop by means of either the mouse or the keyboard makes it far more versatile. Those users who have a mouse will very quickly adopt a personal operating style that more than likely will make use of both the mouse and the keyboard. Once the File menu has been accessed—either by clicking the name with the mouse or by using the ALT-F combination keystroke—any option in the menu may be selected by typing the first letter of that option. This is often quicker than moving the mouse, clicking and dragging, and then clicking again. For instance, to go to the DOS shell, all that is necessary is to press ALT-F and then the "D" key. When permanently exiting the platform, it's easier to press the ALT-X combination than it is to click and drag with the mouse.

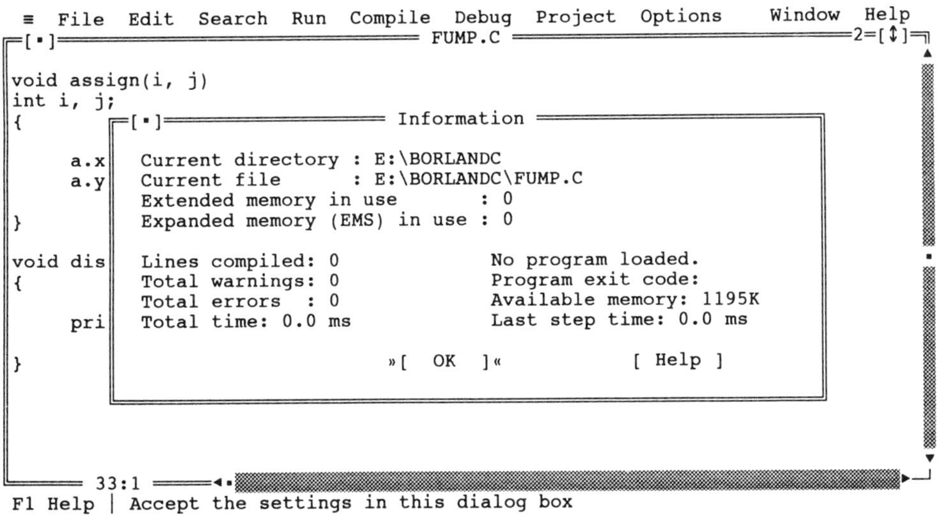

Figure 2-17. The Get Info dialog box.

Edit Menu

Figure 2-18 shows the Edit menu, which may be accessed by means of the ALT-E combination keystroke. As was previously mentioned, this menu allows for standard editing functions, such as Cut, Paste, Copy, Undo, and Redo.

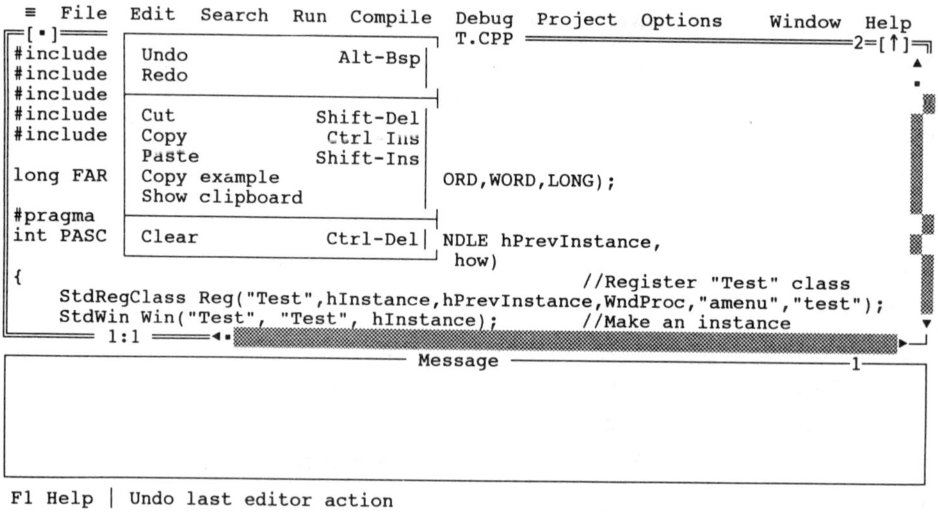

Figure 2-18. Screen showing the Edit menu.

In order to perform most editing functions, it is important to remember that the text must be highlighted before an option from the Edit menu is selected. Again, this can be accomplished using either the mouse or the keyboard.

The Undo option is used to undo the most recent action taken, although there are some restrictions that apply. Put simply, Undo allows you to undo the most recent edit or cursor movement. Redo is the reverse of Undo; that is, Redo reverses the most recent Undo action.

The Cut option is used to remove highlighted text from the current document. Text that is removed using this option is automatically pasted into the Clipboard, where it remains until another selection is Cut. This allows you to place, by means of the Paste option (which will be discussed next), the contents of the Clipboard in multiple locations, as many times as desired.

The Copy option is similar to the Cut option, except that a copy of the highlighted text is placed in the Clipboard and the original document remains the same. As described above, this text is placed in another location by means of the Paste option, and this can be repeated at will until another selection is placed in the Clipboard using either the Cut or Copy options.

The Paste option is used together with the Cut or Copy options to place text in single or multiple locations. It is important to remember that when Paste is selected, it is text that was last cut or copied to the Clipboard that is then pasted. Multiple Pastes of the same text are accomplished by simply reselecting this option.

The Show Clipboard option is used to open the Clipboard, in the form of a window, to review its current contents (often done prior to selecting Paste). You might want to refresh your memory as to what text was last cut or copied before you perform a Paste operation, and to ensure that you do not paste erroneously. However, even if you do use the Paste option mistakenly, the Undo option can always be selected to cancel the Paste and re-highlight and re-Cut or re-Copy the correct text.

When the Clipboard is opened using the Show Clipboard option, it becomes a window like all other windows, which means you can manipulate it in the same manner as any other window; you can move it, resize it, scroll within it, and even edit its contents. You can also open the Clipboard, highlight a portion of the text, and then perform a standard Cut or Copy. Thus you can move large blocks of text to the Clipboard and then paste only the highlighted portion in another location.

The Clear option is similar to Cut, in that it removes highlighted text from the current document. The only difference is that the "cleared" text is not placed automatically in the Clipboard. Instead, it is deleted. You can also use the Clear option to clear the contents of the Clipboard in the same fashion: Open the clipboard, highlight the text, and select the Clear option.

Search Menu

The Search menu provides you with a variety of ways to search for text, function declarations, and error locations. The options provided under this menu are both versatile and powerful, allowing you to perform global search-and-replace operations rapidly. The Search menu options are shown in Figure 2-19.

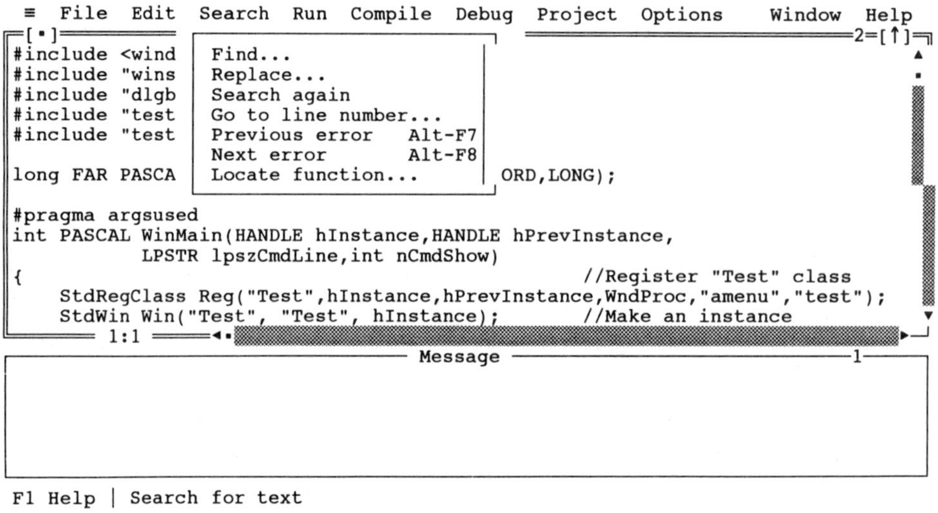

Figure 2-19. Screen showing Search menu options.

The simplest form of search is accessed with the Find option. When this option is selected, a dialog box is displayed, as shown in Figure 2-20. Note that a variety of options can be selected that will establish the criteria for the search that you want to perform.

To establish the search criteria, first enter the text at the very top of the dialog box, then move through the options, selecting those you desire. It is possible to specify, for example, that the search is case-sensitive—that is, if you want the program to locate the text exactly as it appears at the top of the dialog box. If the text was entered entirely in lowercase, for example, and you only wanted to find occurrences of this text in lowercase, you would check the Case-Sensitive option. All default values may be set with the Borland C++ utility TCINST.exe.

You can further define the scope of the search with other options that include a whole-word-only option, a forward-or-backward option, and a global-versus-selected-text search.

The Replace option is used to locate the specified text and replace it—also with specified text—at the same time. The dialog box that is displayed when this option is selected is shown in Figure 2-21. As you can see, this dialog box is a bit different from the previous one; note that there are two areas at the top, one for the text to be found, and another for the text that is to be used as the replacement. Below this area are the same search options, with one important addition: the prompt on the Replace option, which gives you the opportunity to approve each replacement before it occurs. If this option is not selected, each Replace operation will occur automatically.

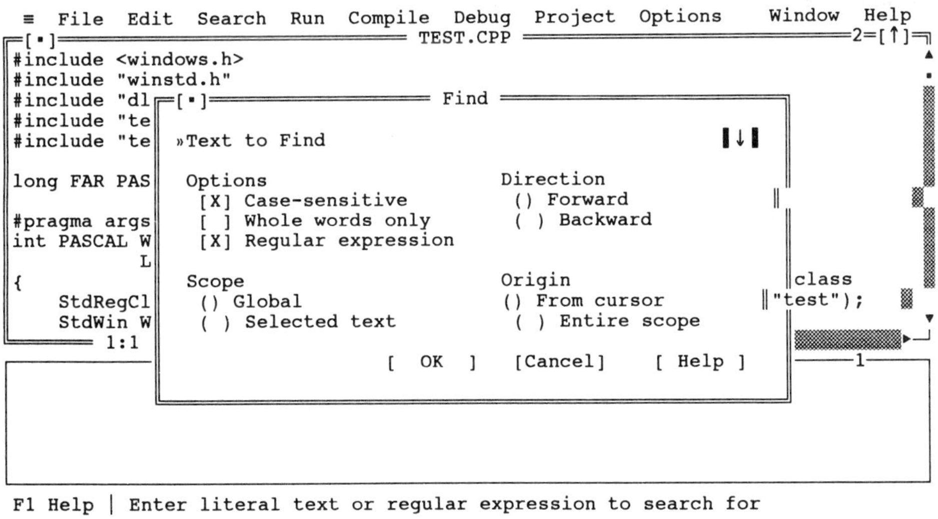

Figure 2-20. The Find option dialog box.

The Again option is used to repeat the last Find or Replace performed. When the Again option is selected, all settings that applied to the last Find or Replace remain in effect.

The Go to Line Number option, as its name implies, allows you to perform a search based on a line number. When this option is selected, a dialog box is displayed, allowing you to enter the line number of the code segment you wish to locate.

The Previous Error option is used to move the cursor to the location of the most recent error or warning message. This option is available only if the error or warning messages have line numbers and are in the Message window. These are normally the types of messages that would be generated by those compile or transfer commands that use a Capture messages filter.

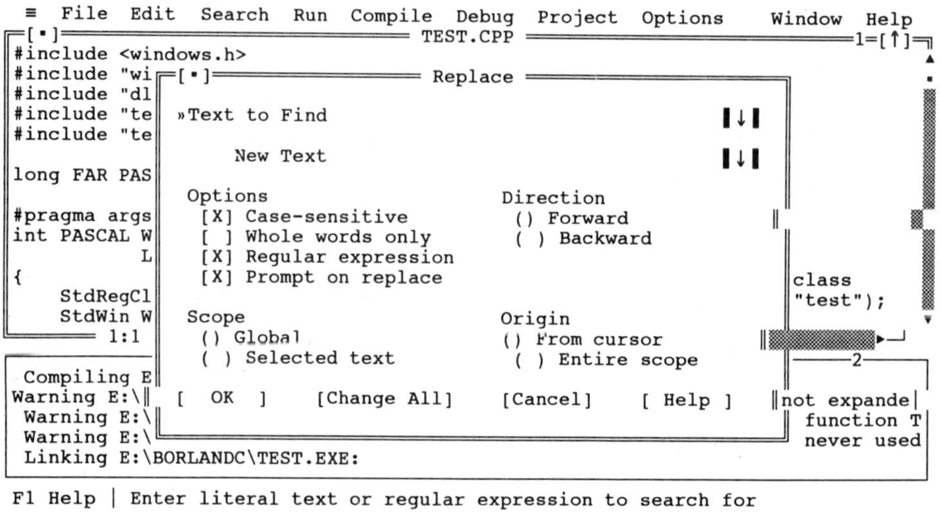

Figure 2-21. The Replace option dialog box.

The Location Function option, when selected, displays a dialog box that allows you to enter the name of a function that is to be located. However, this option is available only during debugging. When the dialog box is displayed, it is possible to either enter the function manually or scroll through a "history" list and make a selection from this list.

Run Menu

The Run menu is selected when the time comes to execute the program you have built under the IDE. This menu is short, sweet, and powerful.

When you select the Run option under the Run menu, whether the program is automatically executed depends on what has taken place previously. For instance, if the source code of the program has been altered since the last compilation and linking, the Run option automatically will lead the Project Manager to recompile and link the program in the active window, and then execute. On the other hand, if the program has not been modified, execution will take place immediately.

If the environment has been set up for source debugging, the executable code will contain debugging information, affecting exactly what the Run option does with your program. First of all, if the source code has not been modified since the last compilation, the program will run to the next breakpoint. If no breakpoints have been set, the program will execute to its logical termination. If the source code has been modified since the last compilation, it will be recompiled and linked prior to execution. If you are in an active debugging session and you are already stepping through your program, the program is recompiled and linked and execution will start at the beginning of the program. (It should be noted here that Windows applications cannot be run within the IDE. To execute Windows programs, you must enter the DOS shell and proceed from there.)

The Program Reset option terminates the current debugging session, releasing all memory allocated to the program. All files are automatically closed. This is an appropriate selection to make when you are debugging a program and there is insufficient memory to run transfer programs or to enter the DOS shell.

The Go to Cursor option under the Run menu is a convenient method of executing a portion of a program that can be quickly set and reset. Using this option, the program will be executed from the Run Bar, the highlighted portion of your source code, to the line the cursor is currently resting on in the Edit window. This operation does not set permanent breakpoints, but it allows the program to stop if a permanent breakpoint is encountered. This is an option that can be conveniently tied to a mouse button using TCINST.exe.

The Trace Into option runs the active program on a statement-by-statement basis. When a function call is encountered, each single statement within the function is executed, as opposed to the function being executed as a single step.

The Step Over option executes the next statement in the current function. This option is used to run the function currently being debugged one statement at a time without branches into other functions.

The last option in the Run menu is the Arguments selection. Choosing this option produces a dialog box in which the user may enter arguments that are to be included when invoking the executable program. Arguments take effect only when the program begins executing.

Compile Menu

The options available in the Compile menu are used to compile the program in the active window or to make or build a project. In order to use the Compile, Make, Build, or Link options, however, a file must be open in an active Edit window or a project must be defined.

The Compile to OBJ option is used to compile the active editor file (a .C or .CPP file to an .OBJ file). Here, the menu will always display the name of the file to be created. Also, as compilation takes place, a status box will be displayed informing you of the progress and results of this process. Also, any errors or warnings that take place will be displayed in the Message window, with the first error highlighted.

The Make EXE File option is used to direct the Project Manager to create an .EXE file. As with the previous option, the menu will always display the name of the file to be created.

The Link EXE File option links the current .OBJ and .LIB files without doing a "make," which produces a new .EXE file. These current files are either the defaults or the files that have been defined in the current project file.

The Build All option is used to rebuild all files in the project. This is similar to the Make EXE File, except that Build All is unconditional. Note that if this option is aborted (either manually or by errors that halt the build), it is possible to continue the build from the point where it was aborted by selecting the Make EXE File option. The Build All-error-correction-MAKE is a very powerful and often overlooked technique.

The final option available on the Compile menu is Remove Messages, which simply removes all messages from the Message window.

Debug Menu

The on-line debugger is accessed via the Debug menu, which offers many powerful features. The first selection available is Inspect. When this option is chosen, an "inspect" window is opened and allows the user to examine and modify values in a data element. Window information changes, depending upon the data element being inspected. Using the integrated debugger, standard data types such as integers, pointers, structures, classes, unions, functions, and arrays can be accessed fully. (For highly detailed and complex debugging operations, users will call on Turbo Debugger.)

The Evaluate/Modify option under the Debug menu evaluates an expression and displays its value in the dialog box. There are three fields in this dialog box: Expression, Result, and New. After the values are displayed, they may be modified where appropriate. This option can be used like a programmer's calculator.

The Call Stack option opens a dialog box that displays the calling sequence of functions in the executed program. At the bottom of the stack is main(). The top of the stack will list the function that is currently being executed.

The Watches option creates a pop-up menu that lists the commands used to control watch expressions. These may be saved across sessions.

The Toggle Breakpoint option allows the user to toggle between setting and unsetting unconditional breakpoints on the line where the cursor rests. A dialog box will be displayed when this option is selected. This box indicates all set breakpoints, their line numbers, and conditions. The condition feature presents a history list that enables users to select breakpoint conditions that have not been used already. The Delete button in this dialog box allows the user to remove breakpoints from the program.

Project Menu

The Project menu is used to perform management-type actions on the projects themselves. The first option, Open Project, displays a dialog box that allows the user to select and load a project or to create a new project. To select an existing project, the user scrolls through the projects displayed in the dialog box and makes a selection. To create a new project, the user enters a name at the very top of the dialog box. The second option, Close Project, is used to close the current project.

The Add Item option is used to add a file to the project list. When this option is selected, a dialog box is displayed, allowing the user to select a current file, which is then added to the Project file. The next option, Delete Item, is the reverse of Add Item, allowing you to delete a file in the Project window.

When Local Options is selected from the Project menu, a variety of options are made available by means of the Override Options dialog box. Here, it is possible to include command-line override options for a project-file module, or to specify a path and a name for the object file as well as a translator for the module. At the bottom of this dialog box are three options that may be selected: Overlay this module, Exclude debug information, and Exclude from link. The first option allows the user to specify the selected module or library to be overlaid. The second option is used to prevent debug information included in the module from going into the .EXE, and the third is used to specify that the module is not to be linked.

The Include Files option is used to obtain a listing of the files that are included by the file chosen from the Project window. As files are compiled, information is collected, which is then displayed using this option.

Options Menu

The Options menu is the largest menu available on the Programmer's Platform and is used primarily to set defaults for the operation of Borland C++. With the options on this menu the user can establish certain minimum environment criteria, determine which memory model C++ compiler will be used, and in general, determine various sets of parameters that will be in effect for program generation. This menu is shown in Figure 2-22.

When the Compiler option is selected, a pop-up menu is displayed. This is shown in Figure 2-23. Selecting the Code Generation option displays a dialog box that allows the selection of the desired memory model and several other options regarding compilation activities. Figure 2-24 shows this dialog box. The radio buttons in the two fields at the left are used to select one of six possible memory model configurations and to determine whether the stack segment (SS) is assumed to be equal to the data segment (DS). The options portion of this dialog box allows the selection of the general performance of the compiler regarding such parameters as word alignment, unsigned character, and precompiled headers. More than one option may be chosen. When an "X" is found in an option box, that option goes into effect. The Defines input box is also available in this dialog box, allowing the user to enter macro definitions to the preprocessor.

```
 ≡  File  Edit  Search  Run  Compile  Debug  Project  Options    Window  Help
[•]                                   TEST.CPP
#include <windows.h>                                  Compiler          ►
#include "winstd.h"                                   Transfer...
#include "dlgbase.h"                                  Make...
#include "test.h"                                     Linker...
#include "testm.h"                                    Application...
                                                      Debugger...
long FAR PASCAL _export WndProc(HWND,WORD,WORD,LONG)  Directories...

#pragma argsused                                      Environment       ►
int PASCAL WinMain(HANDLE hInstance,HANDLE hPrevInst
           LPSTR lpszCmdLine,int nCmdShow)            Save...
{                                              //R
    StdRegClass Reg("Test",hInstance,hPrevInstance,WndProc,"amenu","test");
    StdWin Win("Test", "Test", hInstance);         //Make an instance
        1:1
                               Message                                    2
 Compiling E:\BORLANDC\TEST.CPP:
Warning E:\BORLANDC\WINBASE.H 107: Functions containing while are not expande
 Warning E:\BORLANDC\TEST.H 32: Parameter 'lParam' is never used in function T
 Warning E:\BORLANDC\TEST.CPP 21: 'Reg' is assigned a value that is never used
 Linking E:\BORLANDC\TEST.EXE:

F1 Help | Set compiler defaults for code generation, error messages, and names
```

Figure 2-22. Example of the Options menu.

```
 ≡  File  Edit  Search  Run  Compile  Debug  Project  Options    Window  Help
[•]                                   TEST.CPP
#include <windows.h>                                  Compiler          ►
#include "winstd.h"
#include "dlgbase.h"                                    Code generation...
#include "test.h"                                       Entry/Exit Code...
#include "testm.h"                                      C++ options...
                                                        Optimizations...
long FAR PASCAL _export WndProc(HWND,WORD,WORD,LONG)    Source...
                                                        Messages...
#pragma argsused                                        Names...
int PASCAL WinMain(HANDLE hInstance,HANDLE hPrevInst
           LPSTR lpszCmdLine,int nCmdShow)            Save...
{                                              //R
    StdRegClass Reg("Test",hInstance,hPrevInstance,WndProc,"amenu","test");
    StdWin Win("Test", "Test", hInstance);         //Make an instance
        1:1
                               Message                                    2
 Compiling E:\BORLANDC\TEST.CPP:
Warning E:\BORLANDC\WINBASE.H 107: Functions containing while are not expande
 Warning E:\BORLANDC\TEST.H 32: Parameter 'lParam' is never used in function T
 Warning E:\BORLANDC\TEST.CPP 21: 'Reg' is assigned a value that is never used
 Linking E:\BORLANDC\TEST.EXE:

F1 Help | Specify how compiler prepares object code (memory models, etc.)
```

Figure 2-23. Example of the Compiler option dialog box.

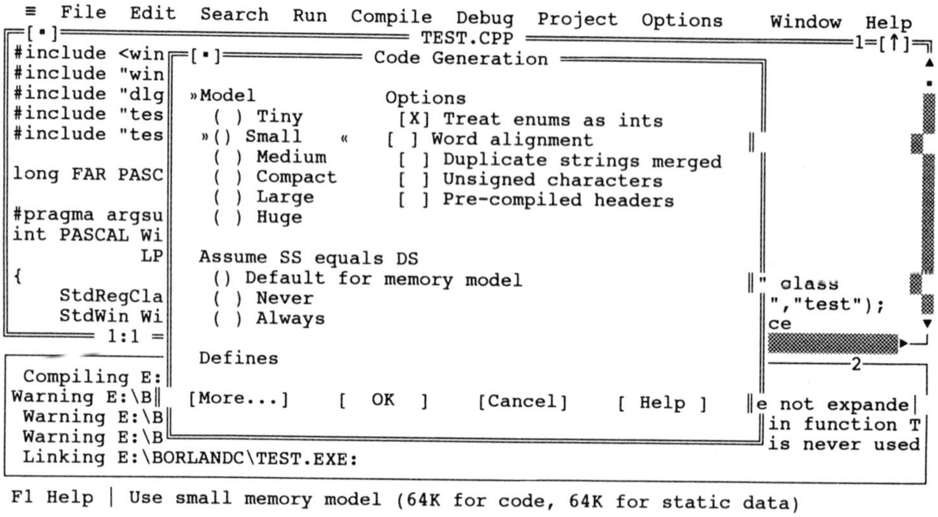

Figure 2-24. Example of the Code Generation dialog box.

The Code Generation dialog box is quickly scrolled into an additional dialog box by clicking the More icon at the lower left. This is the Advanced Code Generation dialog box shown in Figure 2-25. Here, the user can select the method by which floating-point math is handled, along with the microprocessor instruction set to be utilized. The Options menu in this dialog box allows the user to select certain program criteria that address debugging operations and the general handling of data.

Other options present under the Compiler heading include the setting of entry/exit code standards. When a program is intended for Windows, the compiler generates a prolog and epilog that are different than would be the case if the program were intended for DOS operation. This and other similar types of adjustments are made with this option.

A C++ Option command allows for default settings that inform the computer how the object code is to be prepared. The dialog box for this option is illustrated in Figure 2-26 and shows that the categories are broken down into C++ Virtual Tables, Use C++ Compiler, and Options. The first category allows the user to control C++ virtual tables and the expansion of inline functions when debugging. The second tells the Borland C++ environment whether to compile programs as C++ code or to default to standard ANSI C code unless the source code contains the .CPP extension.

```
 ≡  File  Edit  Search  Run  Compile  Debug  Project  Options    Window  Help
 [•]══════════════════════════════ TEST.CPP ═══════════════════════════1=[↑]
 #include <win[•]═══════════ Code Generation ══════════════
 #include "win
 #include "dlg[•]═══════ Advanced Code Generation ═══════════
 #include "tes
 #include "tes  »Floating Point     Options
                  ( ) None            [X] Generate underbars
 long FAR PASC  »() Emulation «     [ ] Line numbers debug info
                  ( ) 8087            [X] Debug info in OBJs
 #pragma argsu    ( ) 80287           [X] Fast floating point
 int PASCAL Wi                        [ ] Fast huge pointers
           LP   Instruction Set       [ ] Generate COMDEFs
 {                () 8088/8086      [ ] Automatic far data      class
     StdRegCla    ( ) 80186                                     ,"test");
     StdWin Wi    ( ) 80286          Far Data Threshold   32767  e
 ══════ 1:1 =
                        [  OK  ]    [Cancel]    [ Help ]        ──────2──────
  Compiling E:
 Warning E:\B                                                    not expande
  Warning E:\B                                                   in function T
  Warning E:\B                                                   is never used
  Linking E:\BORLANDC\TEST.EXE:

 F1 Help | Detect and use coprocessor, otherwise emulate the 8087/80287
```

Figure 2-25. The Advanced Code Generation dialog box.

```
 ≡  File  Edit  Search  Run  Compile  Debug  Project  Options    Window  Help
 [•]══════════════════════════════ TEST.CPP ═══════════════════════════1=[↑]
 #include <windows.h>
 #include "winstd.h"
 #include "dlgbase.h"
 #include "test[•]══════════ C++ Options ═══════════════
 #include "test
                  »C++ Virtual Tables  Use C++ Compiler
 long FAR PASCA    »() Smart      «    () CPP extension only
                    ( ) Local            ( ) C++ always
 #pragma argsus     ( ) External
 int PASCAL Win     ( ) Public
            LPS
 {                 Options                                   t" class
     StdRegClas     [X] Out-of-line inline functions         u","test");
     StdWin Win     [ ] Far virtual tables                   nce
 ══════ 1:1 =
                        [  OK  ]    [Cancel]    [ Help ]     ──────2──────
  Compiling E:\
 Warning E:\BO                                               re not expande
  Warning E:\BORLANDC\TEST.H 32: Parameter 'lParam' is never used in function T
  Warning E:\BORLANDC\TEST.CPP 21: 'Reg' is assigned a value that is never used
  Linking E:\BORLANDC\TEST.EXE:

 F1 Help | Let compiler choose placement of virtual tables
```

Figure 2-26. A default settings dialog box.

The Source selection gives the user the option of allowing for nested comments in C++ source files. Normally, nested comments are not allowed in standard C implementations, and they are not portable. The Keyword radio buttons tell the compiler the standard under which keywords in source code are recognized.

Choosing the Messages command allows for the setting of options that affect compiler error messages within the platform. Using this option, you can choose to stop after so many errors, to stop after warnings, and whether or not to display warnings. There are also other options that address ANSI violations, portability, C++ warnings, and frequent errors.

The Names command lets the user change the default segment, group, and class names for code, data, and BSS sections. These options are part of the professional-level performance offered by the Borland C++ package and deal directly with memory management.

The Transfer selection allows the user to add or remove to and from the System Menu the names of executable programs that may be run from the Programmer's Platform. When selected, a dialog box appears wherein names can be edited or deleted. When placed in the Transfer dialog box, these names will become options on the System menu. Control may be transferred to these programs at any time.

Under the general heading of the Options menu there are many other submenus and nested submenus that address the linker, the debugger, default directories, and the environment in general. In most cases, the Options menu is the menu that is accessed upon initial installation of the Borland C++ programming environment. It is from this menu that many of the operational characteristics of the Programmer's Platform and the programs it accesses are determined.

Window Menu

The Window menu is used to manage windows. As a matter of fact, because all the options are related to windows, all windows that are opened with this menu feature standard window elements with which you are already familiar.

The Size/Move option is selected when you want to change the size or location of a window. To move a window, the arrow keys are activated, with Enter pressed after the window is in the appropriate location on the screen. Alternately, the window can be moved simply by dragging its title bar. To change a window's size, the Shift key is held down while pressing an arrow key. Again, if the window has a resize corner, it is possible to simply drag that corner or any other corner in order to resize.

The Zoom option is used to enlarge the active window to the maximum size allowed. If the window is already at maximum size, choosing this option will restore the window to its previous size. The user can also double-click on the top of the window to zoom or reverse a zoom.

The next series of options allow further actions related to windows: *Tile* tiles all open windows; *Cascade* stacks all open windows; *Next* makes the next window active; *Close* closes the active window; *Message* opens the Message window; *Output* opens the Output window; and *Watch* opens the Watch window.

The User Screen option is selected when you want to view a program's full-screen output. To view output in a Borland C++ window, select the Output command. To return to the Programmer's Platform, click or press any key.

Additional windows that you may open by means of the Window menu include the Register window, the Project window, the Project Notes window (which allows you to record information about the project), and the List window (which displays a list of all open windows).

Help Menu

The Help menu provides on-line help in a separate window. The on-line help provided is very extensive and is accessed via either the keyboard or the mouse. The Help window presents key words that can be scrolled through to locate the topic on which you need assistance. When the appropriate key word is located, simply press Enter to obtain detailed information on that topic.

Using the Contents option, you can scroll through the a table of contents and make a selection from the help listing. Alternately, you can select the Index option and scroll through a complete list of key words or select the Topic Search option to obtain a listing of language help on the currently selected item. It is also possible, by means of the Previous Topic option, to reopen the Help window and obtain a display of the last topic reviewed. The final command on this menu, Help on Help, displays a text window that contains instructions on how to use the Help system.

Summary

The Borland C++ IDE/Programmer's Platform is the heart of the programming power of this new environment. This chapter has provided an overview of its features, but it would take an entire text (or several) to fully explain all the capabilities of this versatile programming tool. Unlike other programming environments, the Borland C++ Programmer's Platform is almost a "be-all, do-all." Once a project is begun, it is rarely necessary to leave (permanently) the IDE for any purpose whatsoever.

Borland's IDE has always been a major asset. The improvements and extensions made on this newest release will make it a hit with even more programmers. It is the glue that binds the entire development package into a single, cohesive unit.

CHAPTER 3

Going from C to C++

Programmers who are already familiar with the C programming language should be very excited about the increased advantages offered by Borland C++. Certainly, learning a new language is not an easy thing, but always bear in mind that C++ is simply a superset of the C programming language. Most C programs already written can be compiled and run under Borland C++, usually with little or no modification. However, it is likely that many of these C programs can be rewritten in a more expressive manner using the additional "toolkit" provided by C++.

Borland C++ implements the ANSI C standard with several extensions. Options may be set within the compiler to warn if any of the extensions are encountered. Borland C++ is also a full implementation of AT&T's C++ Version 2.0.

Let's begin this study of Borland C++ by discussing some of the differences and additions that the C++ language presents when compared with standard C.

Comments

Borland C++ supports two types of comments. Standard comment lines such as

```
/* This is a standard C comment line */
```

are fully supported, as they are in standard C. The compiler will ignore everything that follows the /* delimiter. This ignore procedure is terminated when the */ delimiter is reached.

Borland C++ offers another type of comment that is a little easier to input on the keyboard. The following line demonstrates the C++ // comment delimiter:

```
// This is a C++ comment line
```

Both types of delimiters are legal and should be utilized by C++ programmers. Generally speaking, the /* version is used for large blocks of comments, while the // delimiter is used for one-line comments.

Casts

In the C language, the cast operator is used to coerce data of one type to another type. If we assume that variable *x* is an integer and change() is a function that requires a double data type, then

```
change((double) x)
```

coerces the value in x to type double. Using C++, a new type of cast syntax may be used, as in:

```
change(long(x))
```

You can see that the cast type name is not enclosed in parentheses, but its object is. This form of casting looks like a function call, and many programmers feel it is more expressive. In any event, C++ offers two methods of accomplishing the same cast operations, and each may be used to its advantage in the same program.

Declarations

In the C programming language, all declarations within a program or function must be made at the beginning of the program or function. If additional declarations are needed, the programmer must return to the declaration block at the beginning of the program or function and make the necessary adjustments. Again, all declarations must be made before any statements are executed.

C++ does not operate with this restriction. Therefore, variables may be declared closer to the program statements in which they are used. The following program demonstrates this feature:

```
void main(void)
{

        int x;
        for (x = 0; x < 99; ++x)
```

```
        printf("%d\n", x);

    double y;
    for (y =1.21415; y < 2.19682; y += .0001)
        printf("%lf\n", y);

}
```

This program would be strictly illegal in ANSI C, but C++ has the capability of making declarations at any point in a program or function. The following program is a rewrite of the one above, showing how declarations may be made legally at any point in the program.

```
void main(void)
{

    for (int x = 0; x < 99; ++x)
        printf("%d\n", x);

    for (double y =1.21415; y < 2.19682; y += .0001)
        printf("%lf\n", y);

}
```

Here, the declarations of the two variables are made within the *for* loops. (This may be an even more expressive way of making the declarations for certain programming applications.)

I especially enjoy this feature of Borland C++, as it greatly increases programmer efficiency when dealing with large programs that may involve thousands of lines of source code. It is no longer necessary to scan through many lines of code to reach the beginning of a program in order to add another declaration. This feature is certainly desirable and can be used to enhance the expressiveness of C++ source code. However, it can also be abused, producing code that is so unwieldy that it becomes nearly impossible to understand or debug. Use the declaration capabilities of C++ as a means to enhance your source code, not as a make-good for sloppy programming practices.

Placing declared variables closer to the point in the logical execution chain where they are to be used greatly aids the programmer in keeping track of variable names. The above program is a simple example of this, but if you add a couple hundred lines of code to separate the two loops in this example, you get a better idea of how valuable this asset really is. This is not to say that declarations should be made arbitrarily throughout a program, but there are many situations where, for the sake of clarity, it makes sense to make additional declarations.

The Scope Resolution Operator (::)

In C++, the scope resolution operator (::) is used to access variables that are declared outside of the current function or program but which may have a local variable of the same name. It is possible to have a global variable and a local variable with the same name and to access each as a different entity through the use of this operator. (This same operator is also used in class method function definitions.) The following program demonstrates the use of the scope resolution operator:

```
int x;  //Global Variable

void main(void)
{

     double x;    // Local variable
     x =2.65916; // Assignment to local variable
     ::x = 14; // Assignment to global variable
     // Continue with rest of program
```

The scope resolution operator in the above example indicates that the variable named x that is being accessed is not the local variable of the same name, but is, rather, the global variable *x* that has been declared outside this scope or function. This same operator is also used in class method function definitions.

Void

The void data type represents a null value. This data type is incorporated in ANSI C, although it was not in the original C programming language. Any function that does not produce a useful return is usually declared to be data type void. At first glance, it might seem ridiculous to have a type for which there are no defined values. In practice, however, void is very useful.

Most C programmers will be familiar with the void data type, because ANSI C incorporates it. In ANSI C, a function that does not have a meaningful return value still returns something. All functions return a value. The default is an integer type. Therefore, a function that is not specifically programmed to return a meaningful value will still return a random integer upon function exit. In C++ (and ANSI C as well), such a function can be declared to return a void value. This eliminates the possibility that such functions could return a useless int value.

Void can be used to define a pointer to a generic item. Prior to the introduction of void, a pointer to a character or int would be used to refer to some part of memory without having to be concerned with the type of data stored there. The original Kernighan & Ritchie version of the malloc memory allocation function returned a char pointer. Under ANSI C and C++, malloc returns a pointer of type void.

There is a significant difference in how C++ and ANSI handle the assignment of void pointers to other pointer types. For example, the simple program that follows works in ANSI C but not in C++.

```
main()
{

      void *x;
      char *y;

      x = y;
      y = x;

}
```

While this works in ANSI C, Borland C++ would signal the second assignment as a type mismatch. A pointer of type void can be assigned any type, but the reverse is not true unless the cast operator is used to coerce the void pointer to the appropriate type (char * in the above example). In C++, the last line of the code fragment should read:

```
y = (char *) x;
```

Const

In both C and C++, any value declared as constant may not be modified by the program in any way. While ANSI C does offer const values, it doesn't implement them in the same manner as C++, where const values can be used with far more flexibility. First of all, in C++, const values can be used in place of any literal constant, allowing the user to create typed constants instead of having to resort to #define to create constants that have no type information.

In ANSI C, const values are global in nature. They are visible outside of the file in which they are declared unless they are also declared static. In C++, all const values are static by default and thus must be considered local.

Enum

Enumerated data types (enum) differ slightly in C++ when compared with those in ANSI C. The enum tag name is considered a type name in C++. ANSI C defines the type of enums to be ints. In C++, each enumerated type is in its own separate type. This means that C++ does not allow for an int value to be automatically converted to an enum value; although an enum value can be used in place of an int.

To this point in the discussion, a handful of differences between C and C++ have been presented in card catalog form. The next discussion will involve other differences in a hands-on manner. This will further aid you in making the transition from C to C++.

When learning a new language, students almost never simply sit down, study the language from a book, and then begin to program from a whole-language standpoint. This doesn't make sense, and it isn't practical. Most often, a new language is learned a tiny bit at a time. After a small amount of knowledge has been garnered from a text, the learned materials are put into practice through actual programming. Through the process of trial and error, a working knowledge of the language is built slowly.

Fortunately, C programmers will move quickly into the realm of C++, learning a new extension of the original C programming language, as opposed to learning a completely different language. Borland C++ is a very attractive compiler package for this learning process, as it may be used as a standard C compiler as well. This gives the student the opportunity to "pull in" old C programs and make C++ modifications as his/her learning proceeds.

For those programmers who have used Borland C compilers in the past, Borland C++ presents a very familiar environment. As a matter of fact, users of Borland Turbo C++, Version 2.0, won't recognize any immediate differences in the Integrated Development Environment. To these users, Borland C++ might be like putting a V8 engine in an automobile that formerly contained an inline six. To all external appearances, the automobile is the same. However, the power of the vehicle is much greater.

We'll begin the step-by-step learning process here with a hands-on discussion, pointing out some additional differences between standard C and Borland C++—differences that offer some major advantages to the programmer.

Streams

One of the first features of Borland C++ of which the C programmer can take advantage is the environment's plethora of streams. A stream is an abstraction referring to any flow of data from a producer to a consumer. In programming terminology, we refer to the producer as the source and the consumer as the sink. We also use words like getting, putting, fetching, storing, reading, and writing when referring to the inputting of characters from a source or the outputting of characters to a sink.

In C++, the iostream library is often used in place of the standard input/output library, especially because of the programming ease it offers in writing to the standard output and reading from the standard input. The iostream.h header file is quite complex, but all we need be concerned with for now are two separate streams.

The first is called *cin*, which corresponds to stdin, the standard input. The second is *cout*, the iostream.h equivalent of stdout. With these two streams, a programmer can often do away completely with the more familiar standard input/output functions that have always been used for writing to and reading from the console using the ANSI C language. Certainly these functions—such as printf(), scanf(), getchar(), and puts() are still fully available in Borland C++. However, once you have grasped the simple techniques of cin and cout, you won't be using them nearly as much. Cin and cout represent an immediate improvement in programming efficiency and are so simple in their operation that they can be learned in a single, short programming session.

It is appropriate for students of a new language to begin with routines that write to the screen, because the results of these operations can be immediately visualized (as opposed to grasping a concept on a purely abstract basis). This is the method that will be used for the next series of discussions.

The following program is the old standard presented by Kernighan and Ritchie in their reference work, *The C Programming Language* (Prentice Hall, 1982). This was the first program many of us wrote when learning the original C language:

```
main()
{

      printf("hello, world\n");

}
```

This program writes the string "hello, world" to the monitor screen, followed by a newline character. To be technically accurate, the stdio.h header file should be included with this program. However, most C compilers automatically included the stdin and stdout with any programs that called such functions.

To write this program in Borland C++ using the iostream streams, the program would read:

```
#include <iostream.h>
void main(void)
{

      cout << "hello, world\n";

}
```

You can see that this program does not call a function at all. It uses the cout stream to write to the screen buffer. Stream output is accomplished with the insertion operator (<<). (This is also called the "put operator" in this application.)

In C, many operators use the same keyboard symbol. For example, the multiplicative operator (*) is also the indirection operator, the latter being used in pointer declarations and to return object values from pointers. This is also true in Borland C++, where what is commonly referred to in C as the left shift operator (<<) serves double duty as the insertion operator.

In the line:

```
cout << "hello, world\n";
```

the left operand (cout) is an object of type class ostream. This is defined in iostream.h and corresponds to the standard output. The right operand is any type for which stream output has been defined. The line above sends the quoted string to the output via cout.

At first glance, one might think that sending strings to the monitor in this fashion is very limited, because it does not offer the formatted output capabilities of printf(). This is not a completely accurate observation, although there are situations where printf() may be more appropriate. To my way of thinking, this is a bit easier in most situations than using printf(), although this function too is fully retained in Borland C++. The program statement above is far more elegant and the use of the insertion operator is a welcome improvement to the language.

In any event, writing to the stream offers many capabilities and possibilities.

The following program is written in ANSI C and will be rewritten in C++ to demonstrate the further capabilities of stream writes.

```
main()
{

        int x;

        x = 1718;

        printf("The value in x is %d\n", x);

}
```

This program uses printf() to write a string to the screen, followed by the value in int x. Using this function, it is necessary to supply the %d conversion specification, which tells printf() to convert the value in x to a decimal integer format prior to display.

A C programmer might conclude that writing to cout would be limited only to quoted string expressions, when looking at the code presented thus far. The following C++ rendition of the above program will disprove this:

```
#include <iostream.h>
void main(void)
{

        int x;

        x = 1718;

        cout << "The value in x is " << x << "\n";

}
```

This program will duplicate the screen output of the previous program. Notice that writing to the output stream does not require any conversion specifications, at least not when decimal notations are involved.

The first value written to the output is the string:

```
"The value in x is "
```

The second value is the numeric value in variable x. The variable name is preceded by another insertion operator. The last value written in this particular line is the newline character (\n), which is enclosed in quotation marks, thus making it a string.

In the above operation, three separate writes to cout have been programmed on the same line. Formatting is accomplished in a direct manner, as opposed to inserting specifiers in the original string. Overall, this will result in less input at the keyboard during the programming stage.

Before leaving (temporarily) this discussion on cout, let's present one more example of C language program for study.

```
main()
{

	int x = 14;
	double y = 2659.7861;
	char *c = "y divided by x = ";

	printf("%s%lf\n", c, y / x);

}
```

This program displays two values using printf(). The first is a string, and the second is a double-precision value based on a mathematical operation. The same thing can be accomplished with the C++ iostream in the following manner:

```
#include <iostream.h>
void main(void)
{

	int x = 14;
	double y = 2659.7861;
	char *c = "y divided by x = ";

	cout << c << y / x;

}
```

This method is far simpler and depends on no function calls to accomplish the write to the screen.

The cout stream feature offered in Borland C++ is a great aid to screen writes. It is very flexible and, to some, offers a more expressive means of accomplishing writes to the standard output without resorting to a function call and the increased complexities associated with printf().

Input Using iostream.h

While using cout is a decided advantage in programming many types of applications that write to the screen, the input features offered by iostream.h may be even more appreciated by C programmers who are moving up to Borland C++. Using the cin stream, inputting data—especially numeric values—from the keyboard is greatly expedited when compared with using C-language function calls to accomplish the same operations.

Stream input is quite similar to the output operations just discussed, but it uses the right shift operator (>>), which becomes the extractor operator in this application. The multiple use of a symbol or symbols as different operators is called overloading. Overloading still maintains the associativity of the operator.

In short, the extractor operator is a low-effort (from a code-input standpoint) alternative to the standard input function, scanf(). The latter is the main function used in the C programming language for the collection of formatted input from the keyboard. However, most C programmers use scanf() almost exclusively for single—and sometimes multiple—numeric returns from the keyboard. Often the string capture feature of this function is not utilized, as the gets() function is incorporated more often for string returns.

The cin stream is used in a format of:

```
cin >> variable
```

where the input from the keyboard is written to variable. The conversion and formatting functions in such an operation will depend on the data type of the variable. By default, >> skips whitespace, and then reads in characters appropriate to the type of the input object.

As with <<, the >> operator is left-associative and returns its left operand. This allows multiple input operations to be combined into one statement.

The following program is written in ANSI C and retrieves an int value from the keyboard:

```
main()
{
        int x;

        scanf("%d", &x);

        printf("%d\n", x);
}
```

The scanf() function is used to scan the keyboard for the integer data. The %d conversion specifier informs scanf() about the input data type to be expected within this scan field. The storage source supplied as part of the argument list to scanf() is a pointer to int x. Once the data has been retrieved and stored in x, it is displayed on the screen by the printf() function.

The Borland C++ equivalent to the above program is:

```
#include <iostream.h>
void main(void)
{

        int x;

        cin >> x;
        cout << x << "\n";

}
```

This program is simpler. It requires less input time when writing the source code, and it better expresses what is actually taking place. The cin stream is the keyboard input. The extractor operator (>>) "aims" the input to variable x. The keyboard capture is assigned to storage allocated to x. Notice that it is not necessary to supply a pointer, as would be the case with scanf().

In the next line, the value in x and the newline character are aimed at the output via cout. From both a programming and conceptual standpoints, this method of reading and writing makes a lot more sense. No conversion specifications are necessary, and the two function calls required in the C language version are done away with.

Both cin and cout allow the conceptualization of targeting. With cin, the input at the keyboard is targeted at the holding variable. In the case of cout, program data is targeted at the monitor. The choice of the operator symbols (<< and >>) reinforce this targeting concept.

Multiple inputs are handled in a logical manner, just as multiple outputs were handled by cout. The following program in C begins the discussion of multiple inputs from the keyboard:

```
main()
{

      char c[40];
      int x, y;

      gets(c);
      scanf("%d%d", &x, &y);

      printf("%c %d %d\n", c, x, y);

}
```

This program declares two int variables and a char array. The gets() function is used to retrieve a string, while scanf() is called to receive the two int values. The collected data is then displayed on the monitor by means of printf().

Using iostream.h, the Borland C++ equivalent is:

```
#include <iostream.h>
void main(void)
{

      char c[40];
      int x, y;
```

```
    cin >> c >> x >> y;
    cout << c << " " << x << " " << y;

}
```

Variables are declared in exactly the same manner as in the previous C++ program we examined. The keyboard input is targeted first at array c[], and then at int x, and finally, at int y. Like scanf(), any keyboard input that does not match the variable type being written to automatically terminates the scan of a field. Although we're not dealing with fields in the case of cin, the apparent operation is the same. A carriage return may be used as a field separator following input of the string, whereas any key other than one that produces a numeric character will stop the specific keyboard scan in regard to the integer variables. Like the gets() function, cin will accept whitespace from the keyboard and incorporate it in the string. The newline that is received as an end to the string input is replaced by a null character, as is the case with gets().

Extractors for the built-in data types fall into three categories: integer, floating-point, and string. For all numeric types, if the first non-whitespace character is not a digit or a sign (or a decimal point for floating-point conversions), the stream fails and no further input will be accepted until the error condition is corrected.

Integer Extractors

When cin is used to load data to ints and long ints, the default action of the extractor is to skip whitespace and convert to an integer value. This is done by reading input characters until one is retrieved that is not a legal part of any integer value—this would be any character other than a numeric type, including, of course, the decimal point, which is not a part of an integer value.

Floating-Point Extractors

When float or double variables are targeted by the extractor operator, whitespace is skipped and numeric characters are converted to a floating-point value. Again, all input characters are read until one is found that is not a legal part of a floating-point representation.

Iostream Conversions

So far, the prospect of using the insertion and extractor operators with cout and cin seems quite pleasant. However, there is the matter of dealing with numeric quantities in something other than decimal notation, and there is the necessity of formatting the display using the insertion operation via the addition of whitespace strings (" "). Can we obtain these features while still maintaining the ease of operation that these new operators provide? The answer is yes, and the method of doing so falls right into place with what has just been discussed.

This is a bit of a pain. The following sections address many of these concerns.

Manipulators

An easy way of changing the stream width and other format variables is to use a special function-like operator called a manipulator. Manipulators take a stream reference as an argument and return a reference to the same stream. This means that manipulators can be embedded in a chain of insertions or extractions in order to alter the format.

The following program will demonstrate the use of manipulators specifically for numbers conversion.

```
#include <iostream.h>
void main(void)
{

      int x = 25;

      cout << dec << x << " "
           << oct << x << " "
           << hex << x << "\n";

}
```

This program will display the value in x (25D) in decimal, octal, and hexadecimal bases. This could have been carried out on one continuous line, but it is stepped for clarity. When executed, this program will display:

```
25 31 19
```

These represent the decimal, octal, and hexadecimal values in x.

We already know that the default format is decimal. Therefore, the dec manipulator is not necessary. However, the immediate effect of the oct and the hex manipulators is apparent. These work in the same manner as the conversion specifications that might be supplied to a printf() function. Each of these manipulators sets a conversion base format flag and provides a convenient means of converting a value in one base to the same value in another base.

Of course, we still have some undesirable elements present in the above program. It's annoying to go to the trouble of enclosing in double quotes each whitespace that is to be displayed. The same applies to the newline character that has also been provided as a string argument.

Addressing the latter problem first: We can do something about the newline character by using another manipulator called endl. The above program can be rewritten in the following manner:

```
#include <iostream.h>
void main(void)
{

      int x = 25;

      cout << dec << x << " "
           << oct << x << " "
           << hex << x << endl;

}
```

The endl manipulator at the end of the expression inserts a newline character and flushes the stream. This takes the place of the more laborious "\n", which has the same number of characters but which requires double use of the Shift key.

In regard to the whitespace characters that must be provided as string arguments, there are several methods to handle this. However, the method I prefer is to revert to the #define preprocessor directive, as demonstrated by the final version of the previous program:

```
#include <iostream.h>
#define sp " "
void main(void)
{

      int x = 25;

      cout << dec << x << sp
           << oct << x << sp
           << hex << x << endl;

}
```

On the input side of this discussion, the manipulators may be used in the same manner. The following program accepts input of a hexadecimal value from the keyboard and then displays this value in decimal, octal, and hexadecimal format.

```
#include <iostream.h>
#define sp " "
void main(void)
{

      int x;

      cin >> hex >> x;

      cout << dec << x << sp
           << oct << x << sp
           << hex << x << endl;

}
```

In this example, the extractor operator targets the output from cin to variable x, with the hex manipulator also targeted in order to set the hexadecimal conversion base format flag. This means that the value input at the keyboard will be a hexadecimal number. This value must be input in pure hex format and without the "0x" specifier used to signify hexadecimal constants incorporated as a part of program source code. Any hex value input via the keyboard will be displayed on the screen in decimal, octal, and hexadecimal formats.

Character Extractors

When the extractor operator targets a char variable, whitespace is skipped and the first non-whitespace character is stored. When it is necessary to read the next character, whether it is whitespace or not, it is probably most prudent to use one of the *get* member functions, as in:

```
char c;
cin.get(c);
```

This operation will get the keyboard input and put the next character into char c. To write this character to the monitor, you may also use the put member function, as in:

```
cout.put(c);
```

This relates to the topic of simple file I/O, a discussion of which follows.

Simple File Operations

The C programming language may offer an unusual syntax, but its I/O functions, whether for file access, console access, or even string access, treat I/O in a very generic manner. For instance, printf(), the standard output formatted write function, is mirrored by fprintf(), the function used for formatted output to a disk file. These two functions operate in the same manner, so the transition to file writes is very easy once you know how to write to the monitor screen.

In Borland C++, the same may be said of streams, and functions, operators, and manipulators. The previous discussion dealt with writing and reading information from the console (stin/stout). We can apply the same principles to simple file I/O without resorting to what are thought of as standard filekeeping functions found in stdio.h.

The header file fstream.h declares the Borland C++ stream classes that support file input and output. The classes defined in this header file inherit the insertion operations and the extraction operations from iostream.h. The fstream.h header file provides constructors and functions for creating and handling simple file I/O. In many instances, these operations can completely take the place of the more conventional file I/O operations commonly used in standard C. These latter functions are fully available in Borland C++ as well, but it may not be necessary, in many cases, to resort to their use.

The following program is written in standard C. It opens a disk file for read operations and another file for write operations. The contents of the first file are then copied, one character at a time, into the second.

```
#include <stdio.h>
main()
{

        FILE *fp *ffp;
        int x;

        if ((fp = fopen("file_one", "r")) == NULL)
             printf("File Open Error\n");
             exit(0);

        if ((fp = fopen("file_two", "r")) == NULL)
             printf("File Open Error\n");
             exit(0);


        while ((x = fgetc(fp)) != EOF)
             fputc(x, ffp);

        fclose(fp);
        fclose(ffp);

}
```

Although this program accomplishes a very simple task, it consumes much overhead because of checking for error returns. Using the fgetc() function, data is extracted from file_one, one character at a time, and then written in the same manner to file_two. When the end-of-file (EOF) is returned, fclose() is called to close the two files.

There is a simpler way of accomplishing the same task using Borland C++. The following program #includes the fstream.h header file to gain access to files in a manner similar to accessing the standard input/output.

```
#include <fstream.h>
main()
{

     char c;

     ifstream fp("file_one");        // open file_one
     if (!fp)                        // test for bad open
          cout << "Cannot open file\n";

     ofstream ffp("file_two");       // open file_two
     if (!ffp)       // test for bad open
          cout << "Cannot open file\n";

     while (ffp && fp.get(c))        // read file_one data
          ffp.put(c);                // write file_two data

}
```

This program accomplishes exactly the same operations as the previous standard C program, but it is infinitely simpler, although the comment lines may seem to add to its visual complexity. Through the definitions in fstream.h, we use ifstream to open a file for input. The filename, "file_one," is a string argument that is tied to fp. This is the file handle. The line

```
if (!fp)
```

is a test for the successful opening of the file whose handle is fp. The not operator (!) is technically overloaded here and may be thought of in this case as "if file not open..." The timesaving aspect of using this stream method lies in the fact that errors are detected during stream I/O, and once a stream is placed in an error state, all attempts to read or write information from the stream will be ignored until the error condition is corrected. In simpler terms, this means that if the file cannot be opened, it is not necessary to directly program in an early termination, as was done with the exit() statement in the C language version. If file_one cannot be opened for any reason, no great harm is done. This is true because an error condition exists, and the file will be ignored; there will be no attempt to read information from a file that does not exist.

In discussing this program, we assume that file_one already exists and that its contents are to be read into file_two, which is yet to be created. The creation process takes place with ostream. This opens file_two and gives it a handle named ffp. Again, if the file cannot be opened, there is no chance of a write taking place. In standard C, it is mandatory that programming checks be written in source code, especially to protect against an attempted write to a file that was unsuccessfully opened. In such a case, data will be written to random parts of memory, a possible cause for machine havoc. In standard C, if a file cannot be opened, the program must be terminated to prevent a random write. Certainly, one still should check to make certain a file has been successfully opened when using the advanced streaming capabilities of Borland C++, but the C++ method discussed above avoids the possibility of a potentially disastrous write to an unopened file.

Using the stream class operators and functions in Borland C++, programmers are provided a safety valve that is not directly input into source code by the programmer.

The last line of the program incorporates a while loop that tests both file handles for a return value of zero. This signals an error condition, usually brought on by an end-of-file (EOF). Within the while clause, the expression:

```
fp.get(c)
```

is found. This uses the get() function to get the character from fp into char c. Within the loop body, the expression:

```
ffp.put(c);
```

puts the character found in char c into the second file. When all data has been read from the first file, an end-of-file condition will be returned to while and the program will terminate.

New Key Words

In order to add features to C, a number of new key words were created for C++. (Any C program that uses identifiers with the same name as these key words will have to be changed before that program can be compiled with Borland C++.) These new key words are:

asm	catch	class	delete	friend
inline	new	operator	private	protected
public	template	this	virtual	throw
try				

Type Compatibilities

C is fairly flexible when it comes to type compatibility. C++, however, is far pickier. For example, C++ defines the types short int, int, and long int as different types. Even if a short int is identical in size and format to a plain int, C++ still considers them to be different types that must be cast when those type values are assigned to one another. This is a safety precaution. Truly portable code must treat these types as being different, because various architectures may define the implementations of these types differently.

The character types are another example of types that the compiler sees as different, even though the programmer may consider them to be the same. Unsigned char, char, and signed char will each have a size equal to 1, but C++ does not consider them to be identical. In C++, the types of values must match exactly for complete compatibility, otherwise, a cast is required.

Sizeof(char)

In C, all char constants are stored as ints. This means that in C:

```
sizeof('1') == sizeof(int);
```

In C++, a single char is treated as a single byte and it is not promoted to the size of an int. So in C++:

```
sizeof('1') == 1;
```

When writing code in C++, the user needs to know the differences in the conventions of this language and those of ANSI C.

Struct and Union Tags

In C++, structs and unions are actually types of classes; they can contain both data definition and functions. However, two changes have been made in C++ that may affect existing C programs, and struct and union tags are considered to be type names, just as if they had been declared by the typedef statement. In C, we would have this code fragment:

```
struct mathe { int a; float b };
struct mathe x;
```

This declares a struct with the tag name mathe and then creates an instance of mathe named x.

In C++, things are simpler:

```
struct mathe { int a; float b };
mathe x;
```

The same conventions apply to unions. To maintain compatibility with ANSI C, C++ will accept the older syntax, but as C++ continues to evolve toward the new (formerly, C language) standard, such compatibilities may be deleted from the language.

Anonymous Unions

A special type of union called an anonymous union has been added by C++. Simply put, it declares a set of items that share the same memory address. This certainly meets the definition of a standard union in ANSI C. However, an anonymous union does not have a tag name. This means that the union elements may be accessed directly. This will mean a great savings in programmer input time when writing programs that rely heavily on unions.

The following example is written in ANSI C and uses a standard union.

```
Union test {
          int x;
          float y;
          double z;
};

void main(void)
{

     union access test;

     test.x = 14;
     test.y = 22.768;
     test.z = 0.87941899654;

}
```

While this example is not at all difficult to understand, the indirect access of union members requires a significant overhead in terms of programmer input at the keyboard.

The following program example is carried out in Borland C++ and uses an anonymous union to accomplish the same operation as that in the ANSI-C example above.

```
Union {
     int x;
     float y;
     double z;
```

```
};

void main(void)
{

    x = 14;
    y = 22.768;
    z = 0.87941899654;

}
```

Variables x, y, and z share the same memory location and data space. Unlike unions that have tags, however, anonymous union values are accessed directly.

Enum Types

Enumerated data types are supported fully in C++, but they are treated in a slightly different manner than those in ANSI C. In C++, the enum tag name is classified as a type name. Also, ANSI C considers all enums to be of type int, but in C++, each enumerated type is its own separate type. This means that C++ does not allow for an int value to be automatically converted to an enum value. However, an enumerated value can be used in place of an int. Study the following segment of code:

```
enum color { Red, Blue, Green, Amber };

int x = Green; // Used in place of an int
color screen = Red;
color background = 16; // ERROR!!!
```

While this construct would be perfectly acceptable in ANSI C, it will generate an error message in C++. This occurs because *color* is now a type name, and the numeric constant, 16, is an int data type. The way to make this work in C++ is to cast the numeric constant to the proper type, as in:

```
color background = (color) 16;
```

This will correct the problem because the value assigned to color background has been cast to type color.

While we're on the subject of casts, C++ will support the standard method of casting used in ANSI C, but an alternate method is offered:

```
color background = color(16);
```

This notation equates to exactly the same thing as the method of casting the numeric constant to integer data type. To some programmers, this method of casting will be preferred. To others, it may be confusing, due to the fact that the above construct might look more like a call to a function named color(). I prefer the earlier method, as it clearly identifies a cast operation without making the search for it and comparing enum tags with function names. Returning to the subject of enum implementation under Borland C++, we find another marked difference. The C++ environment supports the creation of anonymous enums (i.e., enums without tags). Such an entity is declared by simply leaving out the tag name. The following code segment is an example of an anonymous enum declaration.

```
enum { Red, Green, Blue, Amber };
```

Used this way, the enum constants may be referenced in the same manner as regular constants, as in:

```
int screen = Red;
int border = amber;
```

Hopefully there is little confusion on the part of the reader about this type of usage, because this equates (from a discussion standpoint) to the anonymous union which was explained earlier in this chapter.

New and Delete

In traditional C programs, all dynamic memory allocation is handled by the UNIX library functions, such as malloc() and free(). The malloc() function sets aside blocks of memory, while free() is used to release these allocated blocks. C++ defines a new method of performing dynamic memory allocation using the new and delete operators.

The following example illustrates the ANSI C method of dynamic memory allocation:

```
void main(void)
{
        int *x;

        x = (int *) malloc(sizeof(int));
        *x = 32456;

        printf("%d", *x);
        free(x);

}
```

In C++, the *new* operator can be used to completely replace the standard C function malloc(). The *delete* operator takes the place of free(). In C++, the previous function could be written as:

```
#include <iostream.h>
void main(void)
{

        int *x;

        x = new int;
        *x = 32456;

        cout << x;

        delete x;

}
```

The C++ method of using the new and delete operators is a simpler and far more direct approach to allocating and freeing up memory for the pointer.

You cannot use a constant value directly with the new operator, as in:

```
c = new 350;   //Incorrect
```

Here, the intent is to set aside 350 bytes of data referenced by the pointer c. Although it is easy to accomplish this with the new operator, the above example is incorrect, and is shown because it represents some of the attempts made by persons learning C++.

The following ANSI C program introduces a discussion that will clear this matter up:

```
/* ANSI C Version */
void main(void)
{

      char *c;

      c = (char *) malloc(350);

      gets(c);

      puts(c);

      free(c);

}
```

To accomplish the same thing in C++, the following program will suffice:

```
/* Borland C++ Version */

#include <iostream.h>
void main(void)
{

      char *c;
```

```
        c = new char[350];

        cin >> c;
        cout << c << "\n";

        delete c;

    }
```

I think the user will agree that this method of dynamic memory allocation is a vast improvement over the ANSI C method.

Note that pointer c is assigned a value of

```
new char[350]
```

This means that total memory allocation will be

```
350 X char
```

or 350 times the number of bytes allocated to a char data type. In most MS-DOS applications, a char is usually allocated 1 byte of storage, so here, a total of 350 x 1 bytes, or 350 bytes, will be allocated.

On the other hand, if the assignment line had been written as

```
c = new int[350]
```

then a total of 700 bytes (350 x 2) would be allocated, assuming that 2bytes are allocated to an int data type.

If new cannot allocate the requested amount of memory, its return value is NULL. This is just like a malloc call, which also returns NULL when a heap error occurs. The above examples are as simple as possible and do not include checks for the NULL return. However, programming practice requires such checks to avoid memory overwrites. A simple check can be made using an if statement, as in:

```
if ((c = new char[350]) == NULL)
     exit(0);
```

The new and delete operators have been added to C++ in order to gain better flexibility for the programmer. Any class can use operator overloading to define its own versions of new and delete. If a class does not define new and/or delete, the default global versions of those operators are used. This allows a class to define its own memory allocation functions for special applications.

Because the new and delete operators can take the place of malloc() and calloc() in the standard function set, and because these operators offer a simpler and more direct approach, it makes sense to use them exclusively. In fact, a problem can arise when mixing the dynamic memory functions with new and delete. It is possible to create custom versions of new and delete on a global, or class, level. A custom memory allocator based on new and delete will probably not use the same memory management techniques as the C library functions. Therefore, if new and delete are replaced, you won't be able to use realloc, malloc, or free with the C++ memory allocators.

In general, it's best to stay with either the C functions (malloc, etc.) or the new and delete C++ operators. Trying to use both dynamic management systems can lead to all sorts of problems and inconsistencies. Also, it tends to make the program confusing when, for example, both malloc and new are used to create objects on the heap.

Functions in C++

While the adoption of the ANSI C standard changed the way many programmers thought about functions, C++ goes a bit farther in improving the programming and calling conventions of these entities. Most of the changes and additions are straightforward, simple, and logical. Many of the function conventions modifications common to C++ were formed through the logical necessity of addressing the object-oriented nature of this new language. They also provide more built-in protection than their ANSI C counterparts while maintaining a high degree of source-code comprehension on the part of the programmer or others who may view the code.

ANSI C does not define a specific format for the main() function.

In many programming applications, there is no concern about returning any sort of status to the operating system. C++, however, explicitly defines main as matching one of the two following prototypes:

```
int main();
int main(int argc, char * argv[]);
```

Because C++ forces main to have a return value, it's good programming practice to actually return a value from main. Simply allowing a program to end by reaching the end of main will result in the return of a random value. Even if the program has no informative return value, having an explicit return 0 statement where the program exits main will indicate that it was successful.

Function Prototypes

C programmers who use any of the modern C compilers have already encountered function prototypes. ANSI C borrowed the concept of function prototypes from C++. A function prototype is a declaration that defines both the return type and the parameters of a function. In ANSI C, functions are declared in the following manner:

```
int funct();
```

Notice that this declaration says nothing about the types of parameters accepted by the function. In pre-ANSI C, a function declaration merely defined the return value type for a function.

In C++, funct() would be declared using a statement like this:

```
int funct(char *c, int i);
```

This means that funct() is a function returning an int value with two parameters: a pointer to a character and an int. The compiler uses the prototype to ensure that the types of arguments passed in a function call are the same as the types of the corresponding parameters. This is known as strong-type checking, something that pre-ANSI C lacked.

Without strong-type checking, it's easier to pass illegal values to functions. A non-prototyped function will allow you to send an int argument to a pointer parameter or to use a float argument when a function expects a long argument. These kinds of errors result in invalid values for the function parameters.

Unlike ANSI C, which permits the use of function prototypes, C++ requires them. In C++, prototypes do more than make sure that arguments and parameters match. An error message is generated if the compiler detects a function that does not contain a prototype either in the program or function proper or in a header file #included with the program or function. C++ internally generates names for functions, including parameter information. The parameter information is used when several functions have the same name.

In the function prototype for funct(), the parameter tags *c* and *i* are not stored in the symbol table, nor do they need to match the names of the corresponding parameters in the function definition. They are present solely to document the purpose of the parameters. They describe what the function parameter is expecting for an argument.

Functions with an unspecified number of parameters of unknown types are declared differently in C++.

To compare, let's consider these two C prototypes:

```
/* C Language Methodology */
int test(void); /* function accepting no parameters */
int func1(); /* function with open parameter list */
```

In C++, you can leave out the void and use a set of empty parameters instead, as shown below:

```
// C++ Methodology
int test(); // function accepting no parameters
int func1(...); // function w/ open parameter list
```

A C++ function that has an empty parameter list cannot accept arguments. In order to have an "open" parameter list, you need to use the ellipses (...).

Again, all C++ functions must be prototyped. This means every function must have its argument list declared, and the actual definition of a function must exactly match its prototype in the number and types of parameters.

Prototyping functions dictate additional work on the part of the programmer when new source code is initially written, but prototypes are invaluable tools in preventing hard-to-find errors. These errors are the ones that may require hours, days, or even weeks of debugging (although the Turbo Debugger included with Borland C++ may be able to cut this time considerably).

Quite frankly, many persons who entered the C programming world initially were sloppy programmers. The C language taught many of us how not to continue this sloppiness, but this was through a route of endless hours of frustration. Many programs executed, but produced unorthodox results. Such occurrences were the result of doing something like passing an int argument to a function that required a double, or vice versa. The original C language served as a training environment by being as rigid as possible and requiring the student to decipher his/her mistakes, often through a long process of trial and elimination. ANSI C took some additional steps in the area of addressing sloppy programming. This was better, but still not good enough. C++ is expressly designed to prevent many of the problems caused by sloppy programmers passing the wrong argument type(s) to functions.

Prototype-like Function Headers

Those of you who began your C programming career working with Kernighan & Ritchie's C-language reference are accustomed to writing functions in the following manner:

```
double multid(i, d)
int i:
double d:
{

      return (d / i);


}
```

While C++ will accept this form, it's considered better programming practice to use a prototype-like format for the function header. Rewriting the above function in proper C++ format would yield the following function:

```
double multid(int i, double d)
{

      return( d / i);


}
```

The C++ style is far more expressive than the now-archaic earlier style. In future versions of Borland C++ and other C++ compilers, the C syntax regarding function definitions may be dropped altogether.

References

One unpleasant aspect of ANSI C is its tendency to be clumsy at times in the hands of clumsy programmers. For example, if you want to write a function that swaps the values of a pair of integers, you could write it like this:

```
void swapint
int *i, *h)
{

      int temp;

      temp = *i;
      *i = *h;
      *h = temp;

}
```

This is the classic example of a swap function first discussed by Kernighan and Ritchie in their *C Programming Language* (Prentice Hall, 1982). Because the purpose of this function is to actually change the values in its argument list, it is mandatory that these arguments be passed to the function as pointers. The call would involve the following program statement in ANSI C:

```
swapint(&x, &y);
```

where variables x and y have been previously declared as int types. The address-of operator preceding each variable name passes a pointer to that variable's storage address to the swapint() function. A prime example of misusing this function involves passing variable values, as in

```
swapint(x, y);
```

Neither is it unheard of for an experienced C programmer to make the same mistake after a long session of grueling programming when the mind may tend to play tricks; it is easy to make such a mistake. In standard C language, this would not result in an error message upon compilation and linking, but the function would not do what is intended to. This example is an error, but the C compiler will not catch it.

Fortunately, C++ helps to overcome such simple (but expensive) mistakes because this language supports a special identifier called a reference. A reference is an alias for another identifier. References can make functions that change the values of their parameters much more elegant. A Borland C++ version of swapint would be:

```
void swapint(int &i, int &h)
{

      int temp;

      temp = i;
      i = h;
      h = temp;

}
```

A reference is indicated by using the address-of (&) operator in the same manner as the indirection operator (*) to indicate a pointer. The difference between a pointer to something and a reference to something is that the pointer needs to be dereferenced and the reference does not. The de-referencing in ANSI C requires the use of the indirection operator to access the object at the memory address contained in the pointer. Because h is a pointer, *h accesses the object at the address contained in the pointer. The Borland C++ version of swapint() does not need to de-reference the i and h in order to change the values of the arguments.

As you can see in the following example, the calling syntax is much simpler too:

```
swapint(x, y);
```

where x and y are standard int data types. Using the C++ reference means that the addresses of variables x and y are automatically passed as arguments to the swapint function.

References are particularly useful when passing large structures and objects to a function. By using a reference for a parameter, only the address is passed, not the entire structure or object. This not only saves time and stack space, but it also makes using the structure/object parameters easier within the function itself.

While references may seem similar to pointers, they are not pointers. They cannot be used to allocate dynamic memory, nor can they be manipulated mathematically. The purpose of references is to make it possible to write functions that change their arguments, as well as to create functions that accept structures and objects as parameters.

Name Mangling

When a C++ module is compiled, function names are generated by the compiler. Such names are comprised of an encoding of the argument types that apply to the function. This process goes by the dubious title of "name mangling" and is what allows the overloading of a function in a C++ program. All the name changes are internal and entail appending parameter information to the function identifier. When a function is overloaded, one name may be used to identify several different functions. The compiler actually changes their names so that each is a discrete entity. Again, this differentiation is made by the compiler and is totally transparent to the programmer. The same process occurs when operators are overloaded.

Inline Functions

In properly written ANSI-C programs, functions are called to provide program structure. Here, what might be called discrete operations are programmed as self-contained code blocks or functions. As useful as functions are, they do impose certain constraints on the overall operation. Arguments to functions must be pushed onto the stack prior to a function call. Next, the call must be executed and the function return value made. This would be followed by the removal of the function parameters from the stack. Owing to the overhead involved in a function call, it is sometimes necessary to duplicate code throughout a program in order to increase efficiency.

This problem may be partially or wholly overcome through the use of the C++ inline function. When a function definition header is preceded by *inline*, that function is not compiled in the same manner as standard functions. Rather, the function code is compiled and inserted into the program wherever a call to that function appears. If the function is used ten times, then the code for this function appears in the program ten times, instead of just once as would be the case with a standard function. This use of the C++ inline eliminates function overhead while still allowing a program to be organized in a structured manner.

Now, if the method of implementing an inline function sounds similar to a preprocessor #define, you're drawing a good parallel. An inline function does not exist as a discrete, callable routine, as is the case with standard functions. It truly is a block of source code. Whenever an inline function is called in a program, the compiled source code for this function is inserted at the call point in the executable program. When compiling a program that uses inline functions, the source code for the function is inserted by the compiler as though it had been placed there in its entirety by the programmer. The following program examples will explain this further:

```
#include <stdio.h>
inline void prnt2sum(int x, int y)
{
      int temp = (x + y) * 2;
      printf("%d\n", temp);

}
void main(void)
{
```

```
        int a, b;

        a = 10;
        b = 20;

        prnt2sum(a, b);

        a = 13;
        b = 8;

        prnt2sum(a, b);

}
```

The inline function named add() simply returns the sum of its two int arguments. This program is certainly a structured program in that functions are used to break the program down into modules. To the programmer examining this source code, there is no difference between the structures of an inline and a standard function. However, when this program is compiled, the following source code is similar to what the compiler does with the inline function:

```
void main(void)
{

        int a, b;

        a = 10;
        b = 20;

        int temp = (a + b) * 2;
        printf("%d\n", temp);

        a = 13;
        b = 8;

        int temp = (a + b) * 2;
        printf("%d\n", temp);


}
```

Admittedly, prnt2sum is a ridiculous function that adds its two arguments, multiplies them by 2 and then writes this value to the screen, but it serves as an example for explaining inline functions. Again, the inline function can be closely equated with a #define preprocessor definition. Naturally, inline functions will increase the size of the compiled program, but this increase is offset by a decrease in processing overhead.

All inline functions must be defined before they are used, due to the obvious fact that their source code must be precompiled before it can be inserted into the program.

As was alluded to earlier, the major drawback when using inline functions is the inherent increase in program size. Simple functions, such as prnt2sum, lend themselves well to inline definitions, but complex inline functions can contain critically large amounts of code. It is necessary for the programmer to be aware of the program size overhead that is a natural by-product of inline functions. In some instances and with some functions, inline definitions are the logical way to go. In other cases, it's simply not worth the program-size overhead to obtain a minimal amount of execution-speed increase. If a program is bogging down in the area of execution speed, it's a simple task to redeclare as inline any suspect functions. It is also necessary to physically move the source code of these functions to a point in the program prior to the function being called. Recompile the program and see what results. If a desirable speed increase is obtained and the program size is not overly burdensome, then the program may be left as is. However, if the desired effects do not result, then the program may be returned to its original state.

As you work with inline functions, you will gain knowledge that will allow you to immediately identify situations and functions that lend themselves readily to inline definitions. Your particular programming style will have a great influence on when and where inline functions are to be utilized. Generally speaking, small functions that are called often will be prime candidates for inline definitions, but this rule will not apply in every case. Often, in classes that define a large number of transient objects, inline constructors and destructors can generate a significantly faster program. Again, it is up to the programmer to analyze the functions in a program to determine which are simple enough and called often enough to be inline functions.

There is a finite limit on the number of inline functions that can be accommodated in a program. The inline key word means that the function will be an inline type only if it can be accommodated. In other words, using the inline key word does not necessarily mean that a particular function will be incorporated as an inline type. It will be if possible. If not, it will be invoked as a standard function. The compiler can ignore inline if and when it finds it necessary to do so. If a program calls too many inline functions, it will stop inlining functions when it runs short on memory. Long inline functions, even those that lack control structures, may be compiled as regular functions. In every case, recursive functions (functions that call themselves) cannot be made inline.

Setting Default Values for Function Arguments

One extremely useful programming feature that C++ offers is that of defining default values for function arguments. In ANSI C, a function that expects an argument must receive one or an error occurs, either upon compilation or when the function is actually executed. This is as it should be in most instances; however, with some assignments, the programming task could be sped up if somehow the compiler were told that if an argument is not provided, it should default to some predetermined value. Borland C++ does this in a very direct manner.

To begin our discussion of default function argument values, examine the following function source code:

```
void beep(int num)
{

    int x, y;
    for (x = 0; x < num; ++x) //number of beeps
        printf("%c", 7); // Beep
        for (y = 0; y < 20000; ++y) //delay
            ;

}
```

This function causes the beep character (ASCII 7) to be written to the console, broadcasting a 1000-Htz tone from the computer speaker. The function accepts an int argument that determines the number of times the beep is sounded. Each time beep() is called, it must be handed an argument to determine the number of beeps that are to be sounded. When using this function in a program, it might be found that only one beep is required in most situations, and it becomes bothersome to constantly supply an argument of 1 in such cases. The solution might be to write a new function called beep1() that requires no argument (void) and will sound a single beep each time it is called. The original beep() function would be called only when numerous beeps are required. However, it is quite practical to use the original beep() function by utilizing the default argument value feature of C++.

Regardless of how the function code is written, in C++ it is mandatory to supply a function prototype prior to beep() being called. The following program calls beep() in the proper manner:

```
#include <stdio.h>

void beep(int num); // beep() prototype
void main(void)
{

      beep(10);

}
void beep(int num)
{

      int x, y;
      for (x = 0; x < num; ++x) //number of beeps
            printf("%c", 7); // Beep
            for (y = 0; y < 20000; ++y) //delay
                  ;

}
```

This program will call beep() to sound 10 beeps.

Now, back to the original problem of supplying an argument to beep(). Because it has been determined that most of the time beep() is called with an argument value of 1, it would facilitate programming if we could somehow tell the function to sound only a single beep if it is supplied no argument, (or, on the other hand) if an argument is supplied, it is to be incorporated into the function. The following program does just this and requires only a single, mundane change to the example above:

```
#include <stdio.h>

void beep(int num = 1); // Default Value prototype
void main(void)
{

      beep();
      beep(10);

}
void beep(int num)
{

      int x, y;
      for (x = 0; x < num; ++x) //number of beeps
            printf("%c", 7); // Beep
            for (y = 0; y < 20000; ++y) //delay
                  ;

}
```

The only change made here (other than an added call in the program block under main()) is the prototype. Here, a value of 1 is assigned as the default for num. This means that any time beep() is called WITHOUT an argument, the default value of 1 will be in effect. In the executable portion of the program, beep() has been called twice. The first call does not pass an argument to the function, therefore the default value of 1 is, in effect, handed to beep(). The second time this same function is called, an argument value of 10 is handed to beep(). This value is incorporated into the function actions.

The result of this simple change to the beep() prototype is that a default value is assigned to the function to be used only in the event that it is called without an argument. The function now accommodates the programmer's preference. It becomes a multiuse function because of the addition of the default value in the prototype.

Remember, setting the default value is accomplished in the function prototype and not in the function definition proper. The Borland C++ compiler will use the function prototype to build a call in the event that the function is called without an argument.

While the previous example shows a function that requires only a single argument, defaults may be as easily established for functions that must be handed multiple arguments. There are some specific rules for such operations, however. In functions that have more than one default parameter, parameters must be grouped consecutively as the only arguments for a function. Alternately, a function may be default prototyped to address some of its argument parameters while allowing others to remain in the non-default (i.e., must have an argument) mode. In this latter instance, the syntax rules are very strict. Examine the following examples in order to see just how multiple defaults may be handled:

```
float trap(int i = 3, int j - 6, double d = 8.239124);
```

This is a multiple default prototype. All argument parameters contain default assignments. This is perfectly legal. The modification that follows is not:

```
float trap(int i = 3, int j, double d = 8.239124);
```

The above example is illegal, because the center parameter is not defaulted *and* the one on the far left is. All parameter defaulting moves from right to left in the argument parameter list. Once there is a break in the default chain (again, from right to left), no further default values may be applied. If we change the above prototype to:

```
float trap(int i, int j, double d = 8.239124);
```

then the prototype is legal again. Note that the default value formerly applied to the first argument parameter has been dropped. This means that the first two arguments to trap() require arguments, while the last one will default if an argument is not provided in the call.

If the last parameter in the above example (or any other) does not contain a default value, then none of the parameters may contain defaults. Remember, when providing multiple default values to a function prototype, you must move from right to left and in sequence. As soon as a parameter is reached that is not given a default value, no others to the left of this parameter may be assigned defaults.

The flexibility of this ability to provide multiple defaults to functions requiring multiple arguments can easily be negated by the confusion generated when many functions of this type are called in a complex program. If all arguments contain default values, the probability of confusion diminishes somewhat. However, when a function is prototyped with some of its parameters containing defaults and some not, the possibility of confusion is magnified.

To explain further, consider the following function prototype:

```
int func(int a, int b = 10, int c = 2, int d = 4, int e = 15);
```

This function has five argument parameters, four of which contain defaults. The following call is legal:

```
func(4, 6, 1, 8, 9);
```

It is legal because each of the five argument parameters do contain arguments in this call. The following call is also legal:

```
func(2);
```

The single constant value will be applied to int *a*, the only argument that did not have a default value. Since this is the only argument provided in the call, the remaining four parameters will be assigned default values.

```
func(2, 4);
func(2, 4, 9);
func(2, 4, 9, 7);
```

All of these are also legal. Whenever an argument is missing, the default value will apply.

The following call is illegal:

```
funct();
```

This is so, because int a in the prototype does not contain a default value. Therefore, this parameter has not been addressed and, because no default value has been provided, the function has been called without the necessary argument(s).

Default arguments can make programs easier to write and maintain. For example, if you have an existing function that needs to have new parameters added, you can use default arguments for these new parameters. This alleviates the need to change existing code. Default arguments can also be used to combine similar functions into one.

Type-safe Linkage

In C, there are no provisions for handling linkage with object modules created by other programming languages. For example, Pascal and FORTRAN generally order parameters on the stack in the opposite order from that used by C. Most Pascal compilers convert all identifiers to uppercase, while C compilers allow both upper- and lowercase. In order to allow multilanguage programming, C compiler designers have added several new key words to identify the calling convention of a particular function or identifier. In many MS-DOS C compilers, the key word "pascal" can be added to the declaration of a function to identify this function as one that uses the Pascal calling sequence. For example:

```
pascal double dbladd(double x, double y);
```

is the prototype for a function named dbladd() that uses Pascal calling conventions. A major drawback to special language key words is that they aren't officially standardized. This could mean compatibility problems in the future and even for the present.

Function Overloading

In ANSI C and most other computer languages, each function is a single entity with a unique name. Most programmers find nothing unusual or restricting about this feature. However, this can be attributed more to a situation of "that's how it has always been" as opposed to a true assessment of the single name rule. There are times when the "one function/one name" aspect of ANSI C can hinder efficient programming by adding unnecessary work for the programmer. As an example, ANSI C has several functions that return the absolute value of a numeric argument. Each of these functions has a different name to reflect the type of numeric value that is returned.

Consider the following set of functions:

```
int sqi(int i)
{

     return(i * i);

}

long sql(long l)
{

     return(l * l);

}

double sqd(double d)
{

     return(d * d);

}
```

The purpose of each function is to return the square of its argument. Three functions are needed, because each is designed to return a different data type and each accepts a different data type as its argument. This is an extremely simple function set, and it seems wasteful to have to call three different functions for such a simple operation. ANSI C would require this type of calling routine. However, C++ does not. In C++, all three functions could be given the same name. Let's assume that the functions above are to be included in a program, and all three are named sq(). All other factors remain the same. The following program will call each of the three functions by the same name:

```
#include <stdio.h>

int sq(int i);
long sq(long l);
double sq(double d);

void main(void)
{

        int x;
        long y;
        double z;

        x = sq(4);
        y = sq(33000);
        z = sq(3.3);

        printf(%d  %ld  %lf\n", x, y, z);

}
int sq(int i)
{

        return(i * i);

}
long sq(long l)
{

        return(l * l);

}
double sq(double d)
```

```
{
     return(d * d);
}
```

This program calls the three different functions whose source code was listed earlier. Again, the only alteration made to the original source code is to change the name of each function to sq().

This program takes advantage of function overloading in C++. The function prototypes specify their return and argument types for each function. This is all the information that Borland C++ needs in order to determine which function is to be called. Borland C++ makes this determination by argument evaluation: If the three-fold function named sq() is called with an int argument, then the function that was originally named sqi() is accessed. Arguments to sq() of type long or type double access the functions formerly named sql() and sqd(), respectively.

In C++, the programmer need not be concerned with function name selection, as the compiler will determine which function is to be accessed. All the programmer need remember is that sq() is a function that returns the square of its argument. Of course, it is absolutely essential that the programmer be aware of the return expected in order for this value to be utilized by the remainder of the program. In the above example, the function returns are assigned to common variables that serve as arguments to printf() for screen display. However, function overloading in no way relieves the programmer of the responsibility of data type knowledge. Overloading simply eliminates the need to use different function names for each function in a group that is established only to address different data types.

If an overloaded function exists having parameters identical to those of the arguments being passed in the call, that particular implementation is accessed. Otherwise, the compiler calls the implementation that provides the easiest series of conversions.

Because all of the argument parameters are "tested" when determining which implementation of an overloaded function name is to be used, the number of arguments can also be an identifying factor. The following program serves as an example:

```
#include <stdio.h>

int sq(int i);
int sq(int i, int j);

main()
{

     printf("%d\n", sq(4));
     printf("%d\n", sq(4, 6));

}

int sq(int i)
{

     return(i * i);

}
int sq(int i, int j)
{

     int temp = i + j;

     return(temp * temp);

}
```

In this program, sq() has been changed a bit. Both functions (seen at the bottom of the program) return a value of type int and accept int arguments. However, the first version accepts only a single argument. Its square is returned. The second version accepts two arguments, both ints. The two are added within the function, which then returns the square of the sum of the two.

The prototypes for sq() that lead the program serve as the reference for the compiler to determine which implementation of sq() is to be called. Since both implementations return an int and both accept int data types for arguments, the determining factor is the number of arguments. If sq() is called with one argument, then the first implementation is used. When called with two arguments, the second implementation of sq() is used. The programmer now has the option of accessing an overloaded function based upon the number of arguments provided in the original call.

Function overloading is not a universal panacea for the many inconveniences programmers experience; there are practical and built-in limitations as to how far this can go and when overloading is proper. The following set of functions demonstrates this:

```
int getnum(void)
{

    int temp;

    cin >> temp;

    return(temp);

}

double getnum(void)
{

    double temp;

    cin >> temp;

    return(temp);

}
```

The idea here is to use a single function name to retrieve two different data types from the keyboard. The prototypes are:

```
int getnum(void);
double getnum(void);
```

Both of the functions above have void arguments. If you try this in a program, Borland C++ will error out and tell you that it can't distinguish between the two functions. This reveals the fact that the return value has nothing to do with the identification of overloaded functions. Overloaded functions must differ in ways other than their return type.

Another incorrect example is shown below by revisions to the sq() function set discussed earlier.

```
int sq(int i)
{

      return(i * i);

}


double sq(int i)
{

      return ((double) i * i);

}
```

The prototypes would read:

```
int sq(int i);
double sq(int i);
```

This won't work, because there would be no way for the compiler to know which implementation of the function was called. It is mandatory that overloaded functions differ in the type and/or number of parameters they accept. The key to identifying functions that can be overloaded lies in the argument parameters and not in the return type, becausethe C language and C++ may choose to ignore the return data type. Don't try to use a typedef to get around the rule of different arguments (in type or number) for overloaded functions. Even if a new name is defined as a data type, this doesn't change the rule. If typedef is used to define *dec* as a replacement for type int, the compiler will still see *dec* as an int declaration wherever it is used. A function that uses an argument of *int i* will not be classified as being different from another function of the same name with an argument parameter of *dec i*. They both will equate to *int i*, and the compiler will not be able to differentiate between the two. An error will occur on compilation.

You should always think of function overloading in Borland C++ as a "luxury" feature, one that is used sparingly and where appropriate. Function overloading has been put to some atrocious uses, completely wrecking source-code comprehension. Remember, function overloading is a logical method of calling several functions that do basically the same thing by the same name.

Unfortunately, there is nothing to stop programmers from overloading two completely diverse functions. The following function group is an example of bad programming practice:

```
int sq(int i)
{

     return(i * i);

}

void sq(double d)
{

     printf("%lf\n", d);

}
```

The first implementation of sq() returns the square of the int argument as an int. The second implementation displays the double precision value of its argument on the screen and returns void (nothing). These two functions have nothing in common, and there is no reason whatsoever for overloading. Instead of making the programmer's job easier, this is more complex and leaves room for more errors. In the above example, the programmer must remember that if he/she calls sq() with an int argument, the square of this value will be returned. However, if sq() is called with a double-precision floating-point argument, the value will be displayed on the screen. There is neither rhyme nor reason to the association of these two functions. Again, this is an example of bad programming, and it generally should not be emulated in actual programming tasks.

There *is* one area of programming that might make excellent use of function overloading for the pure purpose of creating confusion: software development of a nature that mandates secrecy or security. This would apply especially where portions of programs must be sent to separate development teams for evaluation and testing. The author has used the convenience of function overloading while software was in the development stage and had to be farmed out to several other developers to see how certain modules meshed with others that had been written by separate teams. All function source code was precompiled into library files. The calling routines formed the portion of the code that was intentionally masked.

The following program serves as a simple example of the confusion that can be purposely built into source code:

```
#include <stdio.h>
#include <math.h>

int printf(int i);
double printf(double d);

void main(void)
{

	int x;
	double y;

	printf("Example of purposely convoluted source code\n");
	x = printf(-12);
	y = printf(6.667);
	printf("%d %lf\n", x, y);

}
```

This program is quite simple and it may be possible to decipher some of what is happening regarding the overloading. Remember, the function source code may be contained in a precompiled module that cannot be deciphered quickly. Knowing the contents of the source code that makes up the functions would be a big help, but if you imagine that this program contains hundreds of lines with nearly every function call using the printf() name, you can begin to imagine the confusion that would be generated.

The above program overloads printf() through three implementations. The original use is defined in the stdio.h header file. The other two uses involve returning the absolute value of an integer(int argument) and returning the square root of a double argument.

Again, function overloading is used 99 percent of the time to call functions that perform similar operations by a single name. Overloading should not be used in a sloppy manner, because it will cause great confusion. Remember, overloaded functions should be a part of a function group, all of which perform the same basic operation(s).

Operator Overloading

A major advantage of C++ is found in a special feature, common to few other programming languages. Operator overloading allows existing operators to be given new definitions, allowing them to perform operations in a user-defined manner. Earlier in this chapter, operator overloading was discussed in regard to those operators that serve multipurpose roles as part of the normal operation of C++. These, however, were predefined as an integral part of the language. The current discussion will center around user-defined operator overloading.

Few programmers consciously realize just how valuable operators are. The mathematical operators such as +, -, *, and / actually represent predefined actions that are carried out through functions. Languages that do not allow for such operators are forced to perform such mathematical operations by means of function calls.

The simple ANSI C assignment line

```
c = a + b;
```

depends on the addition operator to call up a function that will add the values in the two variables and return this sum to the third. Without these operators, the above assignment might look like

```
c = add(a, b);
```

Even the assignment operator (=) performs a relatively complex function by writing the object value into the memory location assigned to a variable.

It is also important to realize that we tend to think of the operators we use most as non-type-specific. In the line above using the addition operator, it makes no difference whether variables *a* and *b* are floats, longs, doubles, chars, or ints. The function would be far more sensitive. The code that is generated by c = a + b—where *a*, *b*, and *c* are int data types—will be quite different than would be the case if the three variables were doubles.

When working with structures and new data types in ANSI C, even simple operations may be quite clumsy. It is in this area that overloaded operators in C++ can be packaged to allow the programmer a more direct approach. The following ANSI C program begins this discussion:

```
#include <stdio.h>
#include <math.h>

struct raise {
     double a;
};


void main(void)
{

     raise x, y, z;

     x.a = 4.15;
     y.a = 6.58;
     z.a = pow(x.a, y.a);
```

```
    printf("%lf\n", z.a);

}
```

This program uses a structure with a single member, assigns values to the member and manipulates these values mathematically. While this is an extremely simple program, member access requires the member-of operator(.) which entails additional work on the part of the programmer when compared with handling standard variables. If the structure were more complex, containing many members, access overhead would be increased substantially.

The following program in C++ accomplishes the same thing but overloads the bitwise exclusive OR operator (^) to perform the *raise-to* operation via the pow() function:

```
#include <stdio.h>
#include <math.h> struct raise {
    double a;
};

raise operator ^ (raise d, raise dd);
void print(raise d);

void main(void)
{

    raise x, y, z;

    x.a = 4.15;
    y.a = 6.58;
    z = x ^ y;

    printf("%lf\n", z.a);
}

raise operator ^ (raise i, raise j)
{

    raise templ;
```

```
        templ.a = pow(i.a, j.a);

        return(templ);
    }
```

The ^ symbol becomes a user-defined operator by using the *operator* key word. The ^ operator is defined as the function that appears at the bottom of the program. To define the operator, the *operator* key word is first used in a manner of:

```
raise operator ^ (raise d, raise dd);
```

where *raise* is the struct label or new data type. This tells the compiler that ^ is an operator of type *raise* and prototypes the arguments to the function that is of the same type. The source code of the function reads:

```
raise operator ^ (raise i, raise j)
{

        raise templ;

        templ.a = pow(i.a, j.a);

        return(templ);
}
```

In the program, the expression x ^ a equates to the return value from the function. While a special function had to be written to call pow() for the desired result, the actual manipulation of the structure member is simplified. In this usage, the ^ symbol now becomes the raise-to operator (as it is used in BASIC); however, this operator applies only to data of type *raise*. For all other operations, it is still the exclusive OR operator unless otherwise overloaded.

Again the operator key word is used in declaring the function. Effectively, this operator is now the function. When it is used in the program, its operands will be passed to the function. What has been accomplished here is the ability to handle nonintrinsic data types with operators. For many programmers, this results in a more natural programming style, one less fraught with complexities.

The above example of overloading the exclusive-OR operator to serve as the exponentiation operator is probably bad practice if used as an example for other types of overloading. For the most part, overloaded operators should stick to the general operations they exhibit as intrinsic operators. While there is a parallel between the ^ symbol and exponentiation, this requires comparison to another programming language (BASIC).

By the same token, we can make the addition operator and overloaded subtraction operator quite legally in C++. But what purpose would that serve? The end result is likely to be mass confusion. This is a factor that operator overloading is designed to eliminate, although overloading can be misused to a point where entire programs are totally convoluted.

The earlier example used a structure with only a single member. The following ANSI-C program adds additional members and operations:

```
#include <stdio.h>

struct test{
     int a, b, c;

};

test assign (int i, int j, int k);
test add(test i, test j);
test sub(test i, test j);
test mult(test i, test j);
void print(test t);

void main(void)
{

     test x, y, z;

     x = assign(4, 6, -7);
     y = assign(21, 3, 8);
```

```
        z = add(x, y);
        print(z);

        z = mult(x, y);
        print(z);

        z = sub(x, y);
        print(z);

}
void print(test t)
{

        printf("%d  %d  %d\n", t.a, t.b, t.c);

}

test add(test d, test e)
{

        test temp1;

        temp1.a = d.a +     e.a;
        temp1.b = d.b +     e.b;
        temp1.c = d.c +     e.c;

        return(temp1);

}

test sub(test d, test e)
{

        test temp1;

        temp1.a = d.a -     e.a;
        temp1.b = d.b -     e.b;
        temp1.c = d.c -     e.c;

        return(temp1);
```

```
}

test mult(test d, test e)
{

     test templ;

     templ.a = d.a *     e.a;
     templ.b = d.b *     e.b;
     templ.c = d.c *     e.c;

     return(templ);

}

test assign(int i, int j, int k)
{

     test templ;

     templ.a = i;
     templ.b = j;
     templ.c = k;

     return(templ);

}
```

This program uses a structure with three members of type int. Five functions have been written to manipulate data in this structure. This overcomes the use of the member-of operator in the calling program and makes things a bit simpler after the functions have been written. The functions are logically named, in that assign() assigns values to all structure members, whereas add(), sub(), and mult() all perform mathematical operations on the group of members. The print() function simply displays all three values on the monitor screen.

This is an efficient means of handling the multimember structure; however, some programmers may see a drawback in the fact that simple math operations must be carried out via function calls. Wouldn't it be nice to handle the math in an operator-oriented manner? This is where C++ comes to the rescue with operator overloading. The following C++ program produces output identical to the previous program, but operator overloading is provided to allow for the mathematical manipulation of the structure data in a more straightforward manner.

```
#include <stdio.h>

struct test{
     int a, b, c;

};

test assign (int i, int j, int k);
test operator + (test i, test j);
test operator -(test i, test j);
test operator * (test i, test j);
void print(test t);

void main(void)
{

     test x, y, z;

     x = assign(4, 6, -7);
     y = assign(21, 3, 8);

     z = x + y;
     print(z);

     z = x * y;
     print(z);

     z = x - y;
     print(z);

}
void print(test t)
{
```

```
    printf("%d  %d  %d\n", t.a, t.b, t.c);

}

test operator + (test d, test e)
{

    test temp1;

    temp1.a = d.a +     e.a;
    temp1.b = d.b +     e.b;
    temp1.c = d.c +     e.c;

    return(temp1);

}

test operator - (test d, test e)
{

    test temp1;

    temp1.a = d.a -     e.a;
    temp1.b = d.b -     e.b;
    temp1.c = d.c -     e.c;

    return(temp1);

}

test operator * (test d, test e)
{

    test temp1;

    temp1.a = d.a *     e.a;
    temp1.b = d.b *     e.b;
    temp1.c = d.c *     e.c;

    return(temp1);
```

```
}

test assign(int i, int j, int k)
{

      test templ;

      templ.a = i;
      templ.b = j;
      templ.c = k;

      return(templ);

}
```

Very few changes have been made to the original program. The operator key word is used to prototype the functions, and the function headers have been altered in the same manner. Within the program, the mathematical functions have been replaced with the common math operators, now overloaded to address the special requirements of the test structure data. The +, -, and * symbols are no longer the addition, subtraction, and multiplicative operators in this usage; they are now operator functions or special operators that address a user-defined data type.

Almost every operator symbol common to ANSI C and to C++ can be overloaded in the manner described above. The only exceptions are

```
.     .*     ?:     ::
```

Referring to the discussion on overloaded functions in this chapter, the compiler chooses the proper operator function using the prototyped argument list. The same restrictions as those for overloaded functions apply. When a nonintrinsic operator is found in source code, the compiler looks for an operator function that has parameters exactly matching the operands that are found.

At this point in the discussion, some readers are certainly thinking about redefining the intrinsic operators. How about using the intrinsic subtraction operator (-) to actually add values; or redefining the multiplicative operator (*) to actually perform division operators? Forget it! This cannot be done, although it would be easy to accomplish such an aberration of operators for nonintrinsic data types. The behavior of intrinsic operators is fixed and cannot be modified by means of the operator overloading process just discussed.

There are other restrictions on operator overloading, depending upon which specific operators are used. Prefix or postfix unary operators may be overloaded, but they will not work as they do in their intrinsic formats. For instance, if the increment operator (++) is overloaded for the same actions on a nonintrinsic data type, the notation

```
x = y++;
```

will mean exactly the same thing as

```
x = ++y;
```

The compiler cannot distinguish between prefix and postfix usage from within the overloaded function as it does with intrinsic data types. Unary operators are defined as having a single argument and should return a value of the same type as their argument.

Binary operators are overloaded by declaring a nonmember function requiring two arguments. These arguments will usually be of the same data type, but this is not a prerequisite.

Assignment operators are defined as having one argument, and there are no restrictions on the argument or return data type.

ANSI C and C++ have several operators not usually thought of as such. Nevertheless, the subscripting brackets used in declaring and accessing arrays [] is an operator as is the double paren (), which is the function call operator. Both may be overloaded in the same manner as most other operators in C++. The function call operator can have any number of arguments (including no arguments) and any type of return value, whereas the subscript operator is used to locate an element from within an array.

Don't look on the operator as a method of redefining all operators for any purpose whatsoever. This won't work. You can't overload a unary operator and treat it as a binary operator or an assignment operator. The basic nature of the operators remains the same. Therefore, a construct of:

```
test operator [] (test x, test y)
{

     test templ;

     templ.a = x.a +     y.a;
     templ.b = x.b +     y.b;
     templ.c = x.c +     y.c;

     return(templ);

}
```

simply will not work. An error message will be generated by Borland C++ and compilation will be halted. Certainly, any of the binary operators could be substituted here, but this is obviously an *add* operation, so the obvious choice would be the binary addition operator.

While operator overloading offers many advantages, rigorous maintenance is a necessity. Make certain that all overloaded operators are fully documented in all programs whose source code is to be used or built on by others.

Summary

Many of the additions to ANSI C that are provided by C++ directly address the object-oriented nature of C++. However, there are just as many additions that can be immediately incorporated by the ANSI C programmer as special features which enhance programming in a non-object-oriented manner. These additions have been discussed in this chapter.

The ANSI C programmer can immediately take advantage of these additional features without performing a major rearrangement of programming style. It might be said that the attributes discussed in this chapter do not alter the overall programming approach by incorporating brand spanking new ideas. Rather, many of these additions are logical extensions of the ANSI C concept.

An alternate title for this chapter might be "Programming Without Objects," as the object-oriented aspects of C++ have been largely ignored to this point. Taking into account only the features covered in this chapter, the ANSI C programmer should immediately see that C++ brings with it an improved set of programming tools. For those making the transition from ANSI C to C++, it would be best to master fully the additional features discussed to this point by modifying (and improving) existing ANSI C programs to include such C++ components as function and operator overloading, reading to and writing from streams (iostream.H), etc. Once a full operating knowledge of these transitional features has been mastered, the reader will be ready to move on to the object-oriented tools.

CHAPTER 4

Object-Oriented Programming in Borland C++: Part 1

Borland C++ is a superset of the original C programming language. With C++, you can do anything you could with standard C. However, you can do much more by taking advantage of the added features of C++.

Many C programmers rewrite much of their original C code using the new C++ features in order to arrive at programs that are simpler and execute more efficiently. Certain programming tasks can be handled in a more logical manner using C++.

Object-Oriented Programming

Object-oriented programming is designed around the data being operated upon as opposed to the operations themselves. Instead of making certain types of data fit specific and rigid computer operations, the computer operations are designed to fit the data. This is as it should be, because the sole purpose of a computer program is to manipulate data.

Object-oriented programming allows us to associate data structures with operations just as we associate data we accumulate in our minds. We associate a specific set of actions with a given type of object, and we base actions on these associations. For example, we know that a dog is a furry animal with four legs and a tail. And we know that a refrigerator is something in which we store items that need to be kept cold. We also know that there are specific things that may be done with a dog that cannot be done with a refrigerator, and vice versa. We cannot use a dog to keep things cold, and we cannot tell a refrigerator to fetch.

Object-oriented programming allows the programmer to use similar mental processes with the abstract concepts used in computer programs. A record can be read, altered, and saved, or high-level mathematical calculations can take place. However, complex numbers cannot be written to files as personnel records, and personnel records cannot be used for mathematical operations—such as multiplying one record by another. Computer languages which are not tailored to object-oriented programming treat personnel records and complex numbers in a similar manner. An object-oriented program does not. The latter specifies acceptable behavior of its data types and allows the programmer to know exactly what he/she may expect from such data types.

With object-oriented programming, it is also possible to create relationships between different data types that exhibit specific similarities. In the real world, objects—and even thoughts—are naturally classified into certain groups and orders. New concepts are compared with existing concepts. Deductions are made based upon the relationships garnered from these comparisons.

Human beings conceptualize the world in a tiered structure with successive levels of detail building upon earlier and less structured relationships. Object-oriented programs work in the same manner, in that they allow new data structures to be built from existing data structures. In such cases, the old structure remains intact within the new, so it is a true tiered building process that retains all of the old while adding the new.

C++ Classes

Moving into the world of object-oriented programming via C++ immediately brings up the subject of classes. While mastering the concept and usage of classes is mandatory to learning C++, this study is not as difficult as it might first appear. To begin this discussion, examine the following C++ program that draws upon concepts learned in the last chapter.

```
#include <stdio.h>
struct alpha {
     int x, y;
};
```

```
alpha assign(int i, int j);
int operator == (alpha i, alpha j);


void main(void)
{

     alpha d, e;
     int i, j;

     d = assign(4, 9);

     printf("alpha.x = %d alpha.y = %d\n\n", alpha.x, alpha.y);

     printf("Input value for member x: ");
     scanf("%d*c", &i);

     printf("\nInput value for member y: ");
     scanf("%d*c", &j);

     e = assign(i, j);


     if (d == e)
          printf("Values Match\n");
     else
          printf("Values do not match\n");

}
void alpha assign(int i, int j)
{

     x = i;
     y = j;


alpha temp1;

temp1.x = i;
temp1.y = j;
```

```
return(temp1);

}
int operator == (alpha a, alpha b)
{

if (a.x == b.x && a.y == b.y)
     return(-1);
else
     return(0);

}
```

This program creates a struct named "alpha" which contains two int members named *x*, and *y*. A function of type alpha named assign() is prototyped and returns a value of type alpha. Using operator overloading, the == operator is handed a function definition that compares the contents of two structs. In typical fashion, it returns a value of zero (0) when the contents are not identical and a value of non-zero (-1) when the contents of two structs are identical. The code for this function definition follows.

```
int operator == (alpha a, alpha b) {


if (a.x == b.x && a.y == b.y)
     return(-1);
else
     return(0);


}
```

The == operator is overloaded using the "operator" key word as discussed in the previous chapter. Note that it returns an int value (0 or -1) and accepts two alpha data types as its argument. Within the function body, the values in the int members of each structure (alpha a and alpha b) are compared. If the value of a.x matches the value in b.x *and* the value in a.y is equal to the value in b.y, then all struct data is identical and a -1 (non-zero) value is returned by the function. If there is a mismatch, then a value of zero is returned. This is the way the intrinsic operator == works.

The assign() function simply makes assignments its struct argument in a format of:

```
struct alpha x = assign(i, j)
```

where *i* and *j* are int variables or constants. This function could have been eliminated easily by resorting to direct assignments as in d.x = 4; d.y = 9. However, the function is more logical in regard to thinking of alpha as an object as opposed to a collection of discrete data.

In the program proper, two struct variables are declared (*d* and *e*) followed by the declaration of two int variables (*i* and *j*). The assign() function is used to load alpha *d* with the constant values of 4 and 9. These values are displayed on the screen as discrete entities using printf(). This non-object-oriented aspect of the program will be addressed (and corrected) later. Next, the user is prompted to input a value for member x in the structure. The scanf() function is used for int data retrieval from the keyboard. Another prompt and scanf() function combination is used to retrieve a value for the y member of the structure. The assign() function is called again to write these values to alpha e.

The overloaded == operator is called in the if-statement construct to test the values in the two structure variables. If a match occurs a TRUE value is returned(-1) and the "match" prompt is displayed. If the values input by the user do not match those in alpha d, then the mismatch prompt is displayed. Input values of 4 and 9 will result in a match, while any other value combination will result in a mismatch.

This discussion has presented nothing that was not learned in the last chapter, but it does serve as a base from which to launch the discussion of C++ classes.

Structs in C++

C++ utilizes structs in the same manner as ANSI C, but there are also additional features which address the object-oriented programming. One of the most important improvements to the struct class in C++ is one which allows the inclusion of functions in structures. As such, these member functions are defined within the structure and can be accessed with the member-of (.) operator. This is a first step in the direction of object-oriented programming, for the reason that a struct may contain not only a group of collective data but also functions with which this data is manipulated and accessed. Such member functions are combined with other struct members to form a collection of code and data that is referenced as a single entity.

C++ structs also offer member-access control. Although the enhanced structs in C++ allow for the bundling of data and functions, such a collection is not as encapsulated as it could be. This leads to the member-access control key words, public, private, and protected.

All members of a struct are public by default. This means that any program statement within the same scope can read data from the members and write data to those same members. This may provide convenient access from all "parties" involved, but it is often an undesirable feature that can lead to serious problems. The general rule in C++ programming is to make all data private, so that it can be manipulated only by public functions. This avoids the possibility of intrinsic functions or member functions from other structs having direct access to data outside of their scopes.

The "private" key word is used in a format of:

```
struct alpha {
     private:
          int x, y;

     //rest of struct template
```

Here the data members int *x, y* are private. This means that they can be accessed only by member functions of the struct alpha.

The following code fragment is an extension to the one above using the "public" key word.

```
struct alpha {
     private:
          int x, y;
```

```
    public:
         // Member function prototypes;
```

Here, the public key word means that the declarations/definitions that follow can be accessed from anywhere within the same scope as the class definition.

Again, by default, all members of a C++ struct are public, unless modified by the private or protected key words. Protected members can be accessed by member functions within the same class (as is the case with the private struct). However, protected data members may also be accessed by member functions of scopes that are derived from the one in which the protected data is declared. (More to come on this a bit later.)

The following program performs in exactly the same manner as the previous example, but the struct-handling functions have been incorporated as member functions.

```
#include <stdio.h>
struct alpha {
     int x, y;
     void assign(int i, int j);
     int operator == (alpha i);
};
void main(void)
{

     alpha d, e;
     int i, j;

     d.assign(4, 9);

     printf("alpha.x = %d  alpha.y = %d\n\n", alpha.x,
alpha.y);

     printf("Input value for member x: ");
     scanf("%d*c", &i);

     printf("\nInput value for member y: ");
     scanf("%d*c", &j);

     e.assign(i, j);
```

```
        if (d == e)
            printf("Values Match\n");
        else
            printf("Values do not match\n");


}

void alpha::assign(int i, int j)
{

        x = i;
        y = j;

}
int alpha::operator == (alpha a)
{

        if (a.x == x && a.y == y)
            return(-1);
        else
            return(0);


}
```

This program does not differ greatly from the last example. The assign() function and the operator function are now a part of the struct; they have become member functions.

The use of member functions necessitates some slight modifications in the function definitions and in the manner in which they are called. Let's begin with the source code of assign().

```
void alpha::assign(int i, int j)
{
```

```
        x = i;
        y = j;

}
```

In the first rendition of the program this example derives from, assign() returned type alpha. In this example, the function returns no value, so it is declared void. The scope resolution operator is used, because this function is a member of a scope.

In this function, we are dealing with an implicit object, struct alpha, which, in turn, is referenced with the scope resolution operator(::) in the function heading. Therefore, we use the name of the instance variables, *x* and *y*, in making the assignments from function arguments *i* and *j*. The compiler assumes that unqualified instance variables are associated with the implicit object alpha. No return is necessary, because these assignments are made in a direct manner.

The operator function code is shown below.

```
int alpha::operator == (alpha a)
{

        if (a.x == x && a.y == y)
             return(-1);
        else
             return(0);

}
```

This heading shows that the function will return an int value and that it is of the alpha scope. There is only a single argument here, as compared to two arguments that were contained in the earlier example. A single argument specifying the struct variable is sufficient because it is *a* of alpha.

Within the function body, the comparisons are made using the values in alpha *a* and the instance variables *x* and *y*. As before, a zero (0) return means a mismatch, while a non-zero (-1) return signals a match.

Now that the member functions have been explained, it is time to move on to the procedure of calling the member function assign. In the first example, the usage was:

```
d = assign(4, 9);
```

However, member functions are of a specific scope. In order to call them in this program, the member of (.) operator is used in a format of:

```
d.assign(4, 9);
```

This is a logical method of accessing a data member of a structure in ANSI C where no member functions are permitted, and it is just as logical in C++ when accessing a member function. The instance variables (*x* and *y*) in alpha *d* are assigned the values of 4 and 9.

This program has gone a long way toward handling data as objects. Member functions are used to handle all data—with one exception. The call to printf() in order to display the contents of alpha *d* is handled in a direct manner, accessing the members of *d* as *d.x* and *d.y*. This is not an object-oriented method. The following program is a slight modification of the previous example that gets rid of the non-object-oriented nature of this one.

```
#include <stdio.h>
struct alpha {
     private:
          int x, y;
     public:
          void assign(int i, int j);
          int operator == (alpha i);
          void display(void);
};
void main(void)
{

     alpha d, e;
     int i, j;

     d.assign(4, 9);

     d.display();

     printf("Input value for member x: ");
```

```
    scanf("%d*c", &i);

    printf("\nInput value for member y: ");
    scanf("%d*c", &j);

    e.assign(i, j);


    if (d == c)
         printf("Values Match\n");
    else
         printf("Values do not match\n");


}

void alpha::assign(int i, int j)
{

    x = i;
    y = j;

}
int alpha::operator == (alpha a)
{

    if (a.x == x && a.y == y)
         return(-1);
    else
         return(0);


}
void alpha::display(void)
{

    printf("%d %d\n", x, y);

}
```

The difference between the last two programs lies in the fact that the latter one declares the struct data members as private while the data member functions are public. This means that the data may be accessed only by functions of the same scope. Whereas printf() was used in previous program examples to display the values in the data members, this won't work when the members have been made private. Only a function of the same scope (alpha) as the data members can access them.

Owing to this, an additional function named display() is added to the program. This is a member function of the same scope as the member data. The source code for this function is shown below.

```
void alpha::display(void)
{
     printf("%d %d\n", x, y);
}
```

This function accepts no arguments and is called in a format of

```
d.display();
```

where *d* is a structure variable of type alpha. This function simply displays the contents of data members *x* and *y*.

With these additions, the program has now become object-oriented in nature, with collections of single data members and function members being treated as a single object or *class*. Additionally, auto members are protected from access via any functions save those specified for that purpose in the class.

What about classes? When do these come into play and how are they used? The following program does the same thing as the previous examples, and it depends upon a class to perform its operations.

```
#include <stdio.h>
class alpha {
          private:
               int x, y;
          public:
               void assign(int i, int j);
               int operator == (alpha i);
```

```
                void display(void);

};
void main(void)
{

     alpha d, e;
     int i, j;

     d.assign(4, 9);

     d.display();

     printf("Input value for member x: ");
     scanf("%d*c", &i);

     printf("\nInput value for member y: ");
     scanf("%d*c", &j);

     e.assign(i, j);


     if (d == e)
          printf("Values Match\n");
     else
          printf("Values do not match\n");


}

void alpha::assign(int i, int j) {

     x = i;
     y = j;

}
int alpha::operator == (alpha a)
{

     if (a.x == x && a.y == y)
          return(-1);
     else
```

```
            return(0);

    }
    void alpha::display(void)
    {

        printf("%d %d\n", x, y);

    }
```

Don't strain yourself trying to spot the differences between the class- and struct-based programs. The only difference lies in the use of the class key word instead of a struct key word. Everything else remains the same. In fact, we have been studying classes all through this discussion on C++ structures.

The fact is that a C++ struct and a C++ class are basically one and the same thing. There are a few minute differences that will be discussed, but structs and classes are treated in almost the same manner (identically, in many operations) and one can usually be used in place of the other with few or no modifications.

In C++, an *object* is an item that has been declared to be of type "class"—and that's all it is. The member functions declared within a class are usually known as "methods." These are functions that have a special relationship with the data members. Instead of accessing data with a function, we say that data access within classes is handled by methods.

The only functional difference between a struct and a class in C++ is that struct members are public by default and class members are private by default. The following struct

```
    struct alpha {
        private:
            int x, y;
            void display(void);

    }
```

is functionally equivalent to

```
class alpha {
     int x, y;
     void display(void);

}
```

We can reverse this and say that

```
class alpha {
     public:
          int x, y;
          void display(void);

}
```

is the functional equivalent of

```
struct alpha {
     int x, y;
     void display(void);

}
```

While all members of a class default to private, it is not unusual to see the private key word used within a class, even when it is not necessary. (The class definition in the last full program example presented in this chapter does just this.)

```
#include <stdio.h>
class alpha {
          private:
               int x, y;
          public:
               void assign(int i, int j);
               int operator == (alpha i);
               void display(void);
```

```
}
```

Here, the private declaration is redundant and the following construct would mean the same as the one above.

```
#include <stdio.h>
class alpha {
            int x, y;
            public:
                  void assign(int i, int j);
                  int operator == (alpha i);
                  void display(void);

}
```

However, the private key word was used for the sake of clarity in making the transition from structs to classes. Using the private key word permits a bit more expression and you will see it often used in this (unnecessary) manner. This is fine, but don't lose sight of the fact that ALL class members are private by default. In both of the above class examples, the public declaration is absolutely essential.

The question always arises as to why class is included in C++ at all. Why not stick to the struct with which all ANSI-C programmers are familiar with? The reason is one of semantics. When data and functions are encapsulated, in object-oriented programming terminology a class is created. The class syntax accurately describes what is taking place within the program, so the class designation is used.

As a rule of thumb, C++ programmers usually resort to structs when working only with collections of data and where no member functions or methods are included. Where there is a combination of both data and function (method) members, class is used. This means that

```
struct alpha {
      int x, y;
      double d;

}
```

is appropriate, because only data members are found, and

```
class alpha {
     int x, y;
     double d;
     void display(void);

}
```

is appropriate in the collection above, because both data and method members exist.

Other rules that apply to classes and structs involve declarations of data members. These cannot be declared extern, register or auto. They may be bit-fields, enums, intrinsic and other user-defined types. Also, objects of previously declared classes can be members of a new class.

Member function (method) definitions have a slightly different header format than do other types of functions. Here, the name of the class that the member function is associated with is added ahead of the member-function name. Since several classes may share methods of the same name, this definition allows the compiler to distinguish between methods associated with the different classes. The following program is a modification of the last program example that defines methods of the same name for two different classes.

```
#include <stdio.h>
class alpha {
     private:
          int x, y;
     public:
          void assign(int i, int j);
          int operator == (alpha i);
               void display(void);

};

class beta {
     private:
          double a, b;
```

```
          public:
               void assign(double e, double r);
               double operator == (beta c);
               void display(void);

     };


     void main(void)
     {

          alpha d, e;
          beta g, h;
          int i, j;
          double x, y;

          d.assign(4, 9);
          g.assign(6.5, -1.3);

          d.display();

          printf("\nInput value for member alpha x: ");
          scanf("%d*c", &i);

          printf("\nInput value for alpha member y: ");
          scanf("%d*c", &j);

          e.assign(i, j);

          printf("\n\n");

          g.display();

          printf("\nInput a value for beta member a: ");
          scanf("%lf*c", &x);

          printf("Input a value for beta member b: ");
          scanf("%lf*c", &y);

          h.assign(x, y);
```

```
    if (d == e)
        printf("\nAlpha Values Match\n");
    else
        printf("\nAlpha Values do not match\n");

    if (g == h)
        printf("\nBeta Values Match\n");
    else
        printf("\nBeta Values do not match\n");



}

void alpha::assign(int i, int j)
{

    x = i;
    y = j;

}
int alpha::operator == (alpha a)
{

    if (a.x == x && a.y == y)
        return(-1);
    else
        return(0);


}
void alpha::display(void)
{

    printf("%d %d\n", x, y);

}
void beta::assign(double c, double w)
{

    a = c;
```

```
        b = w;

}
double beta::operator == (beta d)
{

        if (d.a == a && d.b == b)
            return(-1);
        else
            return(0);


}
void beta::display(void)
{

        printf("%lf %lf\n", a, b);

}
```

This program is lengthy, because it must be spread over more than one book page, but it is simply the previous program doubled. An additional class named beta is set up to mirror the alpha class, with the exception that beta's data members are doubles and the beta methods have the same name as alpha methods, i.e., assign, display, and the overloaded operator function ==. The second set of functions simply addresses the double data members of class beta. These functions work in exactly the same manner as alpha's methods, except for the alteration from int to double.

The source code for the operator function == follows.

```
double beta::operator == (beta d)
{

        if (d.a == a && d.b == b)
            return(-1);
        else
            return(0);
```

```
}
```

This is a member function (method) of class beta, so the implicit object becomes the argument to the left of the operator symbol. Therefore, the operator function needs only to define one explicit argument, which is the object to the right of the symbol represented in the function by beta *d*. The implicit object has replaced the first argument in the two-argument equivalent of this operator function presented in the first (non-object-oriented) program example in this chapter.

At this point in the discussion, it is good to say a bit more about scope and access. In a class definition, the default access is private, whereas a struct defaults to public access. This access specifier—be it private, public, or protected—controls the accessibility of class members outside of the class scope. Scope refers to the program area where a particular identifier is accessible. Scope controls access to data and methods.

It is not unusual to encounter multiple access specifiers in class definitions. Once a specifier is used, the access specified remains in force, unless modified by another access specifier. While it is practical to group all data/methods in a class according to access, it may be more expressive to group data and methods in a more logical manner, irregardless of access level. Take the following example for instance:

```
class animal {
     private:
          char *bird[50];
          char *reptile[30];
          char *mammal[60];
          char *amphib[25];
     public:
          void setbird(char *b);
          void setrep(char *r);
          void setmam(char *m);
          void setamp(char * b);
          void sortbird(void);
          void sortrep(void);
          void sortmam(void);
          void sortamp(void);
```

```
};
```

All the data members are declared private, while all the methods are public. All class members are grouped according to access. However, it might be more expressive to write this class in the following manner:

```
class animal {
      private:
            char *bird[50];
      public:
            void setbird(char *b);
            void sortbird(void);


      private:
            char *reptile[30];
      public:
            void setrep(char *r);
            void sortrep(void);


      private:
            char *mammal[60];
      public:
            void setmam(char *m);
            void sortmam(void);


      private:
            char *amphib[25];
      public:
            void setamp(char * b);
            void sortamp(void);
};
```

Both methods do exactly the same thing, and with a relatively small number of total class members (as in the above examples), perhaps one is just as good as another. However, the latter method may prove to be far more expressive, especially when classes with a large number of data/method members are involved.

The point in the latter example is that the access specifier continues in force with regard to all class members that follow until and unless another access specifier is encountered.

As previous program examples have shown, when data members of a class are private (default), they may be accessed only via methods (member functions) of the same class. No other means of access is possible. None of the standard C++ functions or implicit operators will be able to access the members of a class that are made private.

Inline Functions

The subject of inline functions in Borland C++ was discussed in the previous chapter. Inline functions in classes are perfectly legal and desirable in certain applications, just as they are in non-object-oriented applications.

The following program is an incomplete version of a previous example that incorporates an inline function.

```
#include <stdio.h>
class alpha {
     private:
          int x, y;
     public:
          void assign(int i, int j);

};

inline void alpha::assign(int i, int j)
{

     x = i;
     y = j;

}

void main(void)
{
```

```
    alpha a;

    a.assign(4, 9);

    // Rest of program
```

All that is necessary is to use the inline key word and, of course, insert the source code at a point in the program prior to the first call. There are no surprises here or special methods that must be used to include an inline function as a class method.

There is, however, another way of accomplishing the same thing, without using the inline key word. Any function that is fully defined with the class structure defaults to inline. The example below is the modified version of the previous code fragment.

```
#include <stdio.h>
class alpha {
    private:
        int x, y;
    public:
        void assign(int i, int j)
        {

            x = i;
            y = j;

        }

};

void main(void)
{

    alpha a;

    a.assign(4, 9);

    // Rest of program
```

Here the entire function body appears within the class. The separate prototype is no longer necessary, because it is combined in the function definition with the function body. Because the entire function is contained within the class definition, a source copy of it will be made each time a class object is declared within the calling program. This accurately defines an inline function. No inline key word is required, because this is a default of functions defined within a class.

Constructors/Destructors

With the introduction of classes in C++ comes the topic of constructors and destructors. Every class has a constructor and a destructor, even if it is not explicitly programmed. In this case, a single constructor and destructor is generated by default.

In C++, a constructor is a special function that is a class member bearing the same name as the class. Its purpose is to build objects. A constructor is called within the program to:

1. Allocate space for an object

2. Assign values to the object's data members

3. Perform general housekeeping tasks

There may be any number of constructors in a given class, but a class will have at least one, even if this is generated by default (i.e., by the compiler). Again, the constructor will have the same name as the class, so, in order to choose which constructor to call, the compiler compares the arguments used in the object declaration with the constructor parameter list. This concept is not new and is the same as the process used to choose between other overloaded functions/operators.

Constructors are just like other functions in almost every way. They may have parameters like any other function, but they cannot return a value. This restriction is imposed because constructors are usually called when defining a new object when there's no way to retrieve or examine any return value from a constructor.

As mentioned earlier, if a constructor is not explicitly programmed, then the compiler creates one (for each class) for you. This is the default constructor and it has no arguments. Its purpose is to place values of zero in every byte of the object's instance variables. When any constructor is supplied by the programmer, the default constructor is not generated.

In previous program examples in this chapter, no constructor was explicitly programmed. This means that data-member assignments were handled by default and were simply initialized to zero. The assign() method was used to initialize the class data members. The following program is an expansion of the last example providing constructors for the alpha and beta classes and allowing initializations to be made upon declaration.

```
#include <stdio.h>
class alpha {
	private:
		int x, y;
	public:
		alpha(int i, int h);
		int operator == (alpha i);
		void display(void);

};

class beta {
	private:
		double a, b;
	public:
		beta(double e, double r);
		double operator == (beta c);
		void display(void);

};


void main(void)
{

	alpha d(4, 9);
	beta g(6.5, -1.3);
	int i, j;
	double x, y;
```

```
    d.display();

    printf("\nInput value for member alpha x: ");
    scanf("%d*c", &i);

    printf("\nInput value for alpha member y: ");
    scanf("%d*c", &j);

    alpha e(i, j);

    printf("\n\n");

    g.display();

    printf("\nInput a value for beta member a: ");
    scanf("%lf*c", &x);

    printf("Input a value for beta member b: ");
    scanf("%lf*c", &y);

    beta h(x, y);

    if (d == e)
        printf("\nAlpha Values Match\n");
    else
        printf("\nAlpha Values do not match\n");

    if (g == h)
        printf("\nBeta Values Match\n");
    else
        printf("\nBeta Values do not match\n");



}

alpha::alpha(int i, int j)
{

    x = i;
```

```
        y = j;

    }
    int alpha::operator == (alpha a)
    {

        if (a.x == x && a.y == y)
            return(-1);
        else
            return(0);


    }
    void alpha::display(void)
    {

        printf("%d %d\n", x, y);

    }
    beta::beta(double c, double w)
    {

        a = c;
        b = w;

    }
    double beta::operator == (beta d)
    {

        if (d.a == a && d.b == b)
            return(-1);
        else
            return(0);


    }
    void beta::display(void)
    {

        printf("%lf %lf\n", a, b);
```

```
}
```

In this version of the program, a constructor is used which *requires* that all initializations of class objects be handled with two arguments. This means that initial assignments are made upon declaration. In this program, the assign() method is no longer necessary, because it is not necessary to reassign class member values after initialization.

The declaration line

```
alpha d(4, 9);
```

initializes alpha object *d* to the values contained within parentheses. With the single explicit constructor in place, it would be an error to simply declare

```
alpha d;
```

The addition of the constructor mandates that any declaration of an object of class alpha contain two parameters. The same applies to beta objects. Later in the program, alpha object *e* is declared and initialized with the values in int *i* and *j*. This is not an assignment line as such; rather, it is a declaration of another alpha class object, and it requires the same argument parameters. Another declaration of beta class is made later on in this program, and again, two values are provided for the mandatory argument parameters.

The original assign() method is replaced by the constructor body which reads

```
alpha::alpha(int i, int j)
{

      x = i;
      y = j;

}
```

You can see immediately that this is the same body that was contained in assign().

The requirement that initialization values be provided with each object declaration can be a liability in some usages and an asset in others. However, there is a convenient way around this requirement. Referring to an earlier discussion on default parameter values, the classes used in the program above may be rewritten in the following manner:

```
#include <stdio.h>
class alpha {
     private:
          int x, y;
     public:
          alpha(int i = 0, int h = 0); //default values of 0
          int operator == (alpha i);
          void display(void);

};

class beta {
     private:
          double a, b;
     public:
          beta(double e = 0.0, double r = 0.0); //default
values of 0.0
          double operator == (beta c);
          void display(void);

};
```

Having the default values in place (int i = 0, int h = 0) means that declarations may be made with two initialization values, with only one or with none, and compiler legality still will be maintained. Whenever an argument is missing, the default values assigned in the class prototypes will prevail. Therefore, a declaration within the calling program of:

```
alpha(12, 88);
```

is perfectly legal. So are

```
alpha(12);
```

and

```
alpha();
```

In the first example, values of 12 and 88 are written to the int data members of class alpha. The second declaration writes a value of 12 to the first int data element and a default of 0 (zero) to the second. The third call is made without parameters, so the values in both data members will be zero.

Destructors

A destructor is the reverse of a constructor, in that it frees up space used to store objects. A destructor is a member function of a class and bears the same name as the class, except that a tilde (~) character precedes this name. A class will have only a single destructor, and this member function will have no arguments and will return no values. The following class contains a constructor and a destructor.

```
class gamma {
     private:
          char *c;
     public:
          gamma(int size) //constructor
          {
               c = new char[size];
          }
          ~gamma(void); //destructor
          {
               delete c;

          }
};
```

A destructor is called implicitly when a variable goes outside of its declared scope. Destructors for local variables are called when the block in which they are declared becomes inactive. However, when pointers to objects go out of scope, a destructor is not implicitly called. This means that the delete operator must be explicitly called to destroy the object. Such is the case in the above example. The constructor allows the object to be declared with a size value. The destructor calls delete to destroy the object (free up memory) when the object goes out of scope.

When a destructor is not defined for a class, one which does absolutely nothing is created by default. For many classes —such as the ones used in previous program examples—the default destructor is all that is necessary. For this reason, you will see many classes that depend upon this default destructor which is evidenced by the absence of any destructor definitions.

Assignments to Classes

Creating our own constructor that initializes declarations of class objects has not entirely relieved us from the necessity of using an assignment method. The constructor used with the operating program example took the place of assign(), but only because each class object received only one assignment. This was handled upon declaration of the object. However, if values within a previously declared object are to be changed, then some sort of assignment method/operator is necessary.

The following program begins our discussion about class data-member assignment operators.

```
#include <stdio.h>

class delta {
     private:
          double a, b;
     public:
          void display(void);
          delta(double x = 0.0,
          double y = 0.0)
          {
                    a = x;
                    b = y;
          }
```

```
};

void main(void)
{

     delta e(9.1, 2.6), f;

     f = e;

     f.display();

}
void delta::display(void)
{

     printf("%lf  %lf\n\n", a, b);

}
```

This simple program establishes a class containing two data members of type double. Two methods are established: One is a constructor while the other is the familiar display() member function that writes the contents of the data members to the monitor screen.

In this program, delta object *e* is explicitly initialized upon declaration, while delta *f* is initialized to the default values of (0, 0). Next, the assignment operator is used to assign the contents of *e* to *f*. Finally, we confirm the data copy by displaying the contents of the data members in *f* on the screen.

But just what is this assignment operator? Class data members *a* and *b* are private, so they cannot be accessed by the intrinsic functions and operators. Isn't the assignment operator an intrinsic operator?

The answer to the last question is "It can be." But in this usage, the intrinsic assignment operator definitely will not work on class assignments handled in this manner. The above program has made use of a special assignment operator method that was not defined in the class definitions. This operator was created by default, because no user-written definition was found by the compiler. The default assignment operator created in this example makes an exact copy of the source on a bit-by-bit basis.

This is a simple program example, and the default assignment operator created by the compiler for this class is adequate. (However, more complex class definitions may require far more.)

The safest method of proceeding when class assignments must be made is to create your own assignment operator function as in:

```
delta::operator = (const delta &classvalue)
{

     a = classvalue.a;
     b = classvalue.b;

}
```

Certainly, complex class definitions will require a more complex operator function definition, but this example presents the overall concept well. The following program makes use of the new operator function member.

```
#include <stdio.h>

class delta {
     private:
          double a, b;
     public:
          void display(void);
          delta(double x = 0.0, double y = 0.0)
          {

                    a = x;
                    b = y;
          }

          void operator = (const delta &base);

};

void main(void)
{
```

```
        delta a(9.1, 2.6), b;

        b = a;

        b.display();

}
void delta::display(void)
{

        printf("%lf  %lf\n\n", a, b);

}
void delta::operator = (const delta &base)
{

                a = base.a;
                b = base.b;

}
```

The displayed results will be the same, and for this simple example, the assignment operator function is unnecessary, because the default operator will do just fine. However, this method can be carried over into more complex class definitions, where the default operator simply will not do the job.

Friends

Treating complex groupings of data as a single object offers many advantages, but it also presents some problems that must be addressed. Here we turn to *friends*. The following program begins a discussion on friend declarations.

```
// This program will not compile due to errors
#include <stdio.h>
class dblpnt {
     private:
          double d;
```

```
    public:
        dblpnt(double f = 0.0)
        {

            d = f;

        }

};
void display(dblpnt a, dblpnt b, dblpnt c);
void main(void)
{

    dblpnt a(15.5), b(8.3), c(1342.86);

    display(a, b, c);

}
void display (dblpnt a, dblpnt b, dblpnt c)
{

    printf("%lf  %lf  %lf\n", a.d, b.d, c.d);

}
```

This program will create three errors when compilation is attempted. The reason for this should be fairly obvious by now. The display() function is set up to write the contents of the class data members to the screen. It accepts three arguments that are all objects of class dblpnt. This is all fine and good until you stop to consider that the class data members are all private. They can only be accessed by functions of the same class.

No problem. We'll just go back and write a display() function that is of the same class:

```
#include <stdio.h>
class dblpnt {
    private:
        double d;
    public:
        dblpnt(double f = 0.0)
```

```
          {
               d = f;
          }
          void display (void)
          {
               printf("%lf  ", d);
          }
};
void main(void)
{
     dblpnt a(15.5), b(8.3), c(1342.86);

     a.display(void);
     b.display(void);
     c.display(void);
}
```

This works, but it requires three calls to display, and it doesn't follow the format of the original intention. What we need here is to write a function that can access private members of a class and will display, in one function call, three values.

The easiest way to accomplish this is to write a separate function that is not a member of class dblpnt. However, this function must, in some manner, be given access to the private data members while not actually being a member of the same class. Fortunately, C++ takes such situations into account; this is where friends come into play. The following program closely mimics the uncompilable first example, but it operates in exactly the manner as was intended by the original program example.

```
#include <stdio.h>
class dblpnt {
     private:
          double d;
     public:
```

```
            dblpnt(double f = 0.0)
            {

                 d = f;

            }
            friend void display (dblpnt a, dblpnt b, dblpnt c);

};
void main(void)
{

     dblpnt a(15.5), b(8.3), c(1342.86);

     display(a, b, c);

}
void display (dblpnt a, dblpnt b, dblpnt c)
{

     printf("%lf  %lf  %lf ", a.d, b.d, c.d);


}
```

In this program, display() is declared a friend function of class dblpnt. This means that the function is granted full access to all of the private members of class dblpnt. Within the definition of class dblpnt, the display() function prototype is found. However, it should be firmly established that display() is in no way a method (member-function) of class dblpnt. It is a discrete function that has been granted special access to the members of dblpnt by means of the friend declaration. Notice that the function header and body is exactly the same as it was in the first uncompilable example that began this discussion.

There is no limit to the number of friend functions that a class may have. For that matter, another class may be granted friend status. When an entire class is to be made a friend of another class, it is necessary that the class which is to receive friend status be declared so *before* the class which designates it a friend. For example:

```
class first {

     //class contents

};

class second {
     private:
          int x, y;
     public:
          second(int i = 0, int j = 0)
          {

               x = i;
               y = j;

          }

          friend class first;

};
```

In this example, class first is designated a friend of class second. Notice that class first was declared prior to class second, which calls the former as a friend. With class first a friend of class second, every member function of class first becomes a friend of class second. When a class is made a friend, access is unimportant; members that are private, public, or protected are completely accessible by the friend class.

Summary

This discussion has taken you through the first step of transition from "C++ without objects" to "C++ with objects." The relationship between a C++-enhanced struct and a C++ class has been clearly demonstrated. This demonstration has shown that a C++ struct and a C++ class are, for all intents and purposes, operationally the same thing. The only difference lies in the default access parameters, with the struct's members defaulting to public while class members default to private.

Persons learning C++ seem to have a lot of initial difficulty in grasping the concept of class data members, member functions (methods), and friend functions. However, this may be more a product of an unclear understanding of ANSI C-struct operations than anything else. From this chapter, it can be seen that a C++ struct is identical to an ANSI C struct in every way. However, in C++ the struct may be enhanced with member functions and access specifiers. Once the concept of the enhanced struct is firmly grasped, the move to classes is almost an afterthought.

CHAPTER 5

Object-Oriented Programming in Borland C++ : Part 2

The previous chapter served as an introduction to the object-oriented aspects of Borland C++. This chapter will delve a little further into class inheritance and the general manipulation of objects using C++.

Inheritance

All of the previous program examples dealt with distinct classes — those which contain their own members and methods to act upon methods. However, much of the power of C++ lies in its ability to spawn other classes from a root or base class. This involves inheritance, where one class may inherit methods and/or members from another class. The class that inherits is called the derived class, while the class inherited from is the base class.

A derived class is identified by its own class name and the name of the class from which it inherits. The following program demonstrates this naming procedure.

```
#include <stdio.h>
class alpha { // base class
      private:
            int x, y;
      public:
            alpha(int i, int j)
            {
                  x = i;
                  y = j;
```

```
            }
            void display(void);

};
class beta : public alpha { //derived class
    public:
            beta(int i, int j)
            : alpha(i, j)
            { /* empty method expression */ }

};

void main(void) // main program
{

    alpha d(2, 6);
    beta e(4, 9);

    d.display();
    e.display(); // beta e uses alpha method
}
void alpha::display(void)
{

    printf("%d %d\n", x, y);

}
```

In this example, the base class is alpha. The beta class is derived from alpha by the inclusion of

```
: public alpha
```

which follows the derived class name. Because the public key word is used in the definition of the derived class, this means that all public members of the base class (alpha) are also public members of beta.

While display() is a public member of the alpha class, this method is inherited by the derived beta class, so the expression:

```
e.display();
```

with *e* being an object of type beta is perfectly legal. In many ways, a derived class treats a base class as if it were an object member.

The following code fragment is the constructor taken from the beta class in the above program.

```
beta(int i, int j)
: alpha(i, j)
{ /* empty method expression */ }
```

Constructors and destructors of the base class are *not* inherited by the derived class. Therefore, the constructor for the derived beta class requires parameter information for the constructor of the base alpha class. In the above fragment, the base-class constructor is called by alpha(i, j). In this example, alpha is the constructor name, while i and j are part of its parameter list. The beta constructor is derived solely from the alpha constructor, as the beta class has no data members. Therefore, there are no additional method statements following the call to the base class constructor. The body of the beta constructor, then, is empty following the call to the base constructor.

What we have here is useless from any but a tutorial standpoint, as it results in the members and methods of the alpha base class being utilized by the derived class. The beta class does nothing but utilize alpha members. It brings nothing new into the program.

However, if the beta class contained two data members, as in

```
class beta : public alpha {
     int a, b;

     // etc.......
```

then the beta constructor might be written as:

```
beta(int i, int j, int q, int r)
: alpha(i, j)
{
```

```
        c = q;
        d = r;

    }
```

This example incorporates the constructor from the alpha base class in addition to the assignments exclusive to the derived (beta) constructor. In other words, beta(7, 12, 45, 22) would assign the first two values to the data members of the alpha base class while the last two values would be assigned to the beta class.

Of course, this would necessitate writing a new version of display() for the beta class only. It might look like the method that follows.

```
class beta : public alpha {      //derived class
        private:
                int a, b;
        public:
                beta(int i, int j, int q, int r)
                : alpha(i, j)
                {

                        a = q;
                        b = r;

                }
                void display();
                {

                        alpha::display();
                        printf("%d %d\n", a, b);


                }

};
```

The overloaded beta display() function calls the alpha display() function which it may access, because beta is a derived class. It then incorporates its own call to printf() in order to write the values in *a* and *b* to the screen.

It is necessary to call the alpha display() function, because this is the only function that can display the values of the private data members in the alpha class. A derived class cannot access the private members of the base class. This is done purposely in order to prevent a derived class from overriding the privacy control of the base class. Certainly, all public members (data, method, etc.) are accessible by the derived class, but that is not the case in the program example provided here. The data members of the alpha base class are private.

Access to members of a class is controlled by the private, public, and protected access specifiers available in C++. When a derived class declares its base class public, then all public members of the base class become public members of the derived class. For this reason, the alpha class constructor and the alpha class display() method becomes public members of the derived beta class in the example that preceded this discussion. If the beta class declares the alpha base class as private, then all public members of the alpha base class become *private* members of the beta derived class.

Either way, only the public members of the base class may be accessed by the derived class. Because multiple inheritance is allowed in C+, it would be quite easy to include an additional class that is derived from beta, which, in turn, is derived from alpha. If the base class is declared public in the beta class definition, the public members of alpha become public members of beta and these also become public members of the class derived from beta. However, if the base class is declared private, then the third class does not inherit any of the members of the alpha base class.

The following program is an expanded version of the first example presented in this chapter. Class alpha is the base class while beta is derived from alpha and chi is derived from beta/alpha.

```
#include <stdio.h>
class alpha {
     private:
          int x, y;
     public:
          alpha(int i, int j)
          {
```

```
                x = i;
                y = j;

            }
            void display(void)
            {

                printf("%d  %d\n", x, y);

            }
            void two_times(void)
            {

                printf("%d  %d\n", x * 2, y * 2);

            }

    };
    class beta : public alpha {
        private:
            int a, b;
        public:
            beta(int i, int j, int q, int r)
            : alpha(i, j)
            {

                a = q;
                b = r;

            }
            void display(void)
            {

                alpha::display();
                printf("%d %d\n", a, b);

            }
    };
```

```
class chi : public beta {
    private:
        double v, w;
    public:
        chi (int i, int j, int q, int r, double x, double y)
        : beta(i, j, q, r)
        {

            v = x;
            w = y;

        }
        void display(void)
        {

            beta::display();
            printf("%lf %lf\n", v, w);

        }

};

void main(void)
{

    alpha d(2, 6);
    beta e(4, 9, 6, 1);
    chi f(8, 6, 135, 76, 35.17, 16.11);

    d.display();
    d.two_times();

    e.display();
    e.two_times();

    f.display();
    f.two_times();

}
```

In this example, the inheritance is a straightforward cascade process. Class chi inherits the constructor and the display() method from class beta from which it is derived in addition to a new method called two_times() which simply displays two times the value in alpha data members x and y. Class chi may share all of the methods in class beta and in class alpha, because the beta derivation from alpha was declared public. However, if we change the declaration of class beta to:

```
class beta : private alpha
```

an error message will be generated by the Borland C++ compiler. The message will tell you that class chi does not have access to alpha method two_times(). The reason for this is the private declaration of the derivation of class beta from alpha: Because the derivation has been made private, the alpha methods that are inherited by beta are private to beta. The chi derivation may not share any of the public methods in alpha, but beta may share them all.

Throughout this text, public and private access specifiers have been used in abundance. However, the third type of access specifier — protected — has been mentioned only occasionally. Now that we are well within the discussion of inheritance (classes derived from classes), the protected-access specifier plays a more dominant role.

Class members that are declared private cannot be accessed outside of the scope of the class. This means that derived classes cannot use the private class members. Members that are public can be accessed from any scope. The protected-access specifier is used to provide additional programming flexibility in C++. Protected members may be accessed from within the class or from within any derived class.

Examine the following program.

```
class alpha {
     private:
          int x, y;
     public:
          alpha(int a, int b)
          {
               x = a;
```

```
                y = b;

            }

};
void main(void)
{

    alpha c(4, 19);

    printf("%d  %d\n", c.x, c.y);

}
```

This program will not compile properly. Error messages stating that alpha::x and alpha::y are not accessible from function main() will appear. The reason for this is that data members *x* and *y* in the alpha class are private. They cannot be accessed outside of the scope of alpha. An alternative that does allow outside access is to declare the data members of class alpha as public:

```
class alpha {
    public:
        int x, y;
        alpha(int a, int b)
        etc..............
```

Now all members of class alpha are accessible by any scope that cares to call them. With this change, alpha::x and alpha::y are accessible by main().

However, doing this completely voids the object-oriented programming process. In most cases, programmers will not want data members and various methods to be accessible outside of the scope of the class in which they are defined. But there are many instances where it is desirable or even mandatory for derived classes to have complete access to such members of the base class.

Previous program examples showing class derivations lamely called on the public display() method in the base class to display the contents of data members. Each display() method writes data to the screen and follows this write with a newline

(\n). Let's assume that we want to use one display function to write a single line of data to the screen. This line would contain the values in each of the data members of the base class and the derived class. The following program continues this discussion:

```
#include <stdio.h>
class alpha {
     protected:
          int x, y;
     public:
          alpha(int i, int j)
          {
               x = i;
               y = j;

          }

};
class beta : public alpha {
     protected:
          int a, b;
     public:
          beta(int i, int j, int q, int r)
          : alpha(i, j)
          {

               a = q;
               b = r;

          }
};

class chi : public beta {
     private:
          double v, w;
     public:
          chi (int i, int j, int q, int r, double x, double y)
          : beta(i, j, q, r)
          {
```

```
                v = x;
                w = y;

            }
            void display(void)
            {

                printf("%d %d %d %d %lf %lf\n", alpha::x, alpha::y,
    beta::a, beta::b, v, w);

            }

    };

    void main(void)
    {
        chi f(8, 6, 135, 76, 35.17, 16.11);

        f.display(); // display values in all class data members
    }
```

In this example, the key point lies in the fact that the data members of the alpha and derived beta classes all are declared protected; the members are upwardly accessible — in other words, the last derived class, chi, may access all members of the classes from which it is derived. Within the main() function, a program statement which tries to access these protected members will result in a compile failure and a "No Access" error message. For instance, changing the main() function in the above example to:

```
void main(void)
{
    alpha c(56, 22);

    printf("%d  %d\n", c.x, c.y);

}
```

will not work, because main() does not have access privileges to the protected data members of the alpha class. Only the alpha objects and objects derived from alpha or from alpha/beta may access the protected data members in these upper classes.

The display() method in the derived chi class in the above example directly accesses the data members in the upper classes. This is possible only when these members are declared public or protected. When they are public, access may be gained to them from any scope. However, because they are protected, only the base class or any derived class may access the data members. The protected mode offers the access needed in many programming applications, but this access is tightly controlled in an object-oriented programming manner: Only scopes that are derived from the class or classes that contain the protected members may access them; all others are excluded from such access.

It should be understood that while derived classes may access data members and methods of the classes from which they are derived (providing such access has been explicitly granted through the access specifiers), the reverse is not true. If alpha is the base class and beta is a derived class, then beta may access members of the alpha class, but the alpha class does not inherit the members of the beta class. Derivation is a one-way street that travels from the base class through all derived classes. The reverse is not true.

An object of a derived class can be used as if it were an object of its base class. The derived class might be thought of as a superset of the base class. Given alpha as the base class and beta as the derived class, we might think of alpha/beta as the superset and alpha as a subset of alpha/beta. Therefore, a base class object cannot be treated as a member of the derived class.

A derived class can—and often does—have more than one base class. The following program will demonstrate this principle:

```
#include <stdio.h>
class base_a {                    // First base class
     private:
          double a, b;
     public:
          base_a(double d, double e)
```

```
            {

                  a = d;
                  b = e;

            }

            double plus()
            {

                  return(a + b);

            }
};

class base_b {                      // Second base class
      protected:
            int x, y;
      public:
            base_b(int i, int j)
            {

                  x = i;
                  y = j;

            }
};


class two_base : private base_a, base_b {  // Doubly derived class
      private:
            long l, m;
      public:
            two_base(long c, long d, double e, double f, int x, int y)
            : base_a(e, f), base_b(x, y)
            {

                  l = c;
                  m = d;
```

```
            }

            void show_roots()    // Method has full access to bases
            {

                    printf("%ld %ld %d %d %lf\n", l, m, base_b::x,
base_b::y, plus());

            }
};

void main(void)
{

        two_base s(115000, 64539, 16.3, 22.17, 28, 37);

        s.show_roots();

}
```

The definition

```
class two_base : private base_a, base_b
```

says that two_base is a class that is derived from classes base_a and base_b. As discussed earlier, two_base will inherit all the public and protected members from the two_base classes. However, the base classes inherit nothing from two_base, nor do the two base classes share in any way their separate resources with each other.

The following code fragment is the constructor for two_base:

```
two_base(long c, long d, double e, double f, int x, int y)
: base_a(e, f), base_b(x, y)
{

        l = c;
        m = d;

}
```

Notice how this constructor gains access to the constructors of its two_base classes. This is handled in the same style as the original declaration of two_base.

Class base_a declares its data members to be private. This means that they cannot be accessed by any other scope. Therefore, two_base, even though it is derived from base_a, cannot obtain the values of these private data members. However, a base_a method named plus() is public and returns the added values of the two data members in base_a. Since plus() is public, it is a simple task for two_base to use this method. The data members of class base_b are declared to be protected. This means that they may be accessed from within the original scope or from any derived class, such as two_base. The code for show_roots() is shown below.

```
void show_roots() // Method has full access to bases
{

     printf("%ld %ld %d %d %lf\n", l, m, base_b::x, base_b::y,
plus());

}
```

Here, the printf() function is handed base_b::x and base_b::y. These data members may be accessed directly in this manner, because they have been declared protected. However, we cannot take the direct access route for the data members in base_a, for they were declared private. On the other hand, the plus() method in base-a is public. It can be directly accessed and plus() is handed to printf() to return the total of the values in the two data members.

The following simple program involves four classes. Class alpha is the base class while beta is derived from alpha. Class chi is also derived from alpha, while class delta is doubly derived from class beta and class chi. The class members are made as simple as possible for tutorial purposes. All members of all classes are public. All derivations are public.

```
#include <stdio.h>

class alpha {
     public:
```

```
        int x;
};

class beta : public alpha {
    public:
        long l;
};

class chi : public alpha {
    public:
        int y;
};

class delta : public beta, chi {
    public:
        double a;
};

void main(void)
{

    delta hier;

    hier.a = 446.9978;
    hier.y = 39;
    hier.l = 76000;
    hier.x = 44;

    printf("%lf %d %ld %d\n", hier.a, hier.y, hier.l, hier.x);

}
```

Examine these class derivations carefully. Class delta presents a problem, due to the manner in which it is used within main(). Class delta is derived from two beta which is derived from alpha. Class delta is also derived from class chi which is also derived from alpha. Therefore, there is a double derivation of delta to alpha; it is "connected" to the base class alpha through beta and also through chi.

If you try to compile this program under Borland C++, you will get an error message stating that the expression

```
hier.x = 44;
```

is ambiguous. This means that the compiler has no idea which alpha::x is being accessed. One path could be listed as

```
delta/beta/alpha
```

while the other is

```
delta/chi/alpha
```

There are two base classes for delta, and the Borland C++ compiler cannot tell whether to make the assignment to the alpha::x inherited through beta or to the one inherited through chi.

This is where virtual base classes come into play. The following modification of the earlier program example will permit the program to compile and execute properly.

```
#include <stdio.h>

class alpha {
     public:
          int x;
};

class beta : virtual public alpha {
     public:
          long l;
};

class chi : virtual public alpha {
     public:
          int y;
};

class delta : public beta, chi {
```

```
    public:
        double a;
};

void main(void)
{

    delta hier;

    hier.a = 446.9978;
    hier.y = 39;
    hier.l = 76000;
    hier.x = 44;

    printf("%lf %d %ld %d\n", hier.a, hier.y, hier.l, hier.x);

}
```

Notice that class beta is derived from class virtual public alpha, as is class chi. Virtual base classes that are the same class type are combined to form a single base class of that type for any derived class that inherits them. With the virtual key word in place (as shown by this latest example), both base alpha classes have become a single alpha class. The end result is that delta has only a single base alpha class. This allows the compiler to make the proper access to the x member. Remember, whenever class objects are created within a program, derived classes will contain unique base classes if the derivation is not declared virtual. In the first program example (the one that would not compile properly), unique copies of the base alpha class were involved. By making these derivations virtual, we are dealing with a single base class alpha.

Polymorphism

Having laid a foundation with our discussions on class inheritance and the various modes of access, we can move on to the more difficult subject of polymorphism. Polymorphism is defined as giving an action one name or symbol that is shared up and down a class hierarchy, with each class in the hierarchy implementing the action in a manner that is appropriate to itself.

Polymorphism is also known as late binding or dynamic binding. In C++, this action is accomplished in a manner whereby the type of an object is unidentified until run time. Polymorphism in C++ is handled through the use of virtual functions which are declared with the "virtual" key word.

The following program example will begin our discussion of polymorphism.

```
#include <stdio.h>

class alpha {
     protected:
          int x, y;
     public:
          alpha(int i = 0, int j = 0)
          {

               x = i;
               y = j;

          }
          void display();

};

class beta : public alpha {
     private:
          double d, e, f;
     public:
          beta()
          {

               d = e = f = 0;

          }

          beta (int q, int r, double a, double b, double c)
          : alpha(q, r)
          {

               d = a;
```

```
                e = b;
                f = c;

            }

            void assign(double a, double b, double c);
            void display();


};

void main(void)
{

    beta a;
    alpha d(26, 134), *e;


    a.assign(23.8, 14.768, 165.2821);
    a.display();

    d.display();


}

void alpha::display(void)
{

    printf("Alpha values = %d, %d\n\n", x, y);

}
void beta::display(void)
{

    printf("Beta values = %lf, %lf, %lf\n\n", d, e, f);

}
void beta:: assign(double x, double y, double z)
{
```

```
        d = x;
        e = y;
        f = z;

    }
```

There is nothing unusual about this program. Although class beta is derived from class alpha, there are few differences between this program and earlier examples explored in the previous chapter.

The following program accomplishes the same thing as the last example, but it does so in a different manner.

```
#include <stdio.h>

class alpha {
     protected:
          int x, y;
     public:
          alpha(int i = 0, int j = 0)
          {

               x = i;
               y = j;

          }
          virtual void display();  //virtual method prototype

};

class beta : public alpha {
     private:
          double d, e, f;
     public:
          beta() {

               d = e = f = 0;

          }
```

```
          beta (int q, int r, double a, double b, double c)
          : alpha(q, r) {

               d = a;
               e = b;
               f = c;

          }

          void assign(double a, double b, double c);
          virtual void display();


};

void main(void)
{

     beta a;
     alpha d(26, 134), *pt;


     a.assign(23.8, 14.768, 165.2821);
     pt = &a;
     pt->display();

     pt = &d;
     pt->display();


}

void alpha::display(void)
{

     printf("Alpha values = %d, %d\n\n", x, y);

}
void beta::display(void)
{
```

```
    printf("Beta values = %lf, %lf, %lf\n\n", d, e, f);
}
void beta:: assign(double x, double y, double z)
{
    d = x;
    e = y;
    f = z;
}
```

In this example, alpha::display has been declared a virtual method. Within the body of main(), pointers to objects are used to access the correct display() method. This means that the object type is not identified until run time. The base class is alpha, and all invocation of display() is accomplished through alpha.

Class alpha is the base, and pt is named a pointer of type class. The assignment e = &a assigns the address of alpha a to the alpha class pointer. The expression e.display() accesses the alpha::display() method by means of the base class pointer. The assignment e = &d hands the address of beta *d* to the alpha class pointer. The expression e.display() now invokes beta::display(). The point here is that any invocation of any of the display methods is invoked with the alpha base class.

Virtual function definitions between base and derived classes must be identical. For instance, you couldn't change the display() function in beta to read:

```
virtual int display(void);
```

The definitions must be the same, which means things such as return type and argument parameters must match. When (supposedly) virtual function definitions are different, they are not virtual functions. The virtual key word is simply ignored by the compiler.

In the last program example, the display() prototype in both the alpha and the beta class used the virtual key word. Because a virtual function relies on the original class for which it is called, it is not necessary to use the virtual key word outside of the base class. The prototype in beta:

```
virtual void display();
```

is redundant in its use of virtual. If the prototype in beta read:

```
void display();
```

this would be fine, as void display() has already been declared virtual in the base class alpha.

Let's return to our definition of polymorphism:

> "Giving an action one name or symbol that is shared up and down a class hierarchy, with each class in the hierarchy implementing the action in a manner that is appropriate to itself."

We can see that the display() function in the previous example fits this criteria. There are two different implementations, each sharing the same name and carrying out appropriate actions. The use of display() is shared throughout the two-part hierarchy (up and down). Polymorphism is a highly complex subject and the use of virtual functions throughout a class hierarchy must be a carefully considered procedure.

Unions

In C++, a union is considered a special class. Member functions, constructors, and destructors may be defined for C++ unions in the same manner as they appear in a class declaration. We have already discussed the relationship between classes and structs in C++, with all members of a struct being public unless they are declared private or protected. All members of a class are private unless access is specifically changed. C++ unions behave like structs, in that all members are public unless changed by the access specifiers. The main difference between classes and unions lies in the fact that all data members of a C++ union reside at the same memory location. This latter trait is exactly the same as that of unions in ANSI C.

While a C++ union may be used as a class where it is desirable for all data members to begin at the same memory address, one rarely sees this type of usage. For the most part, programming practice regarding C++ unions treat them in exactly the same manner as ANSI C unions which contain only data members.

Summary

At this point, hopefully the reader understands the general concept of class inheritance. A class may be derived from one or several other classes. A class may also be derived from a class which is itself derived from other classes. Derived classes are automatically granted access to the public members of the base class. A derived class never has access to the private members of the base class. A derived class does have access to protected members of the base class. For derived classes, protected base class members are treated as public. However, they are not, in fact, public, as only derived classes may have access to protected base class members. Other non-derived scopes may not access protected members of a class.

CHAPTER 6

The C++ Turbo Profiler

Borland C++ comes bundled with Borland's Turbo Profiler. Profiling is a very misunderstood area of software development. This misunderstanding is unfortunate because it is an extremely useful tool for the development of high-quality software.

Profiling a program can increase its overall performance by augmenting the programmer's ability to produce the most efficient code possible. Profilers monitor critical computer resources, such as processor time, keyboard input, disk access activities, printer output, and interrupt activities.

Using a profiler, you can locate potential bottlenecks in performance. The Turbo Profiler can tell you how many times a routine is called, how many times a line executes, and where your program, in general, spends its time. A profiler, then, allows programs that are in a stage of near-completion to be fine-tuned.

For instance, a program profile may indicate that a considerable amount of execution time is being tied up in one particular custom function. If execution speed is considered marginal, then this indicates to the programmer that he/she may need to concentrate on improving the execution efficiency of this particular function.

Borland believes in the power of their Turbo Profiler. The praise of this product is not all hype. Interactive profiling quickly reveals inefficient code in a program while allowing you to read and edit any text file during profiling sessions. Turbo Profiler is quite versatile, because it will profile any size program that runs under DOS.

Some programmers confuse profiling and optimizing. The difference lies in the fact that an optimizer can sometimes make a program run slightly faster by replacing time-consuming machine instructions with less expensive ones. However, optimizing does nothing to correct inefficient coding. A profiler works with the programmer detecting inefficient portions of code. It also helps to point to algorithms that can be modified and rewritten in a more efficient manner—some common program bottlenecks that were referred to earlier.

Turbo Profiler is designed to work with other languages offered by Borland—including Turbo Pascal, Turbo C, and Turbo Assembler—in addition to C++. It will also work with programs compiled under Microsoft C and MASM. It tracks a complete call-path history for all routines, analyzing the frequency of calls. It also monitors DOS file activity and logs the number of bytes read and written. Turbo Profiler reports execution time and execution count for routines and individual lines in a program.

The hardware overhead required for Turbo Profiler is minimal. All that is needed is any MS-DOS-compatible machine, from the lowly PC-XT to the current 486 machines running under DOS 2.0 or higher, with 384K or more of RAM. The Turbo Profiler will run on a system that contains only two floppy-disk drives, but a hard disk is recommended. From a practical standpoint, no software developer is going to be using such a minimum system. Therefore, the programmer's system is certainly already configured to utilize Turbo Profiler.

Profiling is an extremely valuable aspect of efficient software development. Because of the misunderstanding of what profiling really is—not to mention what it does—this useful utility is often not utilized to its fullest extent. For example, suppose you have written a fairly elaborate program that simply executes too slowly. The Turbo Profiler can identify the bottlenecks and determine where additional programmer work is required. I used the Profiler to greatly increase the efficiency of a commercial software package I had written some years ago, discovering in the process that a particular function that was being utilized by many other functions was extremely slow. By restructuring the source code for this single function, the program became about 100 times more efficient in terms of execution speed. This improvement in efficiency was carried over to affect all the other functions that called it and resulted in a 25 percent improvement in overall program execution speed. The discovery process took less than two minutes, while the recoding consumed slightly more than an hour of programming time—a very inexpensive price to pay for a significant improvement in execution speed.

Profiling a program involves four basic steps. First of all, the program is set up prior to profiling. Secondly, data is collected while the program executes. The third step is to analyze the collected data, and the final step is to modify the source-code, along with recompiling and linking based upon the report of the Profiler.

After a program has been profiled, modified, recompiled, and relinked, it should be profiled again in order to ascertain exactly what was accomplished by this modification. This series of steps may have to be repeated several times in order to achieve the desired product. Nevertheless, the process is far shorter than what one would be required to do without the Profiler; the latter process might involve a hit-or-miss search pattern that attempts to identify the program elements that are creating or adding to a particular problem. Profiling enables the programmer to obtain an overall look at all program elements and to considerably narrow the search for offending functions and routines at the end of each profiling.

The Turbo Profiler Environment

If you already know how to use the Programmer's Platform in Borland C++, the Profiler environment will not present too many surprises. All of Borland's Integrated Development Environments (IDEs) work in a similar manner, although different options are offered. In any event, those users accustomed to using Borland's earlier C and C++ compilers will have little difficulty navigating the Profiler environment.

Figure 6-1 shows the basic environment, which is composed of the standard menu bar at the top, the window area at the center, and a status line at the bottom. All of the profiling activities are accomplished in a window or in several windows, because Turbo Profiler offers an abundance of these. In the customary Borland windowing manner, the active window (or window with the focus) will have a Close box and double-barred borders.

Due to the operation of Turbo Profiler and the many things it may be called upon to accomplish, multiwindow displays of activities and reports are commonplace. There is also the usual assortment of dialog boxes, radio buttons, and the various controls for moving and enlarging or shrinking windows.

```
 ≡  File  View  Run  Statistics  Print  Options  Window  Help              READY
[•]=Module: BEEP  File: BEEP.CPP 3======================================1=[↑][↓]
  void  beep(int num)
  {
=►
        int x;
        for (x = 0; x < num; ++x)
=►           printf("%c", 7);

=► }

=►

 Execution Profile                                                     2
 Total time: 0 sec            Display: Time
 % of total: 100%              Filter: All
       Runs: 0 of 1              Sort: Frequency

Alt: F1-Last Help F2-Mark function F3-Close F5-User F6-Undo F10-Local menu
```

Figure 6-1. Example of the basic Turbo Profiler environment.

In most instances, the Turbo Profiler will be called from the Borland C++ Programmer's Platform using the Transfer option from the System menu. This makes sense, because a profiling session normally involves returning to the Borland C++ Programmer's Platform (or IDE), making changes to the source code, recompiling and linking, and then profiling again. This is an interactive process between the Profiler and the Borland C++ programming environment. However, Turbo Profiler may be called from the DOS command line using TPROF. This will cause the Turbo Profiler environment to appear on the screen. Alternately, TPROF may be followed by the name of a file to profile, as in:

```
TPROF filename
```

The extension is not given, because Turbo Profiler assumes a source file and a compiled and linked executable file. While this discussion centers around Borland C++, Turbo Profiler can also be used to profile Turbo Pascal programs.

To insure that your Borland C++ program contains the full symbolic data needed for a profiling session, it is necessary for the Source Debugging option to be set to Standalone. This option is found under Options on the Main menu. When Borland C++ is used to compile from the command line, use the -v option.

To facilitate understanding the use of Turbo Profiler, the following discussion takes you through a simple profiling session. In this session, you will see how different features of Turbo Profiler are called to indicate the program's internal activity.

The program that will be profiled is a simple alphabetizing routine written in Borland C++ and compiled with the Standalone option activated from the Option|Debugger menu. If the Profiler is entered from Borland C++ using the Transfer option, the code that currently resides in the main window will also appear in the main window of Turbo Profiler. Alternately, the Profiler could have been run by issuing TPROF from the DOS command line, followed by the name of the file to be profiled. In this case, our file is named ALPHA.CPP. The source code for this program is shown in Figure 6-2. This program accepts the name of a source file, loads the file from disk, sorts the contents in ascending order, and then rewrites the file.

```
#include <stdio.h>
#include <stdlib.h>
#include <string.h>
#include <ctype.h>
#include <conio.h>

#define cls() system("cls")
main()
{

     FILE *fp;
     int x, p;
     char c[250], *alpha[3000], finame[20];
     void sort(char *[], int);

     cls();
     printf("Name of File To Alphabetize: ");
     gets(finame);

     cls();

     if ((fp = fopen(finame, "r+")) == NULL) {
          puts("Can't Open File");
```

```
                exit(0);
        }

        p = 0;
        while ((fgets(c, 240, fp)) != NULL) {
          if ((alpha[p] = (char *) malloc(strlen(c) + 1)) == NULL) {
                       puts("Not Enough Memory to Alphabetize List");
                       exit(0);
                }

           strcpy(alpha[p++], c);
        }

        cls();

        printf("Alphabetizing List\n");

        sort(alpha, p);

        fseek(fp, 0L, 0);
        for (x = 0; x < p; ++x) {
                fprintf(fp, "%s", alpha[x]);
                free(alpha[x]);
        }

        fclose(fp);

        cls();

        printf("Alphabetizing Completed\n");
        printf("%d Lines Sorted\n", p);
}
void sort(char *x[], int i)
{
        char *y;
        int z, a, b;

        for (z = i / 2; z > 0; z /= 2)
                for (b = z; b < i; b++)
                        for (a = b - z; a >= 0; a -= z){
                                if (strcmp(x[a], x[a + z]) <= 0)
```

```
                break;
            y = x[a];
            x[a] = x[a + z];
            x[a + z] = y;
        }

}
```

Figure 6-2. The source code for ALPHA.CPP.

Figure 6-3 shows the Profiler IDE and the Execution Profile window. The source code for ALPHA.CPP appears in the Module window. The Execution Profile window will display statistics after ALPHA.CPP is executed. The program is set up prior to profiling in the Module window, and the profile data is collected in the Execution Profile window. This latter window will be used to analyze the characteristics of the program.

```
  ≡  File  View  Run  Statistics  Print  Options  Window  Help              READ
[•]=Module: ALPHA  File: ALPHA.CPP 8==============================1=[↑][↓]=
    #include <stdio.h>
    #include <stdlib.h>
    #include <string.h>
    #include <ctype.h>
    #include <conio.h>

    #define cls() system("cls")
=►  main()
    {

            FILE *fp;

 Execution Profile--------------------------------------------------2------
 Total time: 0 sec            Display: Time
 % of total: 100%              Filter: All
       Runs: 0 of 1              Sort: Frequency



F1-Help F2-Area F3-Mod F5-Zoom F6-Next F9-Run F10-Menu
```

Figure 6-3. Example of the Profiler IDE and the Execution Profile window.

Prior to actual execution, it is necessary to specify the area or areas of the program that are to be profiled. The "profile entry point" is the program location where data collection is to begin. In order to perform an analysis on certain portions of the program, it is necessary to know how often each program line is called in the execution chain. In order to do this, every line in the program must be marked as an area. To accomplish this, the Local menu for the Module window must be accessed (Alt-F10). From this menu, select Add Areas. This will bring up a sub-menu, from which the Every Line option is selected. This will set area markers for each line in the code contained in the Module window. After these operations are executed, every executable line in the program source code will be tagged with a marker symbol.

Now we are ready to begin the active profiling process. The easiest way to begin the profile program execution is to press the F9 key. At this point, the program will run and the user will be asked to input the name of the text file to be sorted. For this discussion, the name of a file that contains 377 lines of unsorted text is provided.

Upon program termination, the Turbo Profiler IDE will appear, as shown in Figure 6-4. The Execution Profile window shows only a small portion of the overall report. Pressing the F5 key will zoom the window and allow us to view a much larger portion of the report. This zoomed screen is shown in Figure 6-5.

```
≡  File  View  Run  Statistics  Print  Options  Window  Help                READY
 ─Module: ALPHA  File: ALPHA.CPP 8──────────────────────────────────────1──
   #include <stdio.h>
   #include <stdlib.h>
   #include <string.h>
   #include <ctype.h>
   #include <conio.h>

   #define cls() system("cls")
=► main()
   {

           FILE *fp;

═[■]=Execution Profile═══════════════════════════════════════════2=[↑][↓]═
 Total time: 5.4745 sec      Display: Time
 % of total: 99 %             Filter: All
       Runs: 1 of 1             Sort: Frequency

#ALPHA#18          5.3203 sec   97% |==========================================
#ALPHA#16          0.0648 sec    1% |
#ALPHA#20          0.0601 sec    1% |
#ALPHA#22          0.0163 sec   <1% |

F1-Help F2-Area F3-Mod F5-Zoom F6-Next F9-Run F10-Menu
```

Figure 6-4. Example of the Turbo Profiler IDE.

```
≡  File  View  Run  Statistics  Print  Options  Window  Help                 READY
[•]=Execution Profile=============================================2====[↕]
 Total time: 3.1710 sec       Display: Time
 % of total: 99 %              Filter: All
       Runs: 1 of 1              Sort: Frequency

#ALPHA#18          2.7970 sec  88% |===========================================
#ALPHA#37          0.0646 sec   2% |
#ALPHA#16          0.0643 sec   2% |
#ALPHA#51          0.0604 sec   1% |
#ALPHA#20          0.0601 sec   1% |
#ALPHA#49          0.0418 sec   1% |
#ALPHA#28          0.0354 sec   1% |
#ALPHA#22          0.0198 sec  <1% |
#ALPHA#17          0.0044 sec  <1% |
#ALPHA#53          0.0036 sec  <1% |
#ALPHA#45          0.0036 sec  <1% |
#ALPHA#39          0.0029 sec  <1% |
#ALPHA#54          0.0025 sec  <1% |
#ALPHA#64          0.0021 sec  <1% |
#ALPHA#29          0.0008 sec  <1% |
#ALPHA#46          0.0004 sec  <1% |
#ALPHA#34          0.0003 sec  <1% |

F1-Help F2-Area F3-Mod F5-Zoom F6-Next F9-Run F10-Menu
```

Figure 6-5. Example of a zoomed screen.

The Execution Profile window is now divided into two windows. The upper portion displays the total time required to execute the program. Information about various data is provided in the lower portion of the window. This lower portion is comprised of four columns. First of all, there is the Area Name column, which assigns a number to each area tagged for profiling. In this case, every executable line in the program has been tagged. The second column contains the number of seconds spent in that area. The third column displays a figure that is the percentage of total execution time spent in that single area. And finally, the fourth column contains a magnitude bar, a chart which reflects the percentage of execution time spent in a particular area.

Notice that the Execution Profile chart lists its areas in descending order. This means that the tagged lines that require the most time to execute are listed first, followed by those that take less time. The bar chart on the right simply reflects what is displayed in the Percent column and provides a quick means of identifying areas that require large amounts of execution time. This is a visual reference that allows the user to get a general grasp of area interrelations.

We can see from this example that area 18, designated as

```
#ALPHA#18
```

has required a total of 1.9947 seconds to execute. This means that 58 percent of program execution time was tied up in this area. The next highest percentage of time was required by area 45, which required 0.6788 seconds, 19 percent of total execution time. Ordinarily, the large amount of time (in proportion to other program lines) required by area 18 would be targeted for further profiling and for possible changes to the source code. However, in this case, line 18 contains the gets() function for string retrieval from the keyboard. The lengthy execution time simply reflects the amount of time required to input the filename. (It is understood that the reader can have no idea at this point just where line 18 occurs in the source code. This will be explained in detail a bit later.)

It is also noticed that a bevy of areas in this profiling session have come in at far less than 1/100th of a second. These are found near the bottom of the Execution Profile window. These areas have required less than 1 percent of total execution time, so they are all lumped together in a single percentage figure of <1%. Even though the percentages are the same, you will note that they are still listed in descending order with regard to specific execution time. It should also be understood that the portion of the report that is shown in the figure above is not the complete report. The Execution Profile window must be scrolled to see the report from each tagged area.

You can see immediately that a report of this nature is very useful. But this is simply one aspect of the report. Turbo Profiler has many other display options that are designed to aid the software developer. The previous report used execution time as its key.

Execution time is not the only factor involved in profiling a program. For instance, it is often necessary to know how many times a line is called. Looking again at the above example, we see that area 18 required nearly 2 seconds throughout the program run, which lasted only 3.4162 seconds. (Even though we already know that the reason for this relatively large consumption of total execution time lies in the fact that information is being retrieved from the keyboard, let's assume that we don't.)

Long execution time can be a perfectly natural and acceptable aspect of a program, depending upon exactly what is taking place. Suppose a program calls a function that is extremely efficient. One would expect a relatively low execution time being attributed to that function. However, suppose the function were called one million times. This would result in a relatively long execution-speed count and might tend to shadow the true efficiency of that area in the program.

To know fully what is going on within many programs, it is necessary to obtain a count of the number of times an area is executed, in addition to knowing the total time allocated to those executions. In order to obtain this count, we simply return to the Main menu of the Module window by pressing Alt-F10. Again, the Display option is selected. From the submenu, we move the Radio button to the Counts option. When you exit this menu, you see the report shown in Figure 6-6.

```
 ≡  File  View  Run  Statistics  Print  Options  Window  Help              READY
 =[•]=Execution Profile==========================================2====[↕]=
 Total time: 2.9312 sec      Display: Counts
 % of total: 99 %             Filter: All
       Runs: 1 of 1             Sort: Frequency

 #ALPHA#64                  171  29%
 #ALPHA#63                  171  29%
 #ALPHA#28                   43   7%
 #ALPHA#34                   42   7%
 #ALPHA#46                   42   7%
 #ALPHA#29                   42   7%
 #ALPHA#45                   42   7%
 #ALPHA#62                    5  <1%
 _main                        1  <1%
 #ALPHA#27                    1  <1%
 #ALPHA#37                    1  <1%
 #ALPHA#39                    1  <1%
 #ALPHA#41                    1  <1%
 #ALPHA#43                    1  <1%
 #ALPHA#44                    1  <1%
 #ALPHA#22                    1  <1%
 #ALPHA#20                    1  <1%

F1-Help F2-Area F3-Mod F5-Zoom F6-Next F9-Run F10-Menu
```

Figure 6-6. Example of execution time report.

This report lists tagged areas in descending order. However, execution time is not the key for this report. Instead, it is the number of calls made. From this report, we see that area 64 was called 5311 times, or 29 percent of the total calls made. Again, the bar chart on the right gives us an overall picture of relative call times. Area 63 runs a poor second at 3108 calls, accounting for 17 percent of total calls made. Again, only a portion of the total report is displayed in this window. The rest can be seen by scrolling the Execution Profile window.

Now that we have a profile of the amount of time required for each area to execute and the number of times each area has been called during the execution chain, we can better rate the overall performance of the program. However, it might be even more beneficial if we could combine the two reports to produce a chart of execution times versus the number of calls. (We have already done this by viewing separately each of the two reports discussed above.) Fortunately, Turbo Profiler is perfectly capable of providing a joint report. Again, the Main menu is accessed. Under the Display option, select Both. This means that both counts and times will be included in the same report. When the menu is exited, the report shown in Figure 6-7 will be displayed.

```
 ≡  File  View  Run  Statistics  Print  Options  Window  Help             READY
╔═[•]═Execution Profile═══════════════════════════════════════════2═══[↕]═╗
║ Total time: 4.4402 sec      Display: Time and counts                     ║
║ % of total: 99 %             Filter: All                                 ║
║       Runs: 1 of 1             Sort: Frequency                           ║
╟──────────────────────────────────────────────────────────────────────────╢
║#ALPHA#18                 1  <1% │                                        ▲
║               3.2704 sec   73% │==========================================•
║#ALPHA#45               377   5% │───                                     ░
║               0.5790 sec   13% │=======                                 ░
║#ALPHA#28               378   5% │───                                     ░
║               0.1456 sec    3% │-                                       ░
║#ALPHA#64              2645  36% │─────────────────────                   ░
║               0.0670 sec    1% │                                        ░
║#ALPHA#16                 1  <1% │                                        ░
║               0.0651 sec    1% │                                        ░
║#ALPHA#37                 1  <1% │                                        ░
║               0.0648 sec    1% │                                        ░
║#ALPHA#51                 1  <1% │                                        ░
║               0.0620 sec    1% │                                        ░
║#ALPHA#20                 1  <1% │                                        ░
║               0.0603 sec    1% │                                        ░
║#ALPHA#49                 1  <1% │                                        ▼
╚══════════════════════════════════════════════════════════════════════════╝
Alt: F1-Last Help F2-Mark function F3-Close F5-User F6-Undo F10-Local menu
```

Figure 6-7. The joint report showing both count and times is displayed.

When times and counts are displayed together, each area contains two values in each column. The first value is execution count, followed by execution time. The percentage figures and the bar charts mirror this two-value format. Here it can be seen that area 18 is called only once in the entire program and that this one call requires 1.9947 seconds for execution. On the other hand, area 45 is called 443 times, for a total of 0.6788 seconds of execution time. This latter figure is not per call, but indicates the total time required to complete all 443 calls. The report is generated on a descending basis, with execution time being the key for this order.

Saving/Printing Statistics

A profiling session may be a standard part of a software development project. For this reason, profiling may be performed several times a day for several weeks, months, or longer. It is necessary to have the capability of storing profile reports to a disk file or in hard-copy form from a printer. Also, the information to this point provided by the reports cannot be fully utilized until we match up the information with the source code lines and areas for which the reports were prepared.

To answer all of these needs, Turbo Profiler offers the Print Main menu selection, which will allow reports to be written to files or output to a printer. To print a report, choose the Print selection. From the pop-up menu, select Options. If you wish to write the report to a file, click the File radio button, and then tab to the Destination File input box and type an appropriate name for the file, such as ALPHA.LST. Most users will choose ASCII as the character set for displaying this listing. Now, simply click OK or press Return to exit this menu. Select Print|Module to write the report to ALPHA.LST.

If you choose to output the report to a printer, click the Printer radio button. When you click OK or press Return, the menu will be exited. The report will be sent to the printer when you select Print|Module. Figure 6-8 shows the printed report of our ALPHA.CPP program. This is the same report that would appear in the file ALPHA.LST if the output had been sent to disk instead of to a printer.

With this report, all the information discussed so far comes together. We now see a listing of the original source code, which has been graphed in keys of times and counts. This shows the programmer exactly where time and count overhead is highest. Turbo Profiler automatically includes the date and time of the write, whether it be to file or to printer. This permits an ongoing log of profiling activities and program advancement to be kept.

```
Turbo Profiler Version 1.1i
Program: D:\ECLIPSE\ALPHA.EXE  File ALPHA.CPP
Time   Counts
                 #include <stdio.h>
                 #include <stdlib.h>
                 #include <string.h>
                 #include <ctype.h>
                 #include <conio.h>

                 #define cls() system("cls")
0.0000 1         main()
                 {

                          FILE *fp;
                          int x, p;
                          char c[250], *alpha[3000], finame[20];
                          void sort(char *[], int);
```

Figure 6-8. Sample section of an ALPHA.CPP report.

If we had space to list the entire report here, you would see that the largest execution time overhead lies in the gets() function call, this is of no concern, because it merely reflects the time required to input the filename. This value will be larger or smaller with each profiling session, depending upon how long the user takes to input the filename. The second largest execution time consumption lies in the call to fprintf() ,where the program line is called 443 times. Therefore, there is no indication here that any problem exists. Overall, the program seems to be efficient and in no need of source-code changes.

If you simply wish to print the statistics of the program (time, count, time/count), set the Execution Profile window up as before and select Print|Statistics from the Main menu. The full statistical report will then be printed, a sample section of which is shown in Figure 6-9. If you wish to save the statistics to disk, choose Statistics|Save. This will automatically save full statistical information to a .TFS file, in this case, ALPHA.TFS.

When all the statistical information has been saved to file, you may quit the Profiler at any time without losing any of the information from the particular execution run which generated the statistical report. When the Profiler is entered at a later time, the information may be reloaded from the TFS file by choosing Statistics|Restore. Before this is done, make certain that the file you wish to profile has already been loaded into the Module window. The Statistics|Restore option will automatically load the TFS file associated with that module.

```
Turbo Profiler Version 1.1
Program: E:\BORLANDC\ALPHA.EXE

Execution Profile
Total Time: 4.1312 sec
% of total: 99%
       Run: 1 of 1

Filter: All
  Show: Time
  Sort: Frequency

#ALPHA#18      2.9235 sec  70% ******************************
#ALPHA#45      0.5694 sec   13% ********
#ALPHA#28      0.1828 sec    4% **
```

Figure 6-9. Sample section of the full statistical report.

This discussion has taken you through the basics of a simple profiling session. The program that was profiled was relatively clean and not in need of any major design changes. However, improving a program's performance by using Turbo Profiler is not usually as simple as the tutorial example above might indicate.

Let's assume we are profiling a program that has shown some undesirable characteristics that we wish to detect and improve upon if possible. The first task is to locate the bottlenecks in the program. These would be program areas where the code causes execution to be bogged down. Perhaps these areas may already be suspected from observation of the source code alone. But often there is some uncertainty in such perfunctory inspections, so Turbo Profiler may be utilized to confirm your suspicions. In many instances, it may not confirm such suspicions and may identify a formerly unsuspected program construct as the true culprit.

To accomplish the initial profiling task, run a profile on the program using the default settings. When the results are reported in the Execution Profile window, you will have an immediate idea of which routines in your program consume the largest amount of execution time. These areas can be inspected further by displaying a time-and-count report. As was the case in the previous discussion, an area that consumes a large amount of execution time may be one that is called thousands of times within the execution chain. This will serve as a further indication as to whether or not an inefficiency exists in this single code area. If a program area requires two seconds to execute and is called only once, it may be inefficient. However, if the same area is called 10,000 times, it may be highly efficient.

Once the initial statistical information has been provided by Turbo Profiler, a report can be generated that matches this information with the program source code. At this point, the user will most likely want to closely analyze the report in hopes of detecting, by visual inspection alone, an easily correctable flaw in the program segment.

With these corrections made, the modified program can be profiled again in much the same manner. At this point, however, you may want to select only the suspect program areas for reporting. This process will continue over and over again until the program has met the user's efficiency requirements.

Summary

This discussion has touched briefly upon the highlights of Borland's Turbo Profiler. It is an extremely powerful tool that should be utilized for any and every new program that is written—another step toward the goal of utilizing the highest possible efficiency in program design. One major aspect of Turbo Profiler that sometimes goes unheralded is its ability to teach programmers to write more efficient code. Turbo Profiler might better have been named "Turbo Critic," for, indeed, its job is to criticize a program, and identify its weak points.

Through the continued use of Turbo Profiler, the programmer begins to become more conscious of inefficiencies that may tend to be created by his/her particular programming style. Through this awareness, styles change and Turbo Profiler makes fewer and fewer critical remarks about the source-code content. It is through exercises such as these that great programmers are made.

CHAPTER 7

Windows Programming

If there is a single factor that distinguishes Borland C++ from Borland Turbo C++, it is Borland C++'s ability to produce applications for Windows 3.0—alone and unaided by additional software. As I stated in an earlier chapter, Borland C++ provides all the necessary tools for building Windows applications. You don't need anything else.

However, writing an application for Windows is not a simple matter of compiling your pet C or C++ source code under Borland C++. Windows programming is a separate discipline unto itself. Existing C or C++ programs require major modification to allow them to exist as Windows entities.

Programmers who are already writing Windows applications using the Microsoft resources and who are familiar with C++ will have little difficulty in making the easy transition to using Borland C++ exclusively for writing all applications. However, those users with no Windows experience will require a comprehensive course in the Windows environment, protocols, and general procedures.

While Borland C++ provides tutorial source code and documentation for C++ programming, it does not address Windows programming in the same manner. There is a documentation file that assists programmers in addressing Windows applications, but it falls far short of being an exhaustive orientation to this subject.

Programming Windows applications using Borland C++ is more a process of calling Windows routines from the C++ programming language, as opposed to writing a typical C++ program and somehow running it in the Windows environment. But C++ is very well adapted to Windows programming due to its object-oriented nature.

Writing a Windows application involves relatively complex data structures which are best addressed as a single unit or class. Windows is a message-based system. The Windows environment communicates with an application via an exchange of messages. Windows tells an application that something has occurred; the application receives this message and then decides on an appropriate response.

A Windows application, as it relates to Borland C++, is a program that is designed to be run under Windows. Such an application can call functions from dynamic link libraries and from static libraries. It can also cause other applications to be run. Dynamic link libraries (DLLs) are library modules that are dynamically linked to an application at the time of execution. A dynamic link can drastically cut down on the size of code, because a single copy of any function called will serve all applications that reference it. The function itself never actually becomes a part of the executable code. It is simply called when it is needed during run time.

Every Windows program or module compiled under Borland C++ must include the windows.h header file. This file contains prototypes of all the Windows functions and makes other definitions necessary for accessing the Windows environment. In effect, this file contains 90 percent of the tools needed to program a Windows application.

If you are new to Windows programming, a first glance at a Windows application written under Borland C++ can be a most interesting and intimidating experience. Although the code resembles other C++ programs in structure, every other aspect seems quite alien. It all appears confusing, because of the Windows routines that are provided by the Borland C++ environment. The windows.h header file contains a wealth of definitions. The best way to begin to overcome this confusion is to perfunctorily glance through the source code of windows.h and identify its various definitions and functions by name. You may not learn much about the exact nature of the definitions and functions, but at least you can familiarize yourself with their predefined names.

The next step is to obtain a basic reference source for Windows programming. There is a wealth of these on the market aimed at readers of varying levels of expertise. What we are dealing with here is, in a sense, two languages. The first is the Microsoft Windows "toolkit," and the second is Borland C++. Borland C++ calls the Windows tools and executes them in the proper order. Programmers who have used adjunct graphics packages with ANSI C and C++ compilers will be quite familiar with the concept of calling discrete routines from within the environment of a specific computer language.

Once a Windows program has been written in Borland C++, the process of compiling and linking appears to be identical to those same operations performed on standard (non-Windows) programs. The compiler builds an object file and then links it with the Borland C++ start-up code, libraries, and the module-definition file.

The object code created during compilation of a Windows module differs (internally) from a standard DOS implementation. The Windows prolog and epilog code surround each function. The exact nature of the prolog and epilog code vary depending on the Windows compilation options that are chosen. Lastly, the Resource Compiler is called on to connect the resources to the EXE module. This is an extra step that does not occur during a standard (non-Windows) compilation.

Because the concept of creating object code and linking it with the start-up code to form an executable module is not foreign to any reader, let's concentrate on the resource files that are necessary to arrive at a module that will execute under Windows.

First of all, "resources" or resource files are such things as dialog boxes, icons, bitmaps, fonts, and cursors that are a part of a typical Microsoft Windows environment or program. Each program written to run under windows is often by a resource file containing a .RC extension. Usually the base name of the resource file is the same as the name of the C++ (.CPP) source file.

Resource files are standard text files that may be composed within the IDE, on a word processor, or by using the DOS Line Editor (EDLIN). Obviously, the easiest method of writing such a file utilizes the Borland C++ IDE.

The resource file with the .RC extension is actually source code that must be compiled by the Resource Compiler. The output from this compiler will be a binary file with a .RES extension with the same base name as the .RC file. Therefore, compiling TEST.RC will result in TEST.RES. The Resource Compiler also binds the .RES file to the .EXE file. The Resource Compiler is the instrument that makes a module become Windows-compatible. It compiles .RC files to .RES files, binds the .RES file to the previously compiled and linked .EXE or .DLL module, and then flags the final output as a Windows module. Using Borland C++, a .RC file is not mandatory for producing Windows applications that do not use any of the special resources. The sample .RC file supplied with the Borland C++ package simply gives the filename of an icon file (.ICO) as a resource for a WHELLO Windows application example.

Using Borland C++, a Windows application will often contain three types of source files. Using the TEST base name, they would be TEST.CPP, TEST.RC, and TEST.DEF. All three of these are source-code files with TEST.CPP containing C++ code and TEST.RC containing the resource code.

TEST.DEF is the module-definition file. This file contains information used by the linker to determine the system requirements for the matching Windows application. The .DEF file contains the name of the application, a user description, the stack and heap size, and the nature of the code type. While the .CPP and .RC files are mandatory for creating a Windows application, the .DEF file is optional. TLINK, the Borland C++ linker, is "intelligent" in that it can determine the required information on its own. For this reason, the .DEF files which have previously been a necessary part of a Windows application, can be ignored (in most instances) when such applications are produced under Borland C++.

All of these features make Borland C++ an ideal environment for beginning Windows programmers, as well as for seasoned pros. The IDE can be used to develop new Windows applications simply by writing a Windows program, and compiling/linking it in a familiar manner—that's all there is to it. Assuming no special icons or other resources are to be used (which is normal during the learning stages of Windows programming), the user-written program is ready to run under Windows as soon as the compilation/linking process is completed. Naturally, as special resources are incorporated during further training sessions, the need for the .RC resource file arises. As the user learns more about resource programming (using the Whitewater Resource Toolkit bundled with Borland C++), these resources will be brought into (formerly) basic Windows applications. (I can think of no better method for bringing programmers into a Windows environment without the overhead of producing a resource and definition file for each application.)

The Compilation/Linking Process

As is the case with standard C++ applications, most Windows applications will be built using the Programmer's Platform (IDE). Certainly, the command-line compiler/linker may be called directly (the main reason for resorting to the command-line options would be constraints on available machine RAM) or with a Make file, but why go to the bother when the IDE will handle the same jobs in a user-interactive manner?

To set up the IDE for Windows applications, you simply open a new project and add the names of the source-code modules that are to form the application. Typically, the project will consist of the C++ source-code module(s) and the appropriate .DEF and .RC files—when the latter two are incorporated. As was stated earlier, these two files are not mandatory for a basic Windows application.

Once the project file has been completed, the user selects Options | Application to open the Set Application Options dialog box. Here there is a choice of procedures that address the various application capabilities of Borland C++. Choose Windows Applications, and you're all set to compile and link a Windows application.

Once the source code for all modules in the project has been entered, the Compile | Build option from the IDE will perform all the necessary operations. Assuming correct source code, the Windows application is complete and ready to be run in the Windows environment.

Let's compare this procedure with building a standard MS-DOS application. First, a project file is written naming all the modules that are to be included. Second, the Option | Application selection from the IDE is chosen and the mode set to DOS Standard. The C++ source code for all modules is entered in the edit window(s) and Compile | Build is selected. Then the modules are compiled and linked, resulting in an executable file running under DOS. The only difference between creating a DOS application and a Windows application lies in the choice of the Borland C++ application mode.

The point here is that a programmer who is familiar with the Borland C++ IDE does not have to do anything significantly different when building a Windows application. The familiar environment is just as friendly with Windows applications as it is with standard C++ programs that run under DOS. Not only has Borland brought Windows programming capability to their C++ compiler but the company has done so in a manner that should not intimidate anyone.

Building Windows Applications from the Command Line

To compile and link a Windows application from the command line, type in the following at the DOS prompt:

```
BCC -W FINNAME.CPP
```

FINAME is the name of the C++ source code file. The -W option tells the compiler/linker that this is a Windows application. With this single command, FINAME.CPP is compiled into FINAME.OBJ. The linker is then called to connect the appropriate libraries and start-up code.

If a resource file is incorporated, the resource compiler must be invoked at this point. The appropriate command is

```
rc -r FINAME.RC
```

where FINAME.RC is the name of the resource source-code file. This will be compiled into FINAME.RES. Next, rc is invoked again to add the binary source code from FINAME.RES to the executable module. The command line for this operation is

```
rc FINAME.RES FINAME.EXE
```

If the executable file has the same base name as the resource file, then all that is necessary is to input

```
rc FINAME
```

on the command line, and the Borland Resource Compiler will do the rest.

There are numerous options available for controlling the command-line compile/link process. These options address compile without doing such things as automatic linking or debugging information generation.

When a Windows module is compiled under Borland C++, the compiler must know what kind of prolog or epilog to create for the functions in each module. The prolog may be defined as the entry code for a module while the epilog is the exit code. Using the IDE, the correct options are selected within the environment. Using the command line, switch settings are selected to determine the type. Under the IDE, choosing Windows App in Options | Application will automatically set the compiler up for Windows All Functions Exportable. If you select Windows DLL, then the compiler entry/exit code defaults to Windows DLL Exportable. In other words, the IDE allows a single-application selection to set up the most appropriate entry/exit code.

The prolog and epilog ensure that the correct data segment is active during callback functions; prologs and epilogs are not exclusive to windows but occur in all executable programs—including those that run in the MS-DOS environment (standard .EXE files). They also mark the near and far stack frames for the Windows stack-crawling mechanism.

When the Option | Application option is set to Windows All Functions Exportable, this is the same as producing the -W option when the compiler is invoked via the command line. Using either method, the Windows object module is created with all far functions. This mode should be considered the default setting for Windows applications, although the code it produces is not always the most efficient type. In this mode of operation, the Borland C++ compiler generates a prolog/epilog set for each far function. This is what makes the module exportable; it does not mean that every far function is or will be exported, only that each *can* be exported.

To export a function, it is necessary to use the _export key word. Alternately, the function name may be entered in the EXPORTS portion of the module-definition file.

Another application option is Windows Explicit Functions Exported. This is selected within the IDE as an alternative to Windows All Functions Exported or via the command line switch -WE. When this mode is invoked, only those functions tagged as _export may be exported. In most applications modules, many functions will not be exported. For this reason, it makes sense to strive for the highest possible efficiency by tagging those functions that are to be exported. The Borland C++ compiler provides tagged functions with the prolog and epilog for exportable functions. Using this mode, all functions not specifically tagged with _export are provided abbreviated prolog/epilog codes. This results in a smaller object module which, in turn, usually brings about an increase in execution speed.

The Windows Explicit Functions Exported mode works only in conjunction with the _export key word. This means that the EXPORTS portion of a definition module is not read for a list of export functions as was described in an earlier discussion. Any attempt to utilize the EXPORTS option results in incompatible prolog/epilog code that will wreak havoc.

Another entry/exit code mode supported by Borland C++ is called Windows Smart Callbacks, which is invoked on the command line with the -WS switch or can be directly selected via the IDE. This produces prolog/epilog code, which assumes that the default data segment is identical to the stack segment, thus eliminating the need for special code that is created for exported functions. Windows Smart Callbacks is a speed-enhancement option that, when invoked, produces function calls that do not have to be passed through the special Window code.

In this mode of operation, exported functions do not require the _export key word, nor do they need to be listed in the EXPORTS section of the definition file. While operating in Smart-Callbacks mode, the linker does not need to create an export entry in the executable file in order for functions to be exported. Dynamic Link Libraries (DLLs) are not supported, because in the Smart-Callbacks mode, the compiler assumes that the data segment and the stack segment (DS == SS) are identical. Also, DS must not be changed explicitly (programmer-changed) in the Windows module. The latter requirement should pose few, if any, problems, because changing the DS is usually avoided, being that it is a potentially hazardous practice in Windows applications in the first place.

Windows applications may be programmed in several—but not all—memory models available in Borland C++. No executable Windows applications may use the tiny- or huge-memory models. If you try to use either of these two models, code will be generated without error messages, but this code will not execute within the Windows environment. Keep all Windows applications confined to the small-, compact-, medium-, or large-memory models.

The previous discussions in this chapter have presented an overview of the processes and options involved in generating Windows applications using Borland C++. It should be obvious by now that, on the surface, compiling and linking a Windows application differs little (externally) from compiling and linking standard MS-DOS applications. Other than changing the application option that is standard with MS-DOS programs, everything else remains about the same. The fact that the programmer needs to make few adjustments when compiling and linking a Windows application (in comparison with a DOS application) means that the process of learning Windows programming is shortened considerably. Seasoned Windows programmers will benefit from this feature as well, because they will be able to concentrate fully on coding the application and won't have to worry about getting it into executable form after this coding has been entered.

Programming Windows Applications

The next section of this chapter deals specifically with source code for Windows applications developed under Borland C++. As we alluded to previously, the Borland C++ package is a complete Windows development environment. However, it is not a Windows tutorial. In the \EXAMPLES directory of Borland C++, you will find several examples of Windows applications that can be used as a guide, but this will be of most use to persons who have previous experience with Windows applications using the Microsoft development kit. Those persons who have no experience in programming Windows applications will need further guidance. (This guidance can be obtained from other Windows tutorial sources.) However, because Borland C++ is a relatively new software offering, it may be some time before a large selection of Borland C++ Windows applications guides are available.

The discussions that follow provide several Windows programs written in Borland C++ and should be adequate for familiarizing new Windows programmers with the basic methods used to write Windows applications. These discussions will also lay the groundwork for using current Windows tutorials and making the necessary modifications to effect the same operations under Borland C++.

When newcomers to Windows programming take a first look at the source code for even a simple application, they discover that there is a fear factor that must be dealt with first: There is so much code, even for a "simple" application. An untutored glance at such source-code examples is sometimes enough to cause a less determined programmer to give up.

To overcome this impression (a false one), let's begin by stating for the record that the majority of code in a simple Windows application is overhead. Such code portions form the basis for getting to a point in the program where the actual work—the specific actions that are to be effected by the application—takes place. Most of this overhead is core material that is repeated verbatim in every Windows application. The programmer need not be overly concerned with this overhead code, at least in the early stages of Windows program development.

We'll enter the world of Windows programs using Borland C++ by first discussing the application(s) in blocks. This will feed information to the reader a logical code block at a time and make the overall process clear and far less intimidating than would be the case if we started with a full-program example.

The first code block extract is shown below, and forms the beginning of the Windows application that is designed to display a single-line message in a window. One must remember that the Windows application must establish (create) a window and prepare to write to it before any message may be displayed. (Most of the overall code in this entire program deals with setting up a particular window and in communicating what has, is, and will take place to the central control block.) The opening code section follows:

```
class core {
     public:
          static int manip;
          static int event(void);
          static HANDLE hInstance;
          static HANDLE hPrevInstance;

};

PAINTSTRUCT pstruct;
RECT rect;
HANDLE core::hInstance = 0;
HANDLE core::hPrevInstance = 0;
int::core::manip = 0;
```

This opening code block declares a class named "core" which contains four static members. In explaining what we have so far, it is necessary to know what a handle is in Windows application programming. Put simply, a handle is a 16-bit number that refers to an object. A handle may reference a particular window, an icon, a cursor or whatever. In the preceding block, HANDLE is a typdef and hInstance is the instance handle. This is a 16-bit number that identifies this program when it is running under Windows. No other program will have this same handle. The instance-handle value assigned to one program is always different from that assigned to another program running under Windows.

The instance handle of the most recent previous instance of this same program is found in the hPrevInstance parameter. If only one copy of this program is running under Windows, then the value of hPrevInstance is NULL. One must remember that Windows is a multitasking environment where the same program may be run several times simultaneously. Even though there is only one copy of a particular program, it may be called, and while it is running, may be called again. In such a case, two copies of this program are currently executing in memory. Each will have a different instance handle. However, the one that is called second will contain the hInstance value of the one run first in its hPrevInstance parameter. The variable named "manip" is assigned a value when the program is run under Windows. This number indicates how the window is to be displayed in the Windows environment. We are speaking here of the window that is set up (in this example) to display the single-line message.

The event() prototype is of a method that keeps tabs on the message queue maintained by Windows. When an event occurs, Windows translates this event into a message that is then placed in the queue. The event() method retrieves messages from the queue. (More on this later.)

Two structs contained in the windows.h header file that must be #included with any Windows application which comes into play at this point in the code fragment are PAINTSTRUCT and RECT. The first declares a structure which contains data used for painting the area of a window known as the client area—the area written to by the application. RECT declares a structure defined in windows.h, which will contain the dimensions of the client area in pixels. Finally, the class members are assigned initial values, and this completes the opening segment of the Windows application. Admittedly, this code block does practically nothing. However, it lays out the "tools" that will be needed to build this application.

The following code block is the method used for retrieving event messages:

```
int core::event(void)
{
     MSG msg;

     while (GetMessage(&msg, NULL, 0, 0)) {
          TranslateMessage(&msg);
          DispatchMessage(&msg);
     }

     return msg.wParam;
}
```

This member function or method of class core contains the routine that accesses the message queue. The contents of event() are quite straightforward and easy to understand. Variable msg is a structure of type MSG which is defined in the windows.h #include file. The GetMessage function called in the "while" loop retrieves the message from the queue. The NULL and 0, 0 parameters indicate that all messages for all windows created by this application are to be retrieved.

The TranslateMessage call passes the loaded contents in msg back to Windows for translation. There is another exchange and DispatchMessage sends the contents in msg back to Windows, which in turn sends the message to the targeted window for processing. wParam is a member of struct MSG. This is a 16-bit number that indicates the meaning of the message that has been retrieved.

The following code fragment defines another class and some additional tools to facilitate Windows programming. Not all of the members/methods will be used for every program, but here we are setting up an environment to facilitate the easy writing of Windows applications. The code follows.

```
class corewin {
     protected:
          HWND wndhandle;
     public:
          virtual long WndProc(WORD message, WORD wParam, LONG
lParam ) = 0;
```

```
        HWND GetHandle(void)
        {
            return(wndhandle);

        }
        int display(int manip)
        {

            return (ShowWindow(wndhandle, manip));

        }

};
corewin *rtnptr(HWND wndhandle)
{

    return (corewin *) GetWindowWord(wndhandle, 0);

}

void SetPointer(HWND wndhandle, corewin *winpntr)
{

    SetWindowWord(wndhandle, 0, (WORD) winpntr);

}
```

The corewin class could be defined as the base class. wndhandle is defined as a structure of type HWND, the handle to a window. As we discussed previously, every window has a unique handle that identifies that window and that window only. The unique value will be contained in wndhandle. This structure name should be thought of as the unique window which is being handled by any block of code that names it.

A function called WndProc is prototyped in this class definition. A Windows procedure may be given any name. This is set up as a virtual function which makes corewin an abstract class. GetHandle is a method that returns the window handle when called on, while display() calls ShowWindow, which causes the designated window to be displayed on the screen. (This method will be called in another program block to follow.)

Two other functions are defined. The first, rntptr(), calls GetWindowWord() and returns a pointer of type corewin, which names the address of the window procedure identified by wndhandle. The second, the SetPointer function, sets the address of a windows procedure. (Their use will be explained a bit later.)

The next block of code establishes yet another class and goes directly into the process of defining the exact type of window that will be generated by this application.

```
class corepgm:public corewin {
    private:
        static char winname[30];
    public:
        static void Register(void)
        {
            WNDCLASS wndclass; // Structure used to register
Windows class.
            wndclass.style        = CS_HREDRAW | CS_VREDRAW;
            wndclass.lpfnWndProc = ::WndProc;
            wndclass.cbClsExtra   = 0;
            wndclass.cbWndExtra   = sizeof(corepgm *);
            wndclass.hInstance    = core::hInstance;
            wndclass.hIcon        = LoadIcon(core::hInstance,
IDI_APPLICATION);
            wndclass.hCursor      = LoadCursor( NULL,
IDC_ARROW);
            wndclass.hbrBackground    = GetStockObject(
WHITE_BRUSH );
            wndclass.lpszMenuName     = NULL;
            wndclass.lpszClassName    = winname;

            if (!RegisterClass(&wndclass))
                exit(0);
        }
```

Class corepgm is derived from class corewin and defines a variable, winname[], which will later be used to provide the window name and the window caption. This block registers the class after proper assignments have been made in another portion of the program. The initial registration assumes that this is the first instance of this window. A previous instance would mean that the class had already been registered. Only one registration is appropriate per class.

Variable wndclass is declared a struct of type WNDCLASS, which is the structure used to register a Windows class. A window is always created based upon a class. This class identifies the various procedures that will be used in processing messages to this window. WNDCLASS has ten fields, the first of which is wndclass.style. This assignment uses two identifiers that are defined in windows.h. Identifier CS_HREDRAW stands for horizontal redraw, while CS_VREDRAW means vertical redraw. The two values are ORed, and this results in a value that tells the Windows environment to completely repaint (reproduce) the window whenever the horizontal window size or the vertical window size changes. This means that the contents of the window will appear in proper position, regardless of how the window may be resized by the user. This window-style setting is standard and will be used with most window classes.

The second field in the WNDCLASS structure sets the window procedure for this class to WndProc. This is a function that processes all messages to the window or windows created, based upon this particular class.

The third and fourth fields in this structure determine the storage space that will be needed by the class. This storage is maintained internally by the Windows environment. If the program is not to make use of this extra space, then the values may be zero. However, in this example, the fourth field is assigned a value that is the size of corepgm. This space will be used to store a pointer to the C++ object that corresponds to this window.The fifth field assigns the instance handle that was discussed earlier. The sixth field is used to specify the icon that is to be used to represent this application. In this example, IDI_APPLICATION is used. This is the default or standard icon that is a part of the Windows environment. The loadIcon function gets the handle of the specified icon. If you have created your own icon (using the Whitewater Resource Toolkit), then the name of the icon file may be given as the argument to LoadIcon.

The above discussion also holds true for the next field assignment, where the LoadCursor function is called to return a handle to the cursor that is to be active with this application. The first argument to this function is NULL. The second argument names one of the three available predefined cursors. The IDI_ARROW definition specifies the common arrow cursor. You may also choose from the crosshair or the hourglass cursor which users of Windows have seen many, many times. The IDI_ARROW cursor is the standard cursor and it will be used in most general Windows applications. The hourglass is usually incorporated during portions of an application where the user must wait while some processing takes place. The crosshair cursor is often seen in graphics drawing applications.

The next field is similar to the previous two, in that GetStockObject is called to return a value that corresponds to the background color in which the window is to be painted. WHITE_BRUSH specifies a solid white background. We could as easily have chosen GRAY_BRUSH, LTGRAY_BRUSH, or BLACK_BRUSH. Each of these will produce a different background color. WHITE_BRUSH might be called the standard, or default, background color designation.

The next field is assigned a value of NULL. This is done, because no menu is to be used with this application. If a menu were to be included with an application, the menu name would be given to this field.

The last field is the classname. This is the same as the name of the program and it is given here in the pointer to the winname[] array.

Lastly, RegisterClass is called within an if-statement construct. This function will return a zero (NULL) value if the class is properly registered. If not, it will return non-zero. If this should occur, an exit statement terminates further execution and sends an error return.

Now that the window class has been successfully registered, it's time to create the window proper. To do this, the CreateWindow function is called. The following code block will detail this procedure. Remember, we are still operating from within the corepgm class.

```
    corepgm(void)
    {
        wndhandle = CreateWindow(winname,
        "BORLAND C++ WINDOWS EXAMPLE",//winname,
        WS_OVERLAPPEDWINDOW,
        CW_USEDEFAULT,
        CW_USEDEFAULT,
        CW_USEDEFAULT,
        CW_USEDEFAULT,
        NULL,
        NULL,
        core::hInstance,
        (LPSTR) this );

        if (!wndhandle)
            exit(0); // Error Return

        display(core::manip);
        UpdateWindow(wndhandle);
    }

    long WndProc(WORD message, WORD wParam, LONG lParam);

}; // End corepgm class definitions
```

This block defines the general characteristics of the window and allows the same window class to be used for other windows. The handle from the window (wndhandle) is assigned the return from the CreateWindow() function which requires ten arguments. The first field is handed a pointer to winname, the char array that was created earlier. Actually, winname could also have been supplied as the second argument, as this is the same as the quoted string constant. The second argument to CreateWindow() should be handed the caption that is to be written at the top center of the window.

The third parameter is handed the WS_OVERLAPPEDWINDOW definition, which is simply a number that indicates the style of the window. This style is the default type, the standard Windows window.

The next four parameters are handed values of CW_USEDEFAULT, which indicates that the default position for an overlapped window is to be used. CW_DEFAULT used four times indicates, in order, the initial x position and the initial y position of the window (location); and the initial x and y size of the window.

The next two parameters of CreateWindow address handles to a parent window and a menu. Since there is no parent window or menu for this example, the fields are assigned NULL values. The 9th argument is the program-instance handle core::hInstance which was discussed earlier. The last argument is a char far pointer to the window object which uses the LPSTR typedef (char far) and the 'this' key word. 'this' is a local variable available in the body of the function and is cast by (LPSTR). This is the creation parameter that sets a pointer to data that will later be referenced.

The next code block defines the overloaded WndProc() function.

```
long FAR PASCAL _export WndProc(HWND wndhandle, WORD message,
WORD wParam,
                             LONG lParam)
{
     corewin *winpntr = rtnptr(wndhandle);

     if (!winpntr) {
          if (message == WM_CREATE) {
               LPCREATESTRUCT lpcs;
               lpcs = (LPCREATESTRUCT) lParam;
               winpntr = (corewin *) lpcs->lpCreateParams;
               SetPointer(wndhandle, winpntr);
               return(winpntr->WndProc(message, wParam, lParam));
          }
          else
               return (DefWindowProc(wndhandle, message, wParam,
lParam));
     }
     else
          return (winpntr->WndProc(message, wParam, lParam));

}
```

This code block uses the _export keyword to indicate that this is an exportable (far) function. The rtnptr() function is called to return a pointer to the C++ object which is the window. Pointer winpntr is valid when it is initialized to zero. The value in winpntr is tested within the if-statement construct. Within this construct is a nested if clause. This tests for a call to WM_CREATE, which is a direct call to actually create the window based on a window class. This function will be discussed as part of a later code fragment. When WM_CREATE is encountered, lpcs is declared a structure of type LPCREATESTRUCT and is assigned the value in lParam, the message parameter. The pointer to the object is stored in the window's extra bytes in order to provide direct access to the object and its member functions.

Next, SetPointer() is called to store a pointer to this object in the window's extra bytes in order to access this object and its member functions. After this, the object is allowed to perform the initialization from its own WndProc. The return from this is handed to winpntr.

The next code block calls the WinMain function. In a Windows application, WinMain takes the place of the main() function in a standard C or C++ program. WinMain() is the main entry point for a Windows application. The code block follows.

```
int PASCAL WinMain(HANDLE hInstance, HANDLE hPrevInstance,
LPSTR lpszCmdLine,int manip)
{
     core::manip = manip;
     core::hInstance = hInstance;
     core::hPrevInstance = hPrevInstance;

     if (core::hPrevInstance == 0)
          corepgm::Register();

     corepgm coreWnd;
     return(core::event());
}
```

This function accepts four arguments which are the instance handle, the previous instance handle, a pointer (far) to a null-terminated command-line string, and an integer which specifies how the application's window is to be displayed. Again WinMain is the entry point for all Windows applications. It is this part of the program that causes all of the previous actions to execute. All program statements are executed under the auspices of WinMain. The return value from WinMain is not currently used by Windows, although it may be in the future. For now, this return is useful for debugging when using Turbo Debugger, which will display the return value upon program termination. WinMain then ties the rest of the program together in an executable package.

There is one additional code fragment that remains to be discussed. This is the fragment where the actual commands that tell Windows exactly what to do in the window are found. This portion was saved for last, because it is the only code portion that differs drastically from application to application. For the most part, all of the previous code fragments are overhead. That is, these fragments will appear in similar form in every basic Windows application. This overhead code represents the minimum "structure" for carrying out programmers' commands.

Bearing this in mind, remember that the previous code may be (and certainly will be) bundled in a header file and incorporated into many different types of Windows applications. Some minor changes will have to be made in values assigned to some of the elements of this overhead code, but it will remain largely unchanged.

The next code fragment is where the actual commands—the commands that tell Windows what to write and how to display it—are found. This is also the point at which we can incorporate code that is more in line with standard C++ procedures, although special Windows functions will be called.

```
long corepgm::WndProc(WORD message, WORD wParam, LONG lParam)
{

     char *wmsg = "The Quick Brown Fox Jumped Over the Lazy
Dog.";
     switch (message) {

          case WM_CREATE:
```

```
                    break;

                case WM_DESTROY:
                    PostQuitMessage(0);
                    break;

                case WM_PAINT:
                    BeginPaint(wndhandle, &pstruct);
                    GetClientRect(wndhandle, (LPRECT) &rect);
                    DrawText(pstruct.hdc, wmsg, -1, &rect,
DT_SINGLELINE
| DT_CENTER | DT_VCENTER);

                    EndPaint(wndhandle, &pstruct);
                    break;

                default:
                    return(DefWindowProc(wndhandle, message, wParam,
lParam));
        }
}
```

Within the body of this function, a char pointer is declared and assigned the string constant that is to be displayed in the window. A simple switch, which uses the value in variable message as its argument. The value in the message will correspond to one of the cases in the switch. WM_CREATE, WM_DESTROY, and WM_PAINT are all int values that signal a specific Windows action.

When WM_CREATE is encountered, a break statement is executed, because this occurrence is picked up on the message queue and handled by a code block which was discussed earlier. When the code encountered is WM_DESTROY, this window application is ended, and the physical window is destroyed (erased). This is accomplished by a call to the PostQuitMessage function that sends the quit message to the queue. The actual writing takes place with WM_PAINT, which executes the BeginPaint function, which initiates the window painting operation. GetClientRect obtains the dimensions of the window's client (user) area, and DrawText displays the text string contained in wmsg[]. The -1 parameter in this last function indicates that the string is terminated by a NULL byte. The DT_SINGLELINE | DT_CENTER | DT_VCENTER combination is an ORed series of bit flags, which indicate that the text is to be displayed as a single line that is horizontally and vertically centered in the window. The EndPaint function terminates the painting process.

Understand that the switch is used to determine which procedure the window is receiving and how to respond accordingly. Any messages that are received and are not to be processed must be passed on to the DefWindowProc which returns a value to the windows procedure.

This last small block of code is not more Windows overhead. This is the portion of code that new Windows programmers will be most concerned with in order to get the "feel" of Windows applications. All the code that went before it simply allowed for these few simple functions to act.

The following full program is a combination of all the code blocks that have been previously presented. This application will display the message "The Quick Brown Fox Jumped Over the Lazy Dog." in the center of an overlapped window.

```
#include <windows.h>
#include <stdlib.h>
#include <string.h>

long FAR PASCAL _export WndProc(HWND wndhandle, WORD message,
                                WORD wParam, LONG lParam);
class core {
     public:
          static int manip;
          static int event(void);
          static HANDLE hInstance;
          static HANDLE hPrevInstance;

};

PAINTSTRUCT pstruct;
RECT rect;
HANDLE core::hInstance = 0;
HANDLE core::hPrevInstance = 0;
int core::manip = 0;
```

```
int core::event(void)
{
     MSG msg;

     while (GetMessage(&msg, NULL, 0, 0)) {
          TranslateMessage(&msg);
          DispatchMessage(&msg);
     }

     return msg.wParam;
}

class corewin {
     protected:
          HWND wndhandle;
     public:
          virtual long WndProc(WORD message, WORD wParam, LONG
lParam ) = 0;

          HWND GetHandle(void)
          {
               return wndhandle;

          }
          int display(int manip)
          {

               return (ShowWindow(wndhandle, manip));

          }

};

corewin *rtnptr(HWND wndhandle)
{

     return (corewin *) GetWindowWord(wndhandle, 0);

}
```

```
void SetPointer(HWND wndhandle, corewin *winpntr)
{

     SetWindowWord(wndhandle, 0, (WORD) winpntr);

}

class corepgm:public corewin {
     private:
          static char winname[30];
     public:
          static void Register(void)
          {
               WNDCLASS wndclass; // Structure used to register
Windows class.
               wndclass.style        = CS_HREDRAW | CS_VREDRAW;
               wndclass.lpfnWndProc  = ::WndProc;
               wndclass.cbClsExtra   = 0;
               wndclass.cbWndExtra   = sizeof(corepgm *);
               wndclass.hInstance    = core::hInstance;
               wndclass.hIcon        = LoadIcon(core::hInstance,
IDI_APPLICATION);
               wndclass.hCursor      = LoadCursor( NULL,
IDC_ARROW);
               wndclass.hbrBackground     = GetStockObject(
WHITE_BRUSH );
               wndclass.lpszMenuName      = NULL;
               wndclass.lpszClassName     = winname;

               if (!RegisterClass(&wndclass))
                    exit(0);
          }

     corepgm(void)
     {
          wndhandle = CreateWindow(winname,
          "BORLAND C++ WINDOWS EXAMPLE",
          WS_OVERLAPPEDWINDOW,
          CW_USEDEFAULT,
          CW_USEDEFAULT,
```

```
            CW_USEDEFAULT,
            CW_USEDEFAULT,
            NULL,
            NULL,
            core::hInstance,
            (LPSTR) this);

            if (!wndhandle)
                exit(0); // Error Return

            display(core::manip);
            UpdateWindow(wndhandle);
        }

        long WndProc(WORD message, WORD wParam, LONG lParam);

};

char corepgm::winname[] = "BORLAND C++ WINDOW EXAMPLE"; // NAME

long corepgm::WndProc(WORD message, WORD wParam, LONG lParam)
{

    char *wmsg = "The Quick Brown Fox Jumped Over the Lazy
Dog.";
    switch (message) {
        case WM_CREATE:
            break;
        case WM_DESTROY:
            PostQuitMessage(0);
            break;
        case WM_PAINT:
            BeginPaint(wndhandle, &pstruct);
            GetClientRect(wndhandle, (LPRECT) &rect);
            DrawText(pstruct.hdc, wmsg, -1, &rect,
DT_SINGLELINE
| DT_CENTER | DT_VCENTER);

            EndPaint(wndhandle, &pstruct);
            break;
```

```
          default:
               return(DefWindowProc(wndhandle, message, wParam,
lParam));
     }
}

long FAR PASCAL _export WndProc(HWND wndhandle, WORD message,
WORD wParam, LONG lParam)
{
     corewin *winpntr = rtnptr(wndhandle);

     if (!winpntr) {
          if (message == WM_CREATE) {
               LPCREATESTRUCT lpcs;
               lpcs = (LPCREATESTRUCT) lParam;
               winpntr = (corewin *) lpcs->lpCreateParams;
               SetPointer(wndhandle, winpntr);
               return(winpntr->WndProc(message, wParam,
lParam));
          }
          else
               return (DefWindowProc(wndhandle, message,
wParam, lParam));
     }
     else
          return (winpntr->WndProc(message, wParam, lParam));

}

/*WinMain is the main entry point for a Windows application */
int PASCAL WinMain(HANDLE hInstance, HANDLE hPrevInstance,
LPSTR lpszCmdLine,
                    int manip) {
     core::manip = manip;
     core::hInstance = hInstance;
     core::hPrevInstance = hPrevInstance;

     if (core::hPrevInstance == 0)
          corepgm::Register();
```

```
        corepgm coreWnd;
        return(core::event());
}
```

Figure 7-1 shows an example of what the screen looks like while the Windows application is executing.

Figure 7-1. Screen showing Windows application.

The first response that one often has to the on-screen display is "So what!" After all, a great deal of source code has been input—and look what the result was. This doesn't seem like much to show for all that programming work. But think about the whole picture for a bit. The window that was produced on the screen just doesn't sit there (unless you want it to). With the mouse, you can move the window all over the screen, maximize or minimize it, change its size by varying degrees, reduce it to an icon—or whatever. It behaves like any other typical Windows window. There is a lot of power here, which has resulted from what now seems like an elaborate source-code procedure.

However, you must also remember that the majority of source code that went into this application was overhead. This overhead code can be repeated verbatim, and almost verbatim, in many applications that do different things with the same window class. Certainly, you already know how to change the window caption and now to display a different single-line message in the window's client area. This can be accomplished by changing two text strings in the program.

Multiple Text Lines

Let's look at another program example that uses the same overhead code, but displays several lines of text on the screen. The program follows:

```
#include <windows.h>
#include <stdlib.h>

struct {
     char *txtline;

} stext[] = {   // Text block to be displayed in window

"Now is the time",
"for all good men",
"to come to the aid of",
"their party."

};

long FAR PASCAL _export WndProc(HWND wndhandle, WORD message,
WORD wParam, LONG lParam);

class core {
     public:
          static int manip;
          static int event(void);
          static HANDLE hInstance;
          static HANDLE hPrevInstance;

};
```

```
PAINTSTRUCT pstruct;
RECT rect;
HANDLE core::hInstance = 0;
HANDLE core::hPrevInstance = 0;
int core::manip = 0;

int core::event(void)
{
      MSG msg;

      while(GetMessage(&msg, NULL, 0, 0))
      {
            TranslateMessage(&msg);
            DispatchMessage(&msg);
      }

      return(msg.wParam);
}

class corewin {
      protected:
            HWND wndhandle;
      public:
            virtual long WndProc(WORD message, WORD wParam, LONG
lParam ) = 0;

            HWND GetHandle(void)
            {
                  return wndhandle;

            }
            int display(int manip)
            {

                  return (ShowWindow(wndhandle, manip));

            }

};
```

```
corewin *rtnptr(HWND wndhandle)
{

     return (corewin *) GetWindowWord(wndhandle, 0);

}

void SetPointer(HWND wndhandle, corewin *winpntr)
{

     SetWindowWord(wndhandle, 0, (WORD) winpntr);

}

class corepgm:public corewin {
     private:
          static char winname[30];
     public:
          static void Register(void)
          {
               WNDCLASS wndclass;
               wndclass.style        = CS_HREDRAW | CS_VREDRAW;
               wndclass.lpfnWndProc = ::WndProc;
               wndclass.cbClsExtra   = 0;
               wndclass.cbWndExtra   = sizeof(corepgm *);
               wndclass.hInstance    = core::hInstance;
               wndclass.hIcon        = LoadIcon(core::hInstance,
IDI_APPLICATION);
               wndclass.hCursor      = LoadCursor( NULL,
IDC_ARROW);
               wndclass.hbrBackground    = GetStockObject(
WHITE_BRUSH );
               wndclass.lpszMenuName     = NULL;
               wndclass.lpszClassName    = winname;

               if (!RegisterClass(&wndclass))
                    exit(0);
          }

     corepgm(void)
```

```
	{
		wndhandle = CreateWindow(winname,
		winname,
		WS_OVERLAPPEDWINDOW,
		CW_USEDEFAULT,
		CW_USEDEFAULT,
		CW_USEDEFAULT,
		CW_USEDEFAULT,
		NULL,
		NULL,
		core::hInstance,
		(LPSTR) this);

		if (!wndhandle)
			exit(0); // Error Return

		display(core::manip);
		UpdateWindow(wndhandle);
	}

	long WndProc(WORD message, WORD wParam, LONG lParam);

};

char corepgm::winname[] = "MULTIPLE TEXT LINE EXAMPLE"; //
Window Caption

long corepgm::WndProc(WORD message, WORD wParam, LONG lParam)
{
	switch (message) {
		case WM_CREATE:
			break;

		case WM_DESTROY:
			PostQuitMessage(0);
			break;
		}

		case WM_PAINT:
			BeginPaint(wndhandle, &pstruct);
```

```
                for (int k = 0; k < 4; ++k) {
                    SetTextAlign(pstruct.hdc, TA_LEFT | TA_TOP);
                    TextOut(pstruct.hdc, 0, 12 * k,
stext[k].txtline, lstrlen(stext[k].txtline));

                }

                EndPaint(wndhandle, &pstruct);
                break;


            return(DefWindowProc(wndhandle, message, wParam,
lParam));

}

long FAR PASCAL _export WndProc(HWND wndhandle, WORD message,
WORD wParam,
                                LONG lParam)
{
    corewin *winpntr = rtnptr(wndhandle);

    if (!winpntr) {
        if (message == WM_CREATE) {
            LPCREATESTRUCT lpcs;
            lpcs = (LPCREATESTRUCT) lParam;
            winpntr = (corewin *) lpcs->lpCreateParams;
            SetPointer(wndhandle, winpntr);
            return(winpntr->WndProc(message, wParam,
lParam));
        }
        else
            return (DefWindowProc(wndhandle, message, wParam,
lParam));
    }
    else
        return (winpntr->WndProc(message, wParam, lParam));

}
```

```
/*WinMain is the main entry point for a Windows application */
int PASCAL WinMain(HANDLE hInstance, HANDLE hPrevInstance,
LPSTR lpszCmdLine,
                    int manip) {
     core::manip = manip;
     core::hInstance = hInstance;
     core::hPrevInstance = hPrevInstance;

     if (core::hPrevInstance == 0)
          corepgm::Register();

     corepgm coreWnd;
     return(core::event());
}
```

This application will produce the window shown in Figure 7-2.

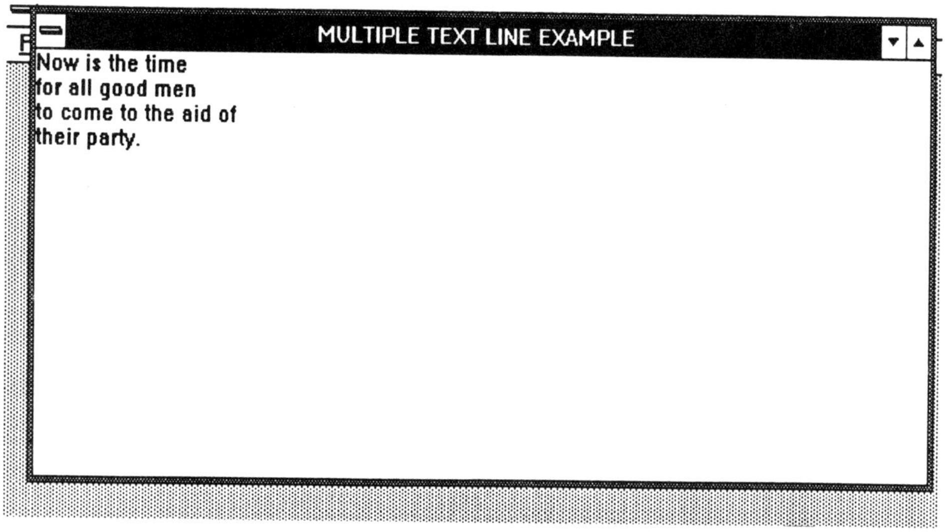

Figure 7-2. Screen showing multiple text lines.

Now, this is still not all that impressive from an on-screen standpoint, but examine this source code closely, and you will see that it is just like the previous program except for the single code block that contains the switch. There is also a struct at the beginning of the program that contains the text lines to be displayed. We still have the same type of window as before, so we can use the same overhead code. What we do in that window is determined by the code block shown below:

```
char corepgm::winname[] = "MULTIPLE TEXT LINE EXAMPLE"; //
Window Caption

long corepgm::WndProc(WORD message, WORD wParam, LONG lParam)
{
      switch (message) {
            case WM_CREATE:
                  break;

            case WM_DESTROY:
                  PostQuitMessage(0);
                  break;
            }

            case WM_PAINT:
                  BeginPaint(wndhandle, &pstruct);
                  for (int k = 0; k < 4; ++k) {
                        SetTextAlign(pstruct.hdc, TA_LEFT | TA_TOP);
                        TextOut(pstruct.hdc, 0, 12 * k,
stext[k].txtline, lstrlen(stext[k].txtline));

                  }

                  EndPaint(wndhandle, &pstruct);
                  break;


            return(DefWindowProc(wndhandle, message, wParam,
lParam));

}
```

In this assignment, the window name and caption have been changed to winname[], and the switch is entered as before. Every case statement in the switch is the same as before, except for case WM_PAINT. This is the operation that must be changed to address the display of multiple lines on the screen.

Within the case statements, we see BeginPaint() as before, but here significant changes from the earlier application are found. First of all, the SetTextAlign function is called with TA_LEFT | TA_TOP definitions. The ORed values determine that window writes are to occur at the left top of the window's client area.

The next operation is a call to TextOut() and we find numeric arguments here of 0, which is the horizontal print position at the far left of the screen. The argument of 12 * k gives us the spacing and the position in the client area. We have allowed 12 pixels for the display of the text and the whitespace line separations. Because variable k is the loop variable, 12 * k gives us the vertical line positions. The first line of text will be located at coordinates:

```
horizontal = 0
vertical = 12 * 0 = 0
```

The second line will be at coordinates

```
horizontal = 0
vertical = 12 * 1 = 12
```

The next argument is the line k from the struct. We must provide TextOut with the line length as well. This is provided by call lstrlen(), which is a Windows function equivalent to strlen() in C++. However, the Windows version returns a far pointer, whereas the C++ version returns a near pointer.

These processes complete all of the necessary mechanisms for displaying four lines of text on the screen. It is obvious that these program examples are made as simple as possible in order to provide the clearest explanations of the basic operations. This is a direct windowing write that uses constants in the "for" loop. However, it would be simple to set up a routine whereby any number of textlines might be displayed with the end of display being determined by an exit clause in the text structure. Also, these simple examples deal with the standard non-proportionally spaced character set as opposed to the special characters generated by the fonts available in Windows. Fortunately, Windows provides functions which can return the specifications of its various character sets and these dimensions can be easily worked into a simple mathematical formula that will determine spacing and length based upon the actual dimensions of the characters being used.

The rest of the switch is identical to the previous program and requires no further explanation. However, the reader can see that writing a different Windows application has required the changing of only a few simple lines of code in order to yield a new type of window write.

Scrolling

You've probably noticed that the window generated by these two applications does not contain the vertical scroll bar commonly seen with many Windows applications. It's not there, because it was not specified in the initial overhead code. However, you can get a scroll window very easily by making a single change to one element in a code block that was discussed earlier. The block is shown below:

```
corepgm(void)
     {
          wndhandle = CreateWindow(winname,
          winname,
          WS_OVERLAPPEDWINDOW | WS_VSCROLL,
          CW_USEDEFAULT,
          CW_USEDEFAULT,
          CW_USEDEFAULT,
          CW_USEDEFAULT,
          NULL,
          NULL,
          core::hInstance,
          (LPSTR) this);

          if (!wndhandle)
               exit(0); // Error Return

          display(core::manip);
          UpdateWindow(wndhandle);
```

All that is necessary to call up a scroll-bar window is to exclusive OR the WS_VSCROLL value with WS_OVERLAPPEDWINDOW. The vertical scroll bar will now appear at the right of the screen. Everything else will remain the same.

The program just discussed only wrote four lines to the client area. There is no need for any scrolling ability, but if the text lines in the struct numbered many more, you would need to scroll in order to see the entire struct contents.

Displaying a window with a scroll bar and scrolling text are two different things, however. You can't simply call up a scrolled window and have scrolling capabilities; scrolling must be programmed. Calling the scrolled window is the first step, but we must then tell Windows what to do in response to a scroll bar hit.

Fortunately, the only change that has to be made in our overhead code has already been made by ORing WS_VSCROLL with OVERLAPPEDWINDOW. All other changes (and they are simple ones) are made within the switch.

The following source code is for an application that displays the text contents of a struct. In this regard, its not much different from the last example. However, the text lines in this example are numerous, and scrolling is required to see all of the lines. The program follows:

```
#include <windows.h>
#include <stdlib.h>
#include <string.h>
#include <stdio.h>

struct {
     char *txtline;

} stext[] = {

"In this lesson you will learn how to successfully manage a
software",
"development project from conception to completion. This will",
"involve learning to apply management tools and skills that are
not",
"exclusive to software development projects only and that have
been",
"proven to be effective in many types of endeavors.",
" ",
"You should already know, from previous lessons in this series,
that",
```

```
"the software development life cycle can take place over
weeks,",
"months, or even years, depending on the scope and nature of
the",
"project. However, regardless of the duration of the project,
the",
"same tools and skills are applicable, with the only real
difference",
"being the manner in which they are applied.",
" ",
"Management Functions",
" ",
"(Insert Fig. 1)",
" ",
"Typical management functions that may take place during a
software",
"development project include such activities as planning,",
"organizing, staffing, directing, budgeting, mediating, and",
"decision-making. Each of these activities has as its ultimate
goal",
"the successful completion of the project on schedule, under
budget,",
"and to the satisfaction of the intended user of the software."
" ",
"It is not unusual for those who study software engineering at
the",
"university level to be required to take some courses that",
"specifically teach management skills. Unfortunately, there are
many",
"software developers who entered the marketplace before this",
"discipline was established and thus were not afforded the
learning",
"opportunities now available to those entering this field
today.",
" ",
"In addition, while software engineering as a discipline does
exist",
"at many colleges and universities, it is certainly accurate to
say",
"that the discipline itself is in an almost continuous state
of",
```

```
"change. This is due to the fact that the role of the soft-
ware",
"engineer continues to be defined and redefined as more and
more is",
"learned about this field, which actually encompasses many",
"disciplines. Certainly, this is to be expected, and while
those",
"already in the marketplace may be deficient in some areas,
newly","",
"educated software engineers will not only possess more
skills",
"themselves, but will be able to share their educational expe-
riences",
"with others. As this process continues, we can expect to see
this",
"manifested in software development projects that are managed
more",
"effectively."

};

long FAR PASCAL _export WndProc(HWND wndhandle, WORD message,
                              WORD wParam, LONG lParam);
class core {
     public:
          static int manip;
          static int event(void);
          static HANDLE hInstance;
          static HANDLE hPrevInstance;

};

PAINTSTRUCT pstruct;
RECT rect;
HANDLE core::hInstance = 0;
HANDLE core::hPrevInstance = 0;
int core::manip = 0;

int core::event(void)
{
     MSG msg;
```

```
    while(GetMessage(&msg, NULL, 0, 0))
    {
        TranslateMessage(&msg);
        DispatchMessage(&msg);
    }

    return(msg.wParam);
}

class corewin
{
    protected:
        HWND wndhandle;
    public:
        virtual long WndProc(WORD message, WORD wParam, LONG
lParam ) = 0;

        HWND GetHandle(void)
        {
            return wndhandle;

        }
        int display(int manip)
        {

            return (ShowWindow( wndhandle, manip ));

        }

};

class corepgm:public corewin {
    private:
        static char winname[30];
    public:
        static void Register(void)
        {
            WNDCLASS wndclass; // Structure used to register
Windows class.
            wndclass.style        = CS_HREDRAW | CS_VREDRAW;
            wndclass.lpfnWndProc = ::WndProc;
```

```
                wndclass.cbClsExtra    = 0;
                wndclass.cbWndExtra    = sizeof(corepgm *);
                wndclass.hInstance     = core::hInstance;
                wndclass.hIcon         = LoadIcon(core::hInstance,
IDI_APPLICATION);
                wndclass.hCursor       = LoadCursor( NULL,
IDC_ARROW);
                wndclass.hbrBackground    = GetStockObject(
WHITE_BRUSH );
                wndclass.lpszMenuName     = NULL;
                wndclass.lpszClassName    = winname;

                if (!RegisterClass(&wndclass))
                     exit(0);
           }

      corepgm(void)
      {
           wndhandle = CreateWindow(winname,
           winname,
           WS_OVERLAPPEDWINDOW | WS_VSCROLL,
           CW_USEDEFAULT,
           CW_USEDEFAULT,
           CW_USEDEFAULT,
           CW_USEDEFAULT,
           NULL,
           NULL,
           core::hInstance,
           (LPSTR) this);

           if (!wndhandle)
                exit(0); // Error Return

           display(core::manip);
           UpdateWindow(wndhandle);
      }

      long WndProc(WORD message, WORD wParam, LONG lParam);

};
```

```
char corepgm::winname[] = "SCROLL TEXT EXAMPLE";  // Window
Caption

long corepgm::WndProc(WORD message, WORD wParam, LONG lParam)
{

    static int vpos;

    switch (message) {
        case WM_CREATE:
            SetScrollRange(wndhandle, SB_VERT, 0, 44, FALSE);
            SetScrollPos(wndhandle, SB_VERT, vpos, TRUE);
            break;

        case WM_VSCROLL:
            switch(wParam) {
                case SB_LINEDOWN:
                    vpos += 1;
                    break;
                case SB_LINEUP:
                    vpos -= 1;
                    break;
                case SB_PAGEUP:
                    vpos = 0;
                    break;
                case SB_PAGEDOWN:
                    vpos = 43;
                    break;
                case SB_THUMBPOSITION:
                    vpos = LOWORD(lParam);
                    break;
                default:
                    break;
            }
            if (vpos > 43)
                vpos = 43;
            if (vpos < 0)
                vpos = 0;

            if (vpos != GetScrollPos(wndhandle, SB_VERT)) {
                SetScrollPos(wndhandle, SB_VERT, vpos,
```

```
TRUE);
                    InvalidateRect(wndhandle, NULL, TRUE);
               }

               break;

          case WM_PAINT:
               BeginPaint(wndhandle, &pstruct);
               for (int k = 0; k < 44; ++k) {
                    SetTextAlign(pstruct.hdc, TA_LEFT | TA_TOP);
                    TextOut(pstruct.hdc, 0, (1 - vpos + k) * 12,
stext[k].txtline, lstrlen(stext[k].txtline));

               }

               EndPaint(wndhandle, &pstruct);
               break;

          case WM_DESTROY:
               PostQuitMessage(0);
               break;
          }

          return(DefWindowProc(wndhandle, message, wParam,
lParam));

}

corewin *rtnptr(HWND wndhandle)
{


     return (corewin *) GetWindowWord(wndhandle, 0);

}

void SetPointer(HWND wndhandle, corewin *winpntr)
{

     SetWindowWord(wndhandle, 0, (WORD) winpntr);
```

```
}

long FAR PASCAL _export WndProc(HWND wndhandle, WORD message,
WORD wParam,
                              LONG lParam)
{
     corewin *winpntr = rtnptr(wndhandle);

     if (!winpntr) {
          if (message == WM_CREATE) {
               LPCREATESTRUCT lpcs;
               lpcs = (LPCREATESTRUCT) lParam;
               winpntr = (corewin *) lpcs->lpCreateParams;
               SetPointer(wndhandle, winpntr);
               return(winpntr->WndProc(message, wParam, lParam));
          }
          else
               return (DefWindowProc(wndhandle, message, wParam,
lParam));
     }
     else
          return (winpntr->WndProc(message, wParam, lParam));

}

/*WinMain is the main entry point for a Windows application */
int PASCAL WinMain(HANDLE hInstance, HANDLE hPrevInstance, LPSTR
lpszCmdLine,
                         int manip) {
     core::manip = manip;
     core::hInstance = hInstance;
     core::hPrevInstance = hPrevInstance;

     if (core::hPrevInstance == 0)
          corepgm::Register();

     corepgm coreWnd;
     return(core::event());
}
```

The structure named stext contains the text lines that are to be written in the window. Note that CreateWindow() is provided a style argument of OVERLAPPEDWINDOW | WS_VSCROLL. This causes the scroll bar to appear at the right of the window. The key to using this scroll bar to actually scroll the window text up or down is found in the following code extract from the previous program.

```
char corepgm::winname[] = "SCROLL TEXT EXAMPLE";  // Window
Caption

long corepgm::WndProc(WORD message, WORD wParam, LONG lParam)
{

    static int vpos;

    switch (message) {
        case WM_CREATE:
            SetScrollRange(wndhandle, SB_VERT, 0, 44, FALSE);
            SetScrollPos(wndhandle, SB_VERT, vpos, TRUE);
            break;

        case WM_VSCROLL:
            switch(wParam) {
                case SB_LINEDOWN:
                    vpos += 1;
                    break;
                case SB_LINEUP:
                    vpos -= 1;
                    break;
                case SB_PAGEUP:
                    vpos = 0;
                    break;
                case SB_PAGEDOWN:
                    vpos = 43;
                    break;
                case SB_THUMBPOSITION:
                    vpos = LOWORD(lParam);
                    break;
```

```
                    default:
                         break;
               }
               if (vpos > 43)
                    vpos = 43;
               if (vpos < 0)
                    vpos = 0;

               if (vpos != GetScrollPos(wndhandle, SB_VERT)) {
                    SetScrollPos(wndhandle, SB_VERT, vpos,
TRUE);
                    InvalidateRect(wndhandle, NULL, TRUE);
               }

               break;

          case WM_PAINT:
               BeginPaint(wndhandle, &pstruct);
               for (int k = 0; k < 44; ++k) {
                    SetTextAlign(pstruct.hdc, TA_LEFT | TA_TOP);
                    TextOut(pstruct.hdc, 0, (1 - vpos + k) * 12,
stext[k].txtline, lstrlen(stext[k].txtline));

               }

               EndPaint(wndhandle, &pstruct);
               break;

          case WM_DESTROY:
               PostQuitMessage(0);
               break;
          }

          return(DefWindowProc(wndhandle, message, wParam,
lParam));
```

There are 44 lines of text in the structure. Under case WM_CREATE, the SetScrollRange function, which sets the scrolling range at values of from 0 to 44, is called. This means that each position of the scroll bar will correspond to the text that is displayed at the top of the window. SetScrollPos() sets the new position that must be within the range specified in the preceding function. The new position value is contained in variable vpos.

A new encapsulating case is encountered in this code block, case WM_VSCROLL. This contains a nested switch that acts on the value in wParam. The value in the definition SB_LINEDOWN indicates that the scroll bar is scrolling down. If this is the case, then the value in vpos is incremented by 1. SB_LINEUP indicates an upward movement of the scroll bar and vpos is decreased by 1.

The SB_PAGEUP value indicates that the scroll bar has been clicked to return to the top of the window page. This is accomplished by setting vpos to its minimum value. SB_PAGEDOWN is effected by setting vpos to its maximum value. SB_THUMBTRACK is a value that the low word (LOWORD) of lparam is the current position of the dragged scroll bar. Variable vpos is set to this value.

The if-statement constructs make certain the values in vpos stay within range and reassign proper values if they fall out of range. This is followed by calls to GetScrollPos(), SetScrollPos, and InvalidateRect (to realign the window to the newly set values of vpos).

Within the WM_PAINT case, the call to TextOut uses the value in vpos to write the text lines at the proper position in the window, the positions that match the scroll-bar position. The notation (1 - vpos + k) * 12 allows the writing of text lines to match the position of the scroll bar. This is the vertical pixel position that accesses the window with the *12 multiplier determining the spacing between text lines.

The end result is the display of more than a full window of text which may be scrolled from top to bottom using the scroll bar and the mouse pointer. Figure 7-3 shows a sample window, while Figure 7-4 shows the same window with text scrolled down.

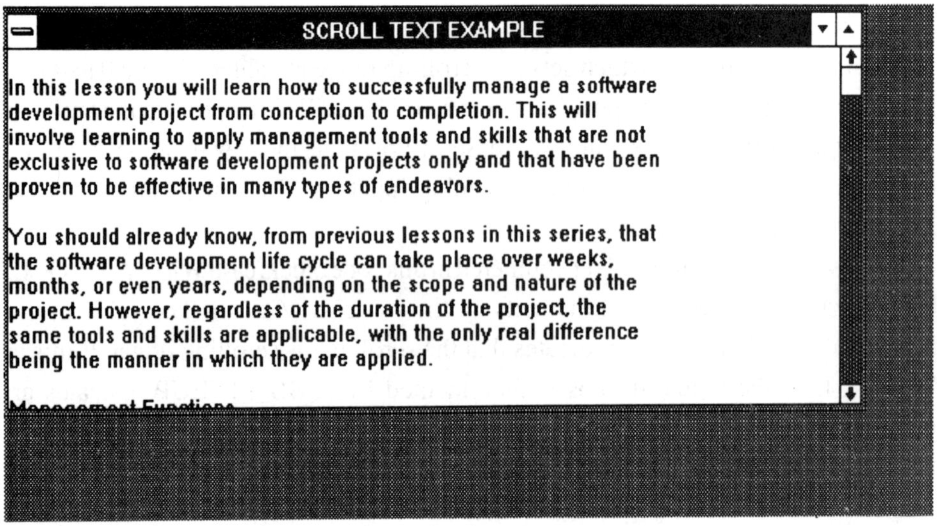

Figure 7-3. Example of screen with a full window of text.

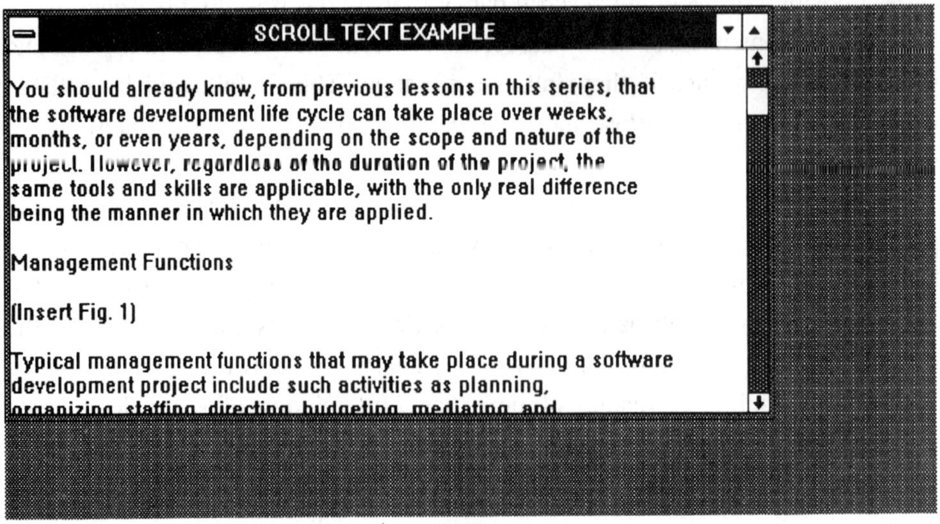

Figure 7-4. Example of screen with text scrolled down.

Horizontal and Vertical Scrolling

The previous program allowed the text lines in the window to be scrolled vertically. This was fine for the text lines contained in the struct, because each was short enough to fit horizontally in an averaged sized window. However, if the window is made considerably smaller or if the length of the text lines in the struct is increased, horizontal scrolling is required in order to see all of the text page. The programming techniques of horizontal scrolling are very similar to those of vertical scrolling. In order to produce the horizontal scroll bar, we need to change the window-style value in CreateWindow and add another case and nested switch to the "action" portion of our source code, just as we did to address vertical scrolling. A modified version of the previous program, one which contains lines of text and provides both horizontal and vertical scrolling is shown below.

```
#include <windows.h>
#include <stdlib.h>
#include <string.h>
#include <stdio.h>

struct {
     char *txtline;

} stext[] = {

"In this lesson you will learn how to successfully manage a
software development project from conception to completion.
This will",
"involve learning to apply management tools and skills that are
not exclusive to software development projects only and that
have been",
"proven to be effective in many types of endeavors.",
" ",
"You should already know, from previous lessons in this series,
that the software development life cycle can take place over
weeks,",
"months, or even years, depending on the scope and nature of
the project. However, regardless of the duration of the
project, the",
```

```
"same tools and skills are applicable, with the only real
difference being the manner in which they are applied.",
" ",
"Management Functions",
" ",
"(Insert Fig. 1)",
" ",
"Typical management functions that may take place during a
software development project include such activities as plan-
ning,",
"organizing, staffing, directing, budgeting, mediating, and
decision-making. Each of these activities has as its ultimate
goal",
"the successful completion of the project on schedule, under
budget, and to the satisfaction of the intended user of the
software."
" ",
"It is not unusual for those who study software engineering at
the university level to be required to take some courses that",
"specifically teach management skills. Unfortunately, there are
many software developers who entered the marketplace before
this",
"discipline was established and thus were not afforded the
learning opportunities now available to those entering this
field today.",
" ",
"In addition, while software engineering as a discipline does
exist at many colleges and universities, it is certainly accu-
rate to say",
"that the discipline itself is in an almost continuous state of
change. This is due to the fact that the role of the software",
"engineer continues to be defined and redefined as more and
more is learned about this field, which actually encompasses
many",
"disciplines. Certainly, this is to be expected, and while
those already in the marketplace may be deficient in some
areas, newly","",
"educated software engineers will not only possess more skills
themselves, but will be able to share their educational experi-
ences",
```

```
"with others. As this process continues, we can expect to see this manifested in software development projects that are managed more",
"effectively.",
" ",
" ",
"There are a number of different approaches that can be applied to a tutorial. One approach is to provide, along with the software, a",
"sample file that is opened and manipulated during use of the tutorial. This sample file should be representative of the user's",
"typical application of the software in its intended environment. Such a tutorial is well-suited for many types of applications,",
"especially if creation of files will not be required for most users of the software. This might be the case if users will be",
"required only to enter, edit and retrieve data— not define or create fields, for example— in a database. Here, the computer department",
"of the user organization might be the only group of persons who has access to these operations, and these more sophisticated users are assumed",
"to have the necessary skills to gain such access.",
" ",
"Another approach is to take the user through actual operation of the software in its intended environment. This type of tutorial",
"would duplicate the procedures that a typical user will follow during normal use of the software. If, for example, users will follow a",
"specific procedure to modify data, this procedure should be duplicated in its entirety in the tutorial.",
" ",
"A good tutorial will take the first-time user through a typical session; that is, it should encompass start up, major functions and",
"operations of the software, creating files, saving files, and ending a session. If on-line help is incorporated in the software,",
```

```
"the tutorial should also describe how the help system works
and how to access help at various points during the operation
of the software."


};

long FAR PASCAL _export WndProc(HWND wndhandle, WORD message,
                        WORD wParam, LONG lParam);
class core {
     public:
          static int manip;
          static int event(void);
          static HANDLE hInstance;
          static HANDLE hPrevInstance;

};

PAINTSTRUCT pstruct;
RECT rect;
HANDLE core::hInstance = 0;
HANDLE core::hPrevInstance = 0;
int core::manip = 0;

int core::event(void)
{
     MSG msg;

     while(GetMessage(&msg, NULL, 0, 0))
     {
          TranslateMessage(&msg);
          DispatchMessage(&msg);
     }

     return(msg.wParam);
}

class corewin
{
     protected:
```

```
        HWND wndhandle;
    public:
        virtual long WndProc(WORD message, WORD wParam, LONG
lParam ) = 0;

        HWND GetHandle(void)
        {
            return wndhandle;

        }
        int display(int manip)
        {

            return (ShowWindow( wndhandle, manip ));

        }

};

class corepgm:public corewin {
    private:
        static char winname[30];
    public:
        static void Register(void)
        {
            WNDCLASS wndclass; // Structure used to register
Windows class.
            wndclass.style        = CS_HREDRAW | CS_VREDRAW;
            wndclass.lpfnWndProc = ::WndProc;
            wndclass.cbClsExtra  = 0;
            wndclass.cbWndExtra  = sizeof(corepgm *);
            wndclass.hInstance   = core::hInstance;
            wndclass.hIcon       = LoadIcon(core::hInstance,
IDI_APPLICATION);
            wndclass.hCursor     = LoadCursor( NULL,
IDC_ARROW);
            wndclass.hbrBackground    = GetStockObject(
WHITE_BRUSH );
            wndclass.lpszMenuName     = NULL;
            wndclass.lpszClassName    = winname;
```

```
            if (!RegisterClass(&wndclass))
                exit(0);
        }

    corepgm(void)
    {
        wndhandle = CreateWindow(winname,
        winname,
        WS_OVERLAPPEDWINDOW | WS_VSCROLL | WS_HSCROLL,
        CW_USEDEFAULT,
        CW_USEDEFAULT,
        CW_USEDEFAULT,
        CW_USEDEFAULT,
        NULL,
        NULL,
        core::hInstance,
        (LPSTR) this);

        if (!wndhandle)
            exit(0); // Error Return

        display(core::manip);
        UpdateWindow(wndhandle);
    }

    long WndProc(WORD message, WORD wParam, LONG lParam);

};

char corepgm::winname[] = "HORIZONTAL SCROLL EXAMPLE"; // Window
Caption

long corepgm::WndProc(WORD message, WORD wParam, LONG lParam)
{

    static int vpos, hpos;

    switch (message) {
        case WM_CREATE:
            SetScrollRange(wndhandle, SB_VERT, 0, 44, FALSE);
```

```
            SetScrollPos(wndhandle, SB_VERT, vpos, TRUE);
            SetScrollRange(wndhandle, SB_HORZ, 0, 75, FALSE);
            SetScrollPos(wndhandle, SB_HORZ, hpos, TRUE);
            break;

        case WM_HSCROLL:
            switch(wParam) {
                case SB_LINEUP:
                    hpos -= 1;
                    break;
                case SB_LINEDOWN:
                    hpos += 1;
                    break;
                case SB_PAGEUP:
                    hpos = 0;
                    break;
                case SB_PAGEDOWN:
                    hpos = 75;
                    break;
                case SB_THUMBPOSITION:
                    hpos = LOWORD (lParam);
                    break;
                default:
                    break;
            }
            if (hpos > 75)
                hpos = 75;
            if (hpos < 0)
                hpos = 0;

            if (hpos != GetScrollPos(wndhandle, SB_HORZ)) {
                SetScrollPos(wndhandle, SB_HORZ, hpos,
TRUE);
                InvalidateRect(wndhandle, NULL, TRUE);
            }

            break;

        case WM_VSCROLL:
            switch(wParam) {
```

```
                    case SB_LINEDOWN:
                         vpos += 1;
                         break;
                    case SB_LINEUP:
                         vpos -= 1;
                         break;
                    case SB_PAGEUP:
                         vpos = 0;
                         break;
                    case SB_PAGEDOWN:
                         vpos = 43;
                         break;
                    case SB_THUMBPOSITION:
                         vpos = LOWORD(lParam);
                         break;
                    default:
                         break;
               }
               if (vpos > 43)
                    vpos = 43;
               if (vpos < 0)
                    vpos = 0;

               if (vpos != GetScrollPos(wndhandle, SB_VERT)) {
                    SetScrollPos(wndhandle, SB_VERT, vpos,
TRUE);
                    InvalidateRect(wndhandle, NULL, TRUE);
               }

               break;

          case WM_PAINT:
               BeginPaint(wndhandle, &pstruct);
               for (int k = 0; k < 44; ++k) {
                    SetTextAlign(pstruct.hdc, TA_LEFT | TA_TOP);
                    TextOut(pstruct.hdc, (1 - hpos) * 10, (1 -
vpos + k) * 12, stext[k].txtline, lstrlen(stext[k].txtline));

               }
```

```
                EndPaint(wndhandle, &pstruct);
                break;

            case WM_DESTROY:
                PostQuitMessage(0);
                break;
            }

            return(DefWindowProc(wndhandle, message, wParam,
lParam));

}

corewin *rtnptr(HWND wndhandle)
{

    return (corewin *) GetWindowWord(wndhandle, 0);

}

void SetPointer(HWND wndhandle, corewin *winpntr)
{

    SetWindowWord(wndhandle, 0, (WORD) winpntr);

}

long FAR PASCAL _export WndProc(HWND wndhandle, WORD message,
WORD wParam,
                    LONG lParam)
{
    corewin *winpntr = rtnptr(wndhandle);

    if (!winpntr) {
        if (message == WM_CREATE) {
            LPCREATESTRUCT lpcs;
            lpcs = (LPCREATESTRUCT) lParam;
            winpntr = (corewin *) lpcs->lpCreateParams;
            SetPointer(wndhandle, winpntr);
            return(winpntr->WndProc(message, wParam,
```

```
lParam));
            }
            else
                  return (DefWindowProc(wndhandle, message,
wParam, lParam));
      }
      else
            return (winpntr->WndProc(message, wParam, lParam));

}

/*WinMain is the main entry point for a Windows application */
int PASCAL WinMain(HANDLE hInstance, HANDLE hPrevInstance,
LPSTR lpszCmdLine,
                        int manip) {
      core::manip = manip;
      core::hInstance = hInstance;
      core::hPrevInstance = hPrevInstance;

      if (core::hPrevInstance == 0)
            corepgm::Register();

      corepgm coreWnd;
      return(core::event());
}
```

The only change in the overhead code is in the window-style definition which now reads:

```
OVERLAPPEDWINDOW | WS_VSCROLL | WS_HSCROLL,
```

By ORing the WS_HSCROLL value with the previous style assignment, the horizontal scroll bar appears at the bottom of the window. The other changes have occurred in the following code block.

```
char corepgm::winname[] = "HORIZONTAL SCROLL EXAMPLE";
long corepgm::WndProc(WORD message, WORD wParam, LONG lParam)
{
```

```
    static int vpos, hpos;

    switch (message) {
         case WM_CREATE:
              SetScrollRange(wndhandle, SB_VERT, 0, 44, FALSE);
              SetScrollPos(wndhandle, SB_VERT, vpos, TRUE);
              SetScrollRange(wndhandle, SB_HORZ, 0, 75, FALSE);
              SetScrollPos(wndhandle, SB_HORZ, hpos, TRUE);
              break;

         case WM_HSCROLL:
              switch(wParam) {
                   case SB_LINEUP:
                        hpos -= 1;
                        break;
                   case SB_LINEDOWN:
                        hpos += 1;
                        break;
                   case SB_PAGEUP:
                        hpos = 0;
                        break;
                   case SB_PAGEDOWN:
                        hpos = 75;
                        break;
                   case SB_THUMBPOSITION:
                        hpos = LOWORD (lParam);
                        break;
                   default:
                        break;
              }
              if (hpos > 75)
                   hpos = 75;
              if (hpos < 0)
                   hpos = 0;

              if (hpos != GetScrollPos(wndhandle, SB_HORZ)) {
                   SetScrollPos(wndhandle, SB_HORZ, hpos,
TRUE);
                   InvalidateRect(wndhandle, NULL, TRUE);
              }
```

```
              break;

          // WM_VSCROLL code goes here

          case WM_PAINT:
              BeginPaint(wndhandle, &pstruct);
              for (int k = 0; k < 44; ++k) {
                  SetTextAlign(pstruct.hdc, TA_LEFT | TA_TOP);
                  TextOut(pstruct.hdc, (1 - hpos) * 10, (1 -
vpos + k) * 12, stext[k].txtline, lstrlen(stext[k].txtline));
              }
```

First of all, the name of the window is changed to HORIZONTAL SCROLL EXAMPLE. This name will also appear in the window-caption box. A new static int variable has been added to this code block. Variable hpos will address the horizontal-scroll screen pixel position. Under case WM_CREATE, we have added an extra call to SetScrollRange() and SetScrollPos. In the additions, SB_HORZ addresses the horizontal scroll bar, whereas SB_VERT was used in the first two calls to these functions to address the range and position of the vertical scroll.

A new case has been added to our master switch, which nests its own switch to address movements of the horizontal scrolling. You will note that the SB definitions match those of the WS_VSCROLL case. However, these values are encountered after a WS_HSCROLL is sent, so they all address the horizontal scroll bar. Therefore SB_PAGEUP may be thought of as PAGELEFT in regard to how this program makes use of these values, just as SB_PAGEDOWN may be thought of as PAGERIGHT.

As was done within the vertical scroll control portion of this program, if-statements are used to keep the values in hops in range.

Skipping down to case WM_PAINT, one argument to TextOut() has been changed. The expression (1 - hpos) * 10 sets the horizontal pixel position for the text write. In the previous program, this value was 0. However, because horizontal scrolling is used in this new program, it is obvious that the horizontal write coordinates have to change. The expression uses a multiplier of 10, because that provides a reasonable rate of scroll. The rate may be increased by increasing the value of the multiplier, or slowed by decreasing its value. Figure 7-5 shows the window with the horizontal and vertical scroll bars at the start of display. Figure 7-6 shows the same window after it has been scrolled horizontally.

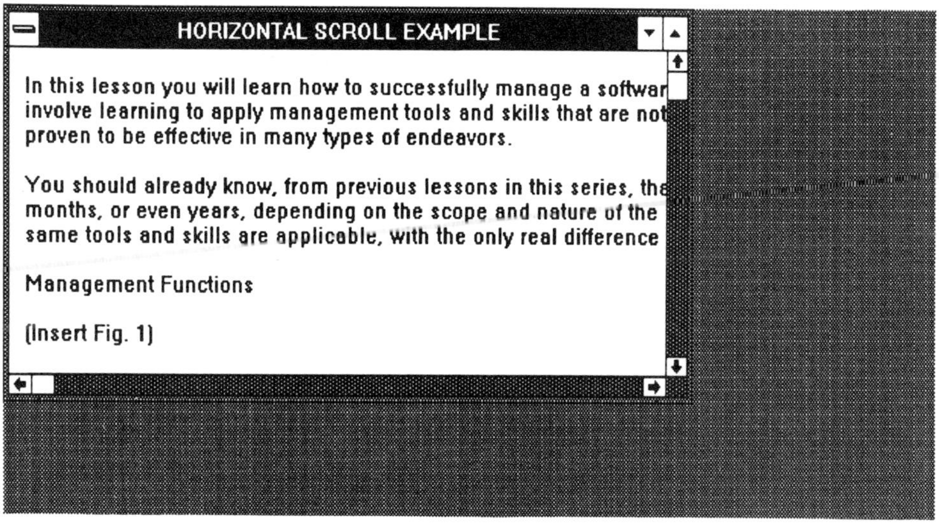

Figure 7-5. Window showing horizontal and vertical scroll bars.

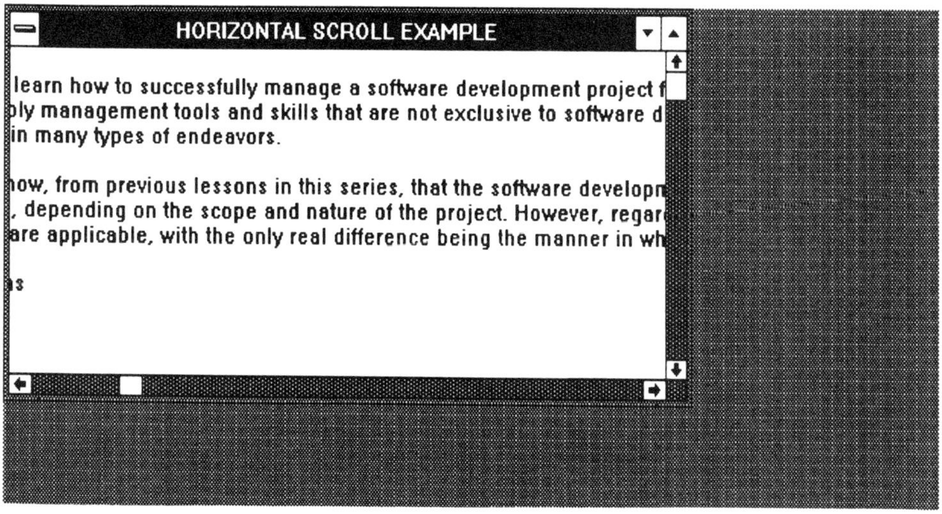

Figure 7-6. Window showing text that has been scrolled horizontally.

A wealth of Windows programming examples may be found by accessing CompuServe (GO BORLAND). It was while roaming around the numerous collections of Borland C++/Microsoft Windows files, uploaded by Windows programmers, that I came across a most interesting offering by Davin S. Hills of Des Moines, Iowa. A recent graduate, Davin is now working as a career chemist, but he continues to develop applications for his father's firm, (a consulting firm in Des Moines that develops office automation systems for physicians) and for persons entering the Windows programming environment.

Davin's offering to the CompuServe file library is a grouping of classes for Windows development, especially aimed at the person who is new to Windows programming under the auspices of Borland C++. Davin writes:

"The decision to begin the task of building a class library for Windows came after trying to use the classes included in Borland's first 'Language Express'. I fully understand how they work and respect the way in which they were implemented, however they seemed to be very complex for a new Windows developer. It is my hope that the classes I have built are a little easier to use."

Included in the source listings that follow are:

```
Test.h     // Defines the dialog class for this application
Testm.h    // Defines menu selections
Test.cpp   // Main program
Winbase.h // Base window class and base registration class
Winstd.h   // A derived class from Window and WinRegClass
Dlgbase.h // Base dialog class
```

Davin continues: "Winbase includes two classes, WindowRegClass and Windows. These are used to build derived classes like StdRegClass and StdWin in Winstd.h and to build a non-standard window. To build a non-standard window, use the base classes to define a window or derive a class from them that defines your window. To build a standard window as I've defined it, use the StdWin class as in Test.cpp. In all the Windows-related classes, you must define your procedure outside of the class and send the name to WindowRegClass.

"The dialog class, however, is different. Instead of sending it the name of your function you MUST build a derived class from it and define the dialogs procedure as a member function (See Test.h for an example).

"This is certainly not a complete class system nor was it intended to be. But, it should get things started if you are new to Windows programming."

The source listings for the Windows classes authored by Davin Hills follow:

```
// Test.h defines the dialog class for this application

#include "dlgbase.h"
#include <windows.h>

class TDlg : public Dialog {

public:
     TDlg(HANDLE hInstance, LPSTR dlgtemp, HWND winparent):
               Dialog(hInstance,dlgtemp,winparent) {
          SetDlgProc(TDlg::DlgProc);
     }
     static BOOL FAR PASCAL _export
DlgProc(HWND,WORD,WORD,LONG);
};

BOOL FAR PASCAL _export TDlg::DlgProc(HWND hDlg, WORD message,
                         WORD wParam, LONG lParam)
     {
          switch(message)
          {
               case WM_INITDIALOG:
                    return TRUE;

               case WM_COMMAND:
                    switch (wParam)
                    {
                         case IDOK:                    // OK Button
                              EndDialog(hDlg, 0);
                              return TRUE;
                    }
                    break;
```

```
        }
        return FALSE;
    }
```

```
// Testm.h defines menu selections

/* D:\BORLANDC\BIN\TESTM.H 3/19/1991 10:32*/
#define IDM_SILLY 3
#define IDM_ABOUT 5
```

```
// Test.cpp- Main program

#include <windows.h>
#include "winstd.h"
#include "dlgbase.h"
#include "test.h"
#include "testm.h"

long FAR PASCAL _export WndProc(HWND,WORD,WORD,LONG);

#pragma argsused
int PASCAL WinMain(HANDLE hInstance,HANDLE hPrevInstance,
        LPSTR lpszCmdLine,int nCmdShow)
{                         //Register "Test" class
StdRegClass
Reg("Test",hInstance,hPrevInstance,WndProc,"amenu","test");
    StdWin Win("Test", "Test", hInstance); //Make an instance

    Win.Create();                           // Create it
```

```
    Win.Display();                          // Show it
    Win.Update();
    Win.MessageLoop();                      // Go Windows.....
    return 0;
}

#pragma argsused
long FAR PASCAL _export WndProc(HWND hwnd,WORD message,WORD
                                wParam, LONG lParam)
{
    HANDLE hInstance;

    switch(message)
    {

    case WM_CREATE:
        hInstance = ((LPCREATESTRUCT)lParam)->hInstance;
        static TDlg Testdlg(hInstance, "aboutbox", hwnd); //
MUST be static !
        return 0;                           // Create dialog

    case WM_COMMAND:
        switch(wParam)
        {
            case IDM_SILLY:
                MessageBox(hwnd,"Feature not
implemented",NULL, MB_OK | MB_ICONQUESTION);
                return 0;

            case IDM_ABOUT:
                Testdlg.Show();             // Show it
                return 0;
        }
    case WM_DESTROY:
        PostQuitMessage(0);
        return 0;
    }
    return DefWindowProc(hwnd,message,wParam, lParam);
}
```

```
// Winbase.h- Base window class and base registration class

#if !defined(WINBASE_H)
class WindowRegClass {
     WORD style;
     LONG (FAR PASCAL *wndproc)( HWND, WORD, WORD, LONG );
     int clsExtra;
     int wndExtra;
     HANDLE hinst;
     HANDLE hprev;
     HICON hicon;
     HCURSOR hcursor;
     HBRUSH backgrd;
     LPSTR menuname;
     LPSTR classname;

public:
     WindowRegClass(LPSTR ClassName, HANDLE hInst, HANDLE hPrev,
                    long (FAR PASCAL *proc)(HWND, WORD, WORD,
LONG )) {
          style     = CS_HREDRAW | CS_VREDRAW;
          wndproc   = proc;
          clsExtra  = 0;
          wndExtra  = 0;
          hinst     = hInst;
          hprev     = hPrev;
          hicon     = LoadIcon(NULL, IDI_APPLICATION);
          hcursor   = LoadCursor(NULL, IDC_ARROW);
          backgrd   = COLOR_WINDOW + 1;
          menuname  = NULL;
          classname = ClassName;
     }
     void SetClassStyle(unsigned newstyle) { style =newstyle; }
     void AddClassStyle(unsigned addstyle) { style |=addstyle; }
     void SetClassBckrnd(HBRUSH newbckrnd) { backgrd =newbckrnd
}
     void SetClassMenu(LPSTR newmenu) { menuname =newmenu; }
     void SetClassWinXbytes(int xtrabytes) { wndExtra=xtrabytes
}
     void SetClassClsXbytes(int xtrabytes) { clsExtra=xtrabytes
```

```
}
    void SetClassIcon(LPSTR iconname) {
        if (hinst)
            hicon=LoadIcon(hinst,iconname);
    }
    void SetClassCursor(LPSTR cursorname) {
        if (hinst)
            hcursor=LoadCursor(hinst, cursorname);
    }
    void SetClassName(LPSTR clsname) { classname = clsname; }
    LPSTR GetClassName(void) { return classname; }
    void Register(void);
};

void WindowRegClass::Register(void) {
    WNDCLASS wndclass;

    if (!hprev)
    {
        wndclass.style          = style;
        wndclass.lpfnWndProc    = wndproc;
        wndclass.cbClsExtra     = clsExtra;
        wndclass.cbWndExtra     = wndExtra;
        wndclass.hInstance      = hinst;
        wndclass.hIcon          = hicon;
        wndclass.hCursor        = hcursor;
        wndclass.hbrBackground  = backgrd;
        wndclass.lpszMenuName   = menuname;
        wndclass.lpszClassName  = classname;

        RegisterClass(&wndclass);
    }
}

class Window {
    MSG msg;
    HWND hwnd;
    LPSTR classname;
    LPSTR windowname;
    DWORD winstyle;
```

```
        int upper_left_x;
        int upper_left_y;
        int winwidth;
        int winheight;
        HWND winParent;
        HMENU menu;
        HANDLE hInstan;
        LPSTR lpParam;

public:
        Window(LPSTR clsname, LPSTR winname, HANDLE hinst) {
                classname = clsname;
                windowname = winname;
                winstyle = 0;
                upper_left_x=upper_left_y=winwidth=winheight=
                                                        CW_USEDEFAULT;
                winParent = NULL;
                menu = NULL;
                hInstan = hinst;
                lpParam = NULL;
        }

        void Display(void) { ShowWindow(GetHandle(),
SW_SHOWNORMAL); }
        void Display(HANDLE hinst, int disp) { ShowWindow(hinst,
disp);
}
        void Update(void) { UpdateWindow(GetHandle()); }
        HWND GetHandle(void) { return hwnd; }
        void Paint(void) {
                PAINTSTRUCT ps;
                RECT rect;
                BeginPaint(GetHandle(), &ps);
                EndPaint(GetHandle(), &ps);
        }
        MessageLoop(void) {
                while (GetMessage(&msg,NULL,0,0))
                {
                        TranslateMessage(&msg);
```

```
            DispatchMessage(&msg);
        }
        return msg.wParam;
    }
    HWND Create(void) {
        hwnd=CreateWindow(classname,
                    windowname,
                    winstyle,
                    upper_left_x,
                    upper_left_y,
                    winwidth,
                    winheight,
                    winParent,
                    menu, hInstan,
                    lpParam);
        return(hwnd);
    }
    void SetWinName(LPSTR winname)       { windowname=winname; }
    void SetWinStyle(DWORD dword)        { winstyle=dword; }
    void AddWinStyle(DWORD dword)        { winstyle |=dword; }
    void SetWinX(int x)                  { upper_left_x=x; }
    void SetWinY(int y)                  { upper_left_y=y; }
    void SetWinWidth(int width)          { winwidth=width; }
    void SetWinHeight(int height)        { winheight=height; }
    void SetWinInstance(HANDLE hinst)    { hInstan=hinst; }
    void SetTitle(LPSTR newtitle)        { SetWindowText(hwnd,
newtitle); }
};
#define WINBASE_H
#endif
```

```
// Winstd.h is a derived class from Window and WinRegClass
```

```
#if !defined(WINSTD_H)
#include <windows.h>
#include "winbase.h"

class StdRegClass : public WindowRegClass {
public:
     StdRegClass(LPSTR ClassName, HANDLE hInst, HANDLE hPrev,
                    long (FAR PASCAL *proc)(HWND, WORD, WORD,
LONG ),
                    LPSTR menu = NULL, LPSTR icon =
IDI_APPLICATION,
                    LPSTR cursorname = IDC_ARROW)
                    :WindowRegClass(ClassName, hInst,
hPrev,proc)
{
          SetClassMenu(menu);
          SetClassIcon(icon);
          SetClassCursor(cursorname);
          Register();
     }
};


class StdWin: public Window {
public:
     StdWin(LPSTR clsname, LPSTR winname, HANDLE hinst)
                              :Window(clsname,winname,hinst) {
          SetWinStyle(WS_OVERLAPPEDWINDOW | WS_CLIPCHILDREN);
          SetWinX(100);
          SetWinY(50);
          SetWinWidth(500);
          SetWinHeight(300);
     }
};
#define WINSTD_H
#endif
```

```
// Dlgbase.h — Base dialog class

#if !defined(DLGBASE_H)
#include <windows.h>

class Dialog {
     FARPROC lpfnDlgProc;
     HANDLE hinst;
     HWND hwnd;
     LPSTR DlgTemplate;
public:
     Dialog(HANDLE hInstance, LPSTR dlgtemp, HWND winparent) {
          hinst = hInstance;
          DlgTemplate = dlgtemp;
          hwnd = winparent;
     }
     int Show(void) {
          int ret;
          ret = DialogBox(hinst,DlgTemplate,hwnd,lpfnDlgProc);
          return(ret);
     }
     void SetDlgProc(BOOL (FAR PASCAL *proc)(HWND, WORD, WORD,
LONG ))
          { lpfnDlgProc =
MakeProcInstance((FARPROC)proc,hinst); }
};
#define DLGBASE_H
#endif
```

As is always the case when humans interact with computer programs, there are many ways of accomplishing the same task. The Windows classes offered by Davin Hills makes it possible to "ease" into Windows programming within the Borland C++ environment. This method removes many of the complexities that face programmers who are in the early stages of tackling the Borland C++/Microsoft Windows programming arena.

Summary

This chapter has explained the overall operation of Borland C++ in regard to its ability to directly program Windows 3.0 applications without the need for any auxiliary software products. The full scope of Borland C++ and Microsoft Windows can and will fill many texts, because we are dealing here with an interface between the Windows programming functions and Borland C++.

The materials in this chapter have barely scratched the surface, but rest assured that Borland C++ can address the full needs of the serious Windows developer. Newcomers to the Windows programming environment will be able to get up and get going with the program examples provided here, while the professional who has been programming Windows outside of the Borland C++ environment will see immediately how Borland C++ and Windows interface. It should be a quick and easy task to bring all former applications up under Borland C++, which offers many shortcuts over what has been the standard development environment.

The examples were designed to be as simple as possible in order to eliminate much of the first-experience learning difficulties. Such subjects as graphics drawings, Windows fonts, and the full production of system resources are a subject unto themselves. The important matter at this point is to supply enough information for the reader to be able to get up and going in the area of Windows programming in Borland C++ and to be able to bring previous knowledge on this subject into the Borland C++ environment.

CHAPTER 8

Turbo Debugger for Windows

The Borland C++ professional developer's package comes with Turbo Debugger, a source-level debugging tool designed specifically for the Borland line of programming languages and for programmers using other types of compilers who now desire a powerful debugging environment. It operates within an integrated development environment quite similar to other IDEs offered by Borland.

Turbo Debugger offers a reconfigurable screen layout and uses expanded memory specifications for debugging large programs. It offers full C, C++, Pascal, and assembler-expression evaluation and features terminate and stay resident, as well as device-driver debugging. It is fully capable of debugging Microsoft Windows applications.

Turbo Debugger includes a number of utilities for interfacing with other types of compilers and software packages. This allows Turbo Debugger to interface with Microsoft compilers, while a small TSR program permits its use with a Periscope I board.

Debugging is a two-step process. First of all, it is necessary to detect an error. Without debugging software, this can take minutes, hours, days, or even months, depending on the complexity of the code in which the error occurs. In commercial software development, it is not unusual to spend considerably more time debugging a large program than that which was required for creating the actual coding.

The second step of debugging occurs after the error has been detected. This involves simply correcting the error. Obviously, error detection is a more difficult and time-consuming process than error correction. Therefore, the trick is to locate the error. From this point on, the process is greatly simplified.

As good as Turbo Debugger is, it is still capable (in most instances) only of giving the programmer an idea of the general location of the error and its nature. A good debugger is more specific in describing the location and nature of an error, but any debugger is still a general tool. Actually, the programmer must use a debugger for some time in order to get a "feel" for its operation. This way, the idiosyncrasies of the debugger are recognized, and the programmer begins to work with it almost as he/she would with a programming team member.

Turbo Debugger assists the programmer with the two hardest parts of the debugging process—first, determining the location of the error, and second, determining the cause of the error. This program does its job by greatly slowing program execution to allow the programmer to examine the specific state of the program at any given point in the execution chain. Variables can even be loaded with new values in order to test the program's reaction, recalling the old adage, "When something's wrong, make a change—any change—and see what happens." Turbo Debugger allows you to do this during execution and tests for changed results. Without a debugger, the programmer has to make such changes in the source code and then wait for the compiling and linking processes to be completed before the program may be rerun with the new values. Having the capability of making these changes during execution saves an inordinate amount of time in almost every debugging effort.

Using Turbo Debugger, the programmer can perform the vital steps of efficient debugging operations—tracing, stepping, viewing, inspecting, changing, and watching.

Tracing means that you can execute one line at a time, noting the results, independent of the remainder of the program. You can even step backward through code that has already been executed, actually reversing the execution as you go.

Stepping entails one-line execution (as does tracing) but you step over any procedure or function call. Stepping over program procedures that have already been debugged shortens the overall debugging process. After all, what is the use of re-executing 400 lines of code that already have been determined to be operationally correct?

Using Turbo Debugger, you can open a special window to view the state of the program being debugged from various perspectives. The programmer can look at variables and their values, stack contents, CPU code, registers, memory, execution history, and program output. The ability to view the execution of a program from varied perspectives greatly enhances the debugging process.

The inspection action of Turbo Debugger allows the nested inner workings of a program to be evaluated. Here, the contents of complicated data structures such as arrays, structs, and classes can be fully examined.

As was mentioned earlier, the ability provided by Turbo Debugger to change the value of a variable either globally or locally with a programmer-supplied value allows the programmer to see how value changes affect program operation. Finally, it is possible to isolate program variables and keep track of their value changes as the program executes.

Turbo Debugger allows a program, no matter how complex, to be broken down into convenient blocks. These blocks can even be broken down into single lines of code or discrete variables. With this microscopic eye on program execution, most bugs are detected within a relatively short period of time.

As efficient as Turbo Debugger is, it is not a panacea for all debugging woes. It can't recompile your program for you. Once an error has been detected, it must be corrected in the source code, which must then be recompiled and linked to arrive at a working program. You cannot change your source code from within Turbo Debugger (assembly code may be changed under the right circumstances in an effort to detect a problem), but you can easily transfer control to the text editor provided with Borland C++. Above all, don't believe for an instant that Turbo Debugger—or any other debugger, for that matter—will allow you to get away with sloppy programming techniques. Turbo Debugger will not think for you. It is a very efficient general indicator of the manner in which the program is executing. Debugging is a technically demanding process, and Turbo Debugger is merely a tool to assist you in acquiring information about a program.

Turbo Debugger for Windows

A chapter or two on Turbo Debugger is a prerequisite for any text involving Borland languages. However, with Turbo Debugger 2.5 and later comes with TDW—Turbo Debugger for Windows, the topic of the rest of this chapter.

In a sentence, TDW is designed to run under Microsoft Windows (3.0 and later) and enables the user to debug Windows applications. TDW is a debugging utility (separate from Turbo Debugger) requiring a computer equipped with at least an 80286 processor and a minimum of 1 megabyte of memory. Even though TDW is different from Turbo Debugger, it is utilized in much the same manner after it is brought up as a Windows application. These shared traits include setting of configuration parameters, ability to address a second monitor attached to the computer, etc. When the TDW screen is first brought up under Windows, it closely resembles the standard Turbo Debugger screen, with the exception that the function key menu does not appear at the bottom of the pane.

However, TDW does not look like a typical Windows 3.0 application when it appears, and it does not support certain features that are available with most applications written to run under Windows. For instance, the Windows hot keys such as ALT-ESC and CTRL-ESC won't function in the usual manner in TDW.

With TDW, you can do anything you can do with Turbo Debugger as well as perform an array of other tasks exclusive only to TDW. These extras involve the debugging of Windows-specific applications, including debugging of the local and global heaps, testing of the messages that are received and sent by an application, and DLL debugging. You can't perform these jobs with the standard Turbo Debugger, so Windows programmers will take to TDW as readily as standard applications programmers have taken to Turbo Debugger.

Again, debugging with TDW is basically the same process as it is with Turbo Debugger. However, a few Turbo Debugger features work differently under TDW, and of course, there are the additional features that directly address Windows applications.

There is no DOS shell available when operating Turbo Debugger under Windows. The Resident feature also is not applicable to TDW, since TDW cannot terminate and stay resident. Device drivers and TSRs cannot be debugged, and keystroke recording is unavailable. Additionally, there is no support for hardware debugging. However, the lack of these features is unimportant when dealing with most Windows applications.

In the new features list for TDW is a view window that shows messages passed to windows in your program. This is called the Windows Messages window in TDW and will be of immediate benefit to Windows programmers during the debugging procedure.

TDW supports the display of three types of data in the Log window. These include the data segments in the local and global heaps, a complete list of modules that comprise the Windows application, and expression type casting from memory handles to far pointers.

Of great importance is the fact that TDW allows for full debugging of dynamic link libraries. A Windows programmer would be hard-pressed to do without some sort of DLL debugging tool. TDW provides this and more.

Windows Messages

Under the View main screen menu is the Windows Messages option. When this option is selected, a three-pane window opens on the work surface. At the top left is the Window-Selection pane, while the Message Class pane is to its immediate right. The Messages pane lies beneath the top two.

It is in the third pane that the messages that are passed from the application to Windows may be recorded. Prior to running the application under TDW, it is necessary to select the VIEW|Windows Messages from the menu. This is done after the application to be debugged has been loaded. In the Window Selection pane, you indicate the window for which messages are to be logged. When using Borland C++, the quickest approach is to input Wndproc, the name of the routine that processes the messages. Alternately, you may input the handle value and click the Handle radio button in the Window Selection menu to indicate that this is a handle value and not the name of a routine.

Again, inputting the name of the routine is usually easiest, as it may be input any time after the application has been loaded. However, if you find it desirable or necessary to input a handle-variable name, it is first necessary to step through the program to a point that lies beyond the line where the handle value is assigned to the handle variable. Should the handle variable be entered in the Window Selection pane prior to stepping past the point where it is assigned in the application, the debugger will not be able to log messages for this window.

You may enter multiple names or handle values as is necessary to intercept all messages for a particular application. This is a great bonus when tracking the Windows messages of a complex, multiwindow application.

The Window Messages option in TDW also allows the user to filter messages according to type. To access the Set Message Filter dialog box, activate the Message Class pane (click it), and choose Add. This will bring up the filter dialog box, which provides the following options:

```
() All Messages
() Mouse
() Window
() Input
() System
() Initialization
() Clipboard
() DDE
() Non-client
() Other
() Single Message
```

The Message filter Dialog Box allows the user to specify the types of messages to be intercepted and informs the user of one of two actions to be performed when this happens. The user may specify a break when a particular message or class of message is tracked as one of these options. The other (default) action is to log the intercepted message.

Choosing All messages results in any message which has the WM_ prefix being intercepted and logged, if the log message option (default) is selected.

If the user selects the Mouse option, then only messages that are generated by a mouse event are logged. Such events would include WM_RBUTTONDOWN, WM_RBUTTONUP, and WM_RBUTTONDBLCLK. The following pane dump shows the message pane of a TDW run with a Windows application when the Mouse filter was chosen.

```
Turbo Debugger Log
Windows messages
Hwnd:1d18 wParam:0000 lParam:007e00c2 (0200) WM_MOUSEMOVE

Hwnd:1d18 wParam:1d18 lParam:02000001 (0020) WM_SETCURSOR

Hwnd:1d18 wParam:0000 lParam:008100be (0200) WM_MOUSEMOVE

Hwnd:1d18 wParam:1d18 lParam:02000001 (0020) WM_SETCURSOR

Hwnd:1d18 wParam:0000 lParam:008700b8 (0200) WM_MOUSEMOVE

Hwnd:1d18 wParam:1d18 lParam:02000001 (0020) WM_SETCURSOR

Hwnd:1d18 wParam:0000 lParam:008c00b4 (0200) WM_MOUSEMOVE

Hwnd:1d18 wParam:1d18 lParam:02000001 (0020) WM_SETCURSOR

Hwnd:1d18 wParam:0000 lParam:009000b0 (0200) WM_MOUSEMOVE

Hwnd:1d18 wParam:1d18 lParam:02000001 (0020) WM_SETCURSOR

Hwnd:1d18 wParam:0000 lParam:009100ac (0200) WM_MOUSEMOVE
```

The Window Message Filter option intercepts only those messages that come from the window manager, such as WM_CREATE. The following messages were displayed while running the same application as above with the Window option selected.

```
Turbo Debugger Log
Terminated, exit code 0
Windows messages
Hwnd:1d18 wParam:0001 lParam:00000000 (0018) WM_SHOWWINDOW

Hwnd:1d18 wParam:0000 lParam:00000000 (030f) WM_QUERYNEWPALETTE

Hwnd:1d18 wParam:0001 lParam:0000048d (001c) WM_ACTIVATEAPP

Hwnd:1d18 wParam:004f lParam:0aed2f00 (000d) WM_GETTEXT
```

```
Hwnd:1d18 wParam:0001 lParam:00001144 (0006) WM_ACTIVATE

Hwnd:1d18 wParam:1458 lParam:00000000 (0007) WM_SETFOCUS

Hwnd:1d18 wParam:0836 lParam:00000000 (0014) WM_ERASEBKGND

Hwnd:1d18 wParam:0000 lParam:00ed02a3 (0005) WM_SIZE

Hwnd:1d18 wParam:0000 lParam:0029001b (0003) WM_MOVE

Hwnd:1d18 wParam:0000 lParam:00000000 (000f) WM_PAINT

Hwnd:1d18 wParam:0000 lParam:05fd07a4 (0024) WM_GETMINMAXINFO

Hwnd:1d18 wParam:0000 lParam:00000000 (0010) WM_CLOSE

Hwnd:1d18 wParam:0000 lParam:00001144 (0006) WM_ACTIVATE

Hwnd:1d18 wParam:0000 lParam:0000048d (001c) WM_ACTIVATEAPP

Hwnd:1d18 wParam:1144 lParam:00000000 (0008) WM_KILLFOCUS

Hwnd:1d18 wParam:0000 lParam:00000000 (0002) WM_DESTROY
```

Messages that are produced by keyboard actions or by the user accessing a System menu, size box, or V/H scroll bar are intercepted by the Input filter option. Such messages include WM_KEYDOWN, WM_KEYUP, and WM_SYSKEYDOWN. The following message list was created while debugging with the Input option in force.

```
Turbo Debugger Log Stopped at WINMAIN Terminated, exit code 0
Windows messages Hwnd:1d18 wParam:001b lParam:00010001 (0100)
WM_KEYDOWN

Hwnd:1d18 wParam:001b lParam:00010001 (0102) WM_CHAR

Hwnd:1d18 wParam:1026 lParam:1022a090 (011f) WM_MENUSELECT

Hwnd:1d18 wParam:f120 lParam:1026a081 (011f) WM_MENUSELECT
```

```
Hwnd:1d18 wParam:f120 lParam:1026a081 (011f) WM_MENUSELECT

Hwnd:1d18 wParam:000e lParam:00001022 (011f) WM_MENUSELECT

Hwnd:1d18 wParam:05fd lParam:0000ffff (011f) WM_MENUSELECT
```

The System option will act upon messages that produce a system-wide change in the window such as WM_FONTCHANGE, WM_SYSCOMMAND, WM_ENTERIDLE, and others shown in the message-window printout below.

```
Turbo Debugger Log
Terminated, exit code 0
Windows messages
Hwnd:1d18 wParam:0002 lParam:00000fd4 (0121) WM_ENTERIDLE

Hwnd:1d18 wParam:f093 lParam:001f0016 (0112) WM_SYSCOMMAND

Hwnd:1d18 wParam:0002 lParam:00000fd4 (0121) WM_ENTERIDLE

Hwnd:1d18 wParam:0002 lParam:00000fd4 (0121) WM_ENTERIDLE

Hwnd:1d18 wParam:0002 lParam:00000fd4 (0121) WM_ENTERIDLE

Hwnd:1d18 wParam:0002 lParam:00000fd4 (0121) WM_ENTERIDLE

Hwnd:1d18 wParam:0002 lParam:00000fd4 (0121) WM_ENTERIDLE

Hwnd:1d18 wParam:f060 lParam:007e0036 (0112) WM_SYSCOMMAND
```

Opting for the Initialization filter results in the tracking of messages that are generated when a window or dialog box are created. A sampling of these messages appears in the pane reprint that follows.

```
Turbo Debugger Log
Terminated, exit code 0
Windows messages
Hwnd:1d18 wParam:1022 lParam:00000000 (0116) WM_INITMENU

Hwnd:1d18 wParam:1026 lParam:00010000 (0117) WM_INITMENUPOPUP
```

The Clipboard option is obvious in that it intercepts the messages that are sent when there is an attempt to access the clipboard.

If there is a need to track the Dynamic Data Exchange (DDE) messages, the DDE option allows this to be accomplished. Such messages are generated when two or more windows are communicating.

The Non-Client filter option intercepts messages such as WM_NCHITTEST which maintain the non-client area in a window. Further examples of such messages as tracked by TDW are shown below.

```
Turbo Debugger Log
Terminated, exit code 0
Windows messages
Hwnd:1d18 wParam:0000 lParam:00130013 (0084) WM_NCHITTEST

Hwnd:1d18 wParam:0000 lParam:00100017 (0084) WM_NCHITTEST

Hwnd:1d18 wParam:0002 lParam:00100017 (00a0) WM_NCMOUSEMOVE

Hwnd:1d18 wParam:0000 lParam:000e0017 (0084) WM_NCHITTEST

Hwnd:1d18 wParam:0002 lParam:000e0017 (00a0) WM_NCMOUSEMOVE

Hwnd:1d18 wParam:0000 lParam:00090011 (0084) WM_NCHITTEST

Hwnd:1d18 wParam:0003 lParam:00090011 (00a0) WM_NCMOUSEMOVE

Hwnd:1d18 wParam:0000 lParam:00080011 (0084) WM_NCHITTEST

Hwnd:1d18 wParam:0003 lParam:00080011 (00a0) WM_NCMOUSEMOVE

Hwnd:1d18 wParam:0000 lParam:0006000d (0084) WM_NCHITTEST

Hwnd:1d18 wParam:0003 lParam:0006000d (00a0) WM_NCMOUSEMOVE

Hwnd:1d18 wParam:0000 lParam:0006000d (0084) WM_NCHITTEST

Hwnd:1d18 wParam:0003 lParam:0006000d (00a1) WM_NCLBUTTONDOWN
```

```
Hwnd:1d18 wParam:09ee lParam:00000000 (0085) WM_NCPAINT

Hwnd:1d18 wParam:0000 lParam:00001144 (0086) WM_NCACTIVATE

Hwnd:1d18 wParam:0000 lParam:00000000 (0082) WM_NCDESTROY
```

The Other option covers all other messages beginning with the WM_ prefix that are not included as a part of any of the other categories. An example of the messages not preceded by the customary WM_ is shown below.

```
Turbo Debugger Log
Stopped at WINMAIN
Terminated, exit code 0
Windows messages
Hwnd:21f8 wParam:0001 lParam:00000000 (0009)

Hwnd:21f8 wParam:0005 lParam:00000001 (0088)

Hwnd:21f8 wParam:0000 lParam:00000000 (0231)

Hwnd:21f8 wParam:0000 lParam:00000000 (0232)

Hwnd:21f8 wParam:0005 lParam:00000001 (0088)

Hwnd:21f8 wParam:0000 lParam:00000000 (0211)

Hwnd:21f8 wParam:0000 lParam:00000000 (0212)
```

Finally, the Single Message option tracks any single message that is to be logged or to create an application break. This message is input by the user and is tracked throughout the debugging run. You may enter a message name or number. If you use a name, then it must be entered in uppercase letters. This option is especially useful when the Break option is used to halt a program upon detection of a specific message that is user-specified. For instance, if you wanted the program run to break upon receipt of a WM_CREATE message, you simply type WM_CREATE in the input window and click Break. During the debugging run, TDW waits for such a message and halts execution when it is received.

The message window can contain up to 200 lines and the contents of this window may be saved to a disk file by dumping the pane to the log, and opening a log-disk file.

Memory/Module Lists

With TDW, it is a simple matter to obtain a listing of the global and local heap along with a list of modules for a particular Windows application. By selecting View|Log, the log window will appear. ALT-F10 brings up the log local menu. The last item in this menu is Display Windows Info. By clicking this option, a Windows Information dialog box appears on the work surface and allows a choice of Global Heap, Local Heap, and Module List. The Global Heap option allows for the list to be displayed from top to bottom, bottom to top, or from a starting location specified by the user. This point of entry must be the name of the global memory handle, which is assigned by a global memory-allocation routine within the application.

Shown below is a Global Heap list generated by TDW and a simple Windows application.

```
Turbo Debugger Log
0476 (0475) 00000020b OEMFONTS PRIV MOVEABLE DISCARDABLE
02FE (02FD) 000000C0b FONTS    PRIV MOVEABLE
061E (061D) 00000020b USER     PRIV MOVEABLE DISCARDABLE
062E (062D) 00000080b USER     PRIV MOVEABLE DISCARDABLE
0626 (0625) 00000080b USER     PRIV MOVEABLE DISCARDABLE
0226 (0225) 00000020b DISPLAY  PRIV MOVEABLE DISCARDABLE
07E6 (07E5) 00000020b PROGMAN  PRIV MOVEABLE
021E (021D) 00000020b DISPLAY  PRIV MOVEABLE DISCARDABLE
0776 (0775) 000000C0b GDI      PRIV MOVEABLE
075E (075D) 00000200b MODERN   PRIV MOVEABLE DISCARDABLE
0166 (0165) 000000C0b KEYBOARD CODE MOVEABLE DISCARDABLE
011E (011D) 000001E0b KEYBOARD PRIV MOVEABLE
09E5        00002680b TDW      DATA FIXED PGLOCKED=0001
0495        00002EA0b KERNEL   PRIV FIXED PGLOCKED=0001
048D        00000200b PDB (048D)
0676 (0675) 00000F80b FONTS    PRIV MOVEABLE DISCARDABLE
LOCKED=0009 PGLOCKED
0605        00000040b GDI      PRIV FIXED PGLOCKED=0001
```

```
060D        00000520b USER     PRIV FIXED PGLOCKED=0001
0615        00000100b USER     PRIV FIXED PGLOCKED=0001
05F5        00000240b USER     DATA FIXED PGLOCKED=0001
04AD        00000D20b USER     PRIV FIXED PGLOCKED=0001
04A5        000092A0b USER     PRIV FIXED PGLOCKED=0001
032D        00000040b GDI      PRIV FIXED PGLOCKED=0001
0345        00005300b GDI      PRIV FIXED PGLOCKED=0001
0315        00000300b COMM     DATA FIXED PGLOCKED=0001
030D        00000400b COMM     PRIV FIXED PGLOCKED=0001
02F5        00000040b SOUND    DATA FIXED PGLOCKED=0001
02ED        000000A0b SOUND    PRIV FIXED PGLOCKED=0001
01F5        000004A0b DISPLAY  DATA FIXED PGLOCKED=0001
01BD        000035C0b DISPLAY  PRIV FIXED PGLOCKED=0001
01A5        00000140b MOUSE    DATA FIXED PGLOCKED=0001
019D        00000220b MOUSE    PRIV FIXED PGLOCKED=0001
018D        00000160b KEYBOARD DATA FIXED PGLOCKED=0001
0185        00000B60b KEYBOARD PRIV FIXED PGLOCKED=0001
0125        000004E0b SYSTEM   PRIV FIXED PGLOCKED=0001
022E (022D) 00000020b DISPLAY  PRIV MOVEABLE DISCARDABLE
0486 (0485) 00000040b DISPLAY  PRIV MOVEABLE DISCARDABLE
014E (014D) 00000240b KEYBOARD CODE MOVEABLE DISCARDABLE
064E (064D) 00000060b USER     PRIV MOVEABLE DISCARDABLE
FREE        000001A0b
0B25        00000100b USER     PRIV FIXED PGLOCKED=0001
0B0D        00000200b PDB (0B0D)
0A0D        00000180b WIN87EM  DATA FIXED PGLOCKED=0001
0875        00000100b USER     PRIV FIXED PGLOCKED=0001
09ED        00000A40b TDW      DATA FIXED PGLOCKED=0001
09D5        000014E0b TDW      DATA FIXED PGLOCKED=0001
085D        00000200b PDB (085D)
0266 (0265) 00000040b GDI      PRIV MOVEABLE LOCKED=0001
PGLOCKED=0001
00FD        00007620b KERNEL   PRIV FIXED PGLOCKED=0001
00F5        000004C0b KERNEL   PRIV FIXED PGLOCKED=0001
```

The maximum number of lines that may be displayed in the log pane is 200, with a default setting of 50.

An area of memory that is set aside for a specific Windows application is called the local heap. This area of memory is private to that application (and to other instances of the same application) and cannot be accessed by other Windows applications. Not all Windows applications will contain a local heap. One is provided if the HEAPSIZE statement is found in the applications definition file. The following list was generated by TDW with the local-heap option in force.

```
Turbo Debugger Log
Local heap
34F8: FFFC BUSY
3198: 035C FREE
3140: 0054 BUSY
3110: 002C BUSY
3104: 0008 BUSY
Terminated, exit code 0
```

The last option in this dialog box causes a list of DLL and task modules to be tracked. The following list displays the modules accessed during execution of a Windows application.

```
Turbo Debugger Log
Module list
00F5 DLL  KERNEL    C:\WINDOWS\SYSTEM\KRNL386.EXE
00ED DLL  SYSTEM    C:\WINDOWS\SYSTEM\SYSTEM.DRV
011D DLL  KEYBOARD  C:\WINDOWS\SYSTEM\KEYBOARD.DRV
0135 DLL  MOUSE     C:\WINDOWS\SYSTEM\MSMOUSE2.DRV
0195 DLL  DISPLAY   C:\WINDOWS\SYSTEM\HERCULES.DRV
01B5 DLL  SOUND     C:\WINDOWS\SYSTEM\SOUND.DRV
01FD DLL  COMM      C:\WINDOWS\SYSTEM\COMM.DRV
02FD DLL  FONTS     C:\WINDOWS\SYSTEM\EGASYS.FON
0325 DLL  OEMFONTS  C:\WINDOWS\SYSTEM\EGAOEM.FON
0335 DLL  GDI       C:\WINDOWS\SYSTEM\GDI.EXE
031D DLL  FIXFONTS  C:\WINDOWS\SYSTEM\EGAFIX.FON
033D DLL  USER      C:\WINDOWS\SYSTEM\USER.EXE
06ED DLL  TMSRB     C:\WINDOWS\SYSTEM\TMSRB.FON
06F5 DLL  SYMBOL    C:\WINDOWS\SYSTEM\SYMBOLB.FON
0705 DLL  HELVB     C:\WINDOWS\SYSTEM\HELVB.FON
0715 DLL  COURB     C:\WINDOWS\SYSTEM\COURB.FON
```

```
0725 DLL  ROMAN     C:\WINDOWS\SYSTEM\ROMAN.FON
0735 DLL  SCRIPT    C:\WINDOWS\SYSTEM\SCRIPT.FON
0745 DLL  MODERN    C:\WINDOWS\SYSTEM\MODERN.FON
049D TASK PROGMAN   C:\WINDOWS\PROGMAN.EXE
0855 TASK TDW       E:\BORLANDC\BIN\TDW.EXE
09F5 DLL  WIN87EM   C:\WINDOWS\SYSTEM\WIN87EM.DLL
0ADD DLL  WINDEBUG  E:\BORLANDC\BIN\WINDEBUG.DLL
0AED TASK HSCROLL   E:\BORLANDC\HSCROLL.EXE
```

On each line, the first value is a handle for the memory segment. This is expressed as a hexadecimal value. The following designation is the module type, which is TASK or DLL. The next designation is the module name followed by the path to that module.

In general, when debugging Windows applications, Borland International recommends that code and message breakpoints should be set where possible. Run the application until it encounters a breakpoint, then step or trace if necessary.

Simply stepping and tracing through an application without established breakpoints is not very useful, in most cases. Owing to the fact that such applications are interactive programs, the procedure of running the application until an interrupt or breakpoint occurs and then stepping through the remainder makes good sense.

DLL Debugging

A Dynamic Link Library, or DLL, is a library of Windows routines and/or resources that is not a stand-alone application. Rather, the DLL is linked to a Windows application during compilation. This allows multiple Windows applications to share a single copy of various data and routines, which can result in a very large savings in regard to RAM usage.

When a Windows application is debugged by TDW, the DLLs in the application are checked for the presence of symbol tables, and TDW uses these to keep track of each DLL. During execution of the application, a call to a DLL entry point results in the symbol table for that DLL being loaded along with the DLL source. The module line marker is placed at the beginning of the DLL routine. Examining the module window will show the DLL. When the DLL is exited, it is replaced by the symbol table and source code for the original application. The line marker is placed on the next statement (following the DLL) and the debugging process continues.

TDW automatically performs the entire DLL debugging routine to this point—nothing special is required of the user in order to address DLLs in the manner described. However, there are additional tasks that can be accomplished by the debugger, and these require some additional user operations.

Using TDW, DLLs may be added to the list of DLLs. The user may also opt to tell TDW not to load certain DLLs where such omissions will enhance the specific debugging task. Additionally, breakpoints may be set within a DLL. You can see that TDW has all of the capabilities necessary to perform efficient tasks aimed at DLL debugging while still maintaining a high degree of simplicity in the user-interface.

To further emphasize the automatic nature of TDW in debugging Microsoft Windows applications and DLLs, it is important to note that there are two error messages that are returned only by TDW. The first is "Invalid Window Handle." This occurs when the user has input an illegal handle-variable name—a handle variable that has not been assigned a handle value. This usually occurs when the user has entered a handle name prior to stepping the application through to a point just past the handle-variable assignment. Remember, a handle name must be specified after the execution point where the variable is assigned a handle.

The second (and last) error message is "Ctrl-Alt-SysRq interrupt. System crash possible. Continue?" This error message is displayed when an attempt is made to reload an application when it has been halted by pressing the key combination, Ctrl-Alt-SysRq. Due to the fact that the Windows kernel code was executing at the time this key combination was made, reloading the application (or trying to exit TDW) can have a broad range of results—often locking the system up, necessitating a reboot.

Summary

If you are familiar with the use of Borland Turbo Debugger, then you will have little difficulty adjusting to Turbo Debugger for Windows. It operates in a manner almost identical to Turbo Debugger, and it offers a full range of debugging capabilities for Windows applications and DLLs. It is an indispensable tool for the Windows professional as well as for those persons who are just now adapting to a Windows programming environment. The automatic nature in which complex Windows applications are addressed means that much of the "debugging set-up" is handled by TDW with little or no user interaction required. However, TDW, like Turbo Debugger, doesn't do it all for you. TDW is a tool which, when used properly, saves many hours of tedious "hit and miss" debugging by Windows programmers of any experience level.

CHAPTER 9

The Whitewater Resource Toolkit

The Whitewater Resource Toolkit is a powerful utility that was developed by The Whitewater Group. Version 3.01 of the WRT is bundled with Borland C++ and aids the programmer in developing resources for Windows applications. With the Toolkit, programmers may visually build, modify, and incorporate resources into Windows applications. These resources may be maintained in .EXE files. Alternately, they may be maintained in resource (.RES), bitmap (.BMT), cursor (.CUR), and icon (.ICO) files. They may also be saved in text files that are compatible with Windows resource script files.

With the Whitewater Resource Toolkit editors, the user may create and manage user interfaces of Windows applications while remaining within the Windows environment. The Toolkit can be used to create, edit, and save dialog boxes, bitmaps, icons, keyboard accelerators, menus, cursors, and strings.

Most of these elements can be created directly in source code, but by defining them as resources, they are removed from the source code. These management tasks are then taken care of by Windows. This results in a more efficient application.

The Whitewater Resource Toolkit is composed of two major parts: the Resource Manager and the Editors. The former provides access to the Toolkit's specialized editors and functions. Its main purpose is to allow the user to navigate through the various features of the Toolkit.

The Whitewater Resource Toolkit must run under Windows Version 3.0 or later and requires a full familiarity with Microsoft Windows operation. The microcomputer must be equipped with 1 megabyte of RAM, a mouse (or other) pointing device, and a graphics display. Borland recommends EGA displays or better, but the program will function adequately in a Hercules-compatible monochrome graphics environment. A bare minimum of 700K of free disk space is required for temporary files. Practical applications will require about 5 megabytes of free disk space. This should be accommodated easily by current systems that have a large hard-disk capacity.

Editors

The Whitewater Resource Toolkit provides a bevy of editors that allow for the efficient building of resources. The Menu Editor supports hierarchic menus used in Windows 3.0. Through the use of hierarchic menus, the user may create a multitude of pop-up menu levels for each menu item.

The Dialog Box Editor allows for the creation of dialog boxes. When a new file is created using this editor, a captioned dialog box is drawn. The user may also create combo boxes, which combine the features of an edit control and a list box.

The Bitmap Editor allows the user to customize palettes, and the Icon and Cursor Editors allow for the creation of multiple images. Such images allow the icons and cursors to be device-independent. Windows automatically loads the appropriate image when an application calls for an icon or cursor. All these editors have a Pixel Size tool that allows the user to draw in one of three pixel sizes: 1 x 1, 4 x 4, and 8 x 8.

The Accelerator Editor allows the user to create and edit accelerator resources. An accelerator is a hot key for issuing commands. This editor allows for the quick establishment of a hot key and for the equally quick modification of existing hot keys.

The String Editor is used to create and edit String resources. These are strings of text used by an application for applying a message or caption to a window.

Starting the Whitewater Resource Toolkit to begin a session under the Whitewater Resource Toolkit (WRT), the user invokes the Toolkit by a command line call when Windows is invoked. The command is:

```
WIN WRT
```

Alternately, the WRT may be called from the Program Manager, File Manager, or MS-DOS Executive.

The Resource Manager

The focal point of the WRT is the Resource Manager, which appears in the main window. All activities are directly or indirectly controlled with this window, which provides access to resources and to each of the resource editors. With the Resource Manager, the user may create new resource files to which other resources are copied. Existing resources can be accessed so that they may be changed, copied, or deleted.

The Resource Manager has a menuless format for quick operation. The main window is shown in Figure 9-1. To activate any selection, the user simply clicks the appropriate button or presses the keyboard key that corresponds to the underlined letter on the button.

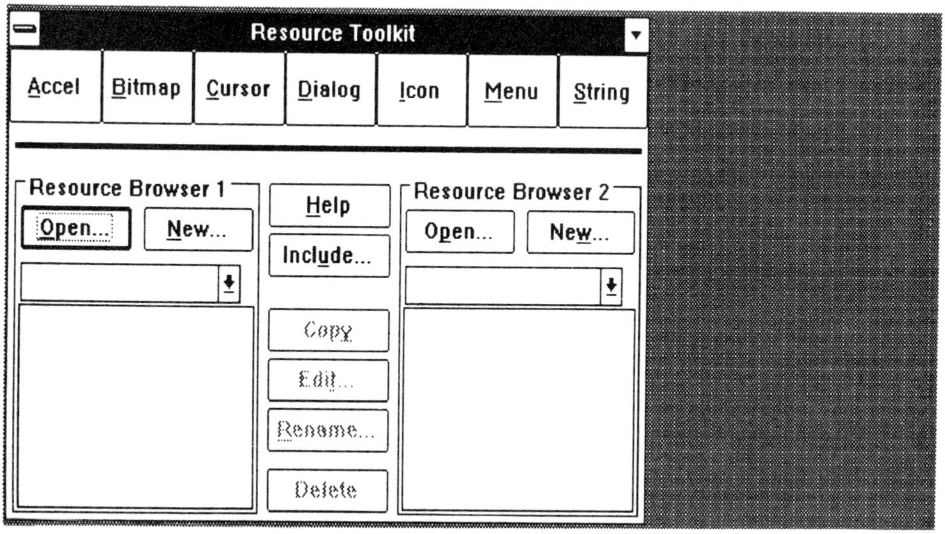

Figure 9-1. Screen showing the Resource Manager.

Across the top of the screen are the editor buttons. These are arranged in alphabetical order and they merely need be clicked to activate the desired editor. Two windows are provided that allow the user to open a file. Two files may be opened simultaneously and resources from one may be copied into the other. To select the resource types to be displayed in these windows, an Include button, which opens a dialog box, is provided. Here, all of the resource types available for editing or copying will be listed. Any combination of resource types may be selected for display.

To enter one of the WRT editors, simply click its button (or press the appropriate keyboard key). Once the editor has been opened, the user may create a new resource or perform editing functions on an existing resource. There are three ways to create a new resource. The first has been discussed already and involves clicking the button of the appropriate editor. If you are currently within an editor, simply select File|New. If you aren't in an editor, the New button that is located above one of the windows may be clicked. This method would be used to create a new file for the purposes of copying a resource to it from an existing file.

To edit a resource, open the file that contains the resource and select a resource type from the window-edit field. Within the list box, double-click the desired resource name or number. This automatically starts the editor and loads the appropriate resource into that editor.

To delete a resource, open the file in which it is contained and select the resource type from the edit field. This lists the resqurces of an individual type in the list box. Select the resource to be deleted and click the Delete button.

Copying a resource involves listing the resource to be copied in one box and opening a file to which the resource is to be copied in the other box. Click the Copy button. This will open the Resource Attributes dialog box so that you can rename the resource. If the resource is not to be renamed, simply click the Okay button.

Each time a file is saved, a backup file that has the same name as the original file, but with the first character of the file extension replaced with a tilde (~), is created. As an example, if changes are made to a file named TEST.CUR, the backup filename will be TEST.~UR. This backup is a safety measure, because occasionally an editing operation may result in the user erasing or hopelessly modifying an existing file in an unsuccessful attempt to accomplished a certain task. The backup feature allows a return to the original state of the file by using the DOS Rename command after the defective file has been erased. With Rename, the backup file is given its original name, and the user may start from square one.

To create a new file, the user enters one of the editors and chooses the FILE|NEW option. Alternately, the New button above either of the browsing boxes may be clicked. This method of new-file creation is best used when it is necessary to copy resources into a new file.

To close the file, simply click the Close button. All of the changes made to the file are saved immediately. Warning: A dialog box to confirm the saving of all changes will not appear when the Close button is clicked. Saving is done automatically on closing a file.

The Accelerator (Hot Key) Editor

The Accelerator Editor is used to create hot keys for issuing application commands. The editor stores accelerator keys and codes in a table that normally contains seven columns that display information about the accelerator. If a header file is opened, then an additional column is used to display the symbolic name of the accelerator.

Accelerator keys are specifically defined within the accelerator table. In general, any virtual key or character key may be defined as an accelerator in any application. The user is cautioned, however, not to define hot keys that will conflict with the established hot keys in the Windows 3.0 environment. In other words, don't activate hot keys that are already in use within the Windows environment.

The hot key table contains seven or eight columns, which are defined as Type, Key, Code, Shift, Ctrl, Value, Invert, and Symbol. The latter column is provided only when a header file is opened. These columns are used to set the data attributable to each hot key.

The Type column indicates whether the hot key is a virtual key or an ASCII code. The term Virtkey names accelerators according to a set of virtual key definitions defined for Windows. ASCII describes the accelerator in terms of ASCII values.

The Key column represents the accelerator key itself. To define the accelerator, simply press the desired key. This column allows you to create direct access to an accelerator key simply by pressing it.

The Code column provides the hot key's scan code. This column is written to automatically when the Key column is filled. The code will depend upon whether the key is designed as a Virtkey or an ASCII in the Type column. This becomes the key's identification number on the keyboard, and is not the same as the ID that is used in the source code, which will be displayed in the Value column.

The Shift column is used to specify whether the Shift key is pressed in order to activate the accelerator that is displayed in the Key column. For example, if the Type column contains Virtkey, this column will cycle between Yes and No, with this value updated when an accelerator is defined in the Key column. If ASCII is displayed in the Type column, this field is blank and the Shift key does not apply to the ASCII accelerator codes.

The Ctrl column is used to specify whether the Ctrl key needs to be pressed in order to activate the accelerator in the Key column. Here, if Virtkey is displayed in the Type column, this column will cycle between Yes and No, and this value will be updated automatically if an accelerator is defined in the Key column. If ASCII is displayed in the Type column, the field will be blank and the Ctrl key will not apply to ASCII accelerator codes.

The Value column displays the ID number for the accelerator that was defined in the Key column. This number is referred to in the application's source code when you wish to load the accelerator into an application. As an alternative, a symbol can be defined for the accelerator by entering its value as it is defined in source code. This value must be an integer. ID values of accelerators can be the same as the IDs of other resources, because Windows always interprets an ID value within the context of the resource that is in use in an application.

The Invert column is used to designate whether the main menu item associated with an accelerator is to be highlighted when the accelerator key is pressed. Here, the value will be Yes or No.

The Symbol column provides the symbol whose ID number in the header file matches the value of the current accelerator. This symbol is referred to in the application's source code when the accelerator is to be loaded into an application.

The Bitmap, Cursor, and Icon Editors

Within the Resource Toolkit there are three separate editors for use with each of the three graphic resource types. These are the Bitmap, Cursor, and Icon Editors. Graphic resources are created within the particular editor with tools from graphics programs. It is possible not only to select a line type or shape to be drawn, but also to select color. In addition, with icons and cursors, it is also possible to view a color, once selected, to see how it will look against a variety of background colors.

A bitmap resource may be thought of as the description of a graphic picture which will be replicated on the monitor screen. Generally speaking, this type of resource has no immediate window-manager function and is used for identification purposes. A good example of this might be a description window that imparts information to the user but that has no effect on the operation of the window's contents.

An icon is a bitmap that represents the available operations that may be carried out within an application. A cursor is another type of specialized bitmap that identifies the position of the mouse pointer. Often, different cursors are used to indicate a particular mode of operation or the presence of a specific application.

The Bitmap Editor is used to create and edit bitmap files, containing device-independent bitmaps. Using the WRT Bitmap Editor, two- or sixteen-color bitmaps may be incorporated. The size of any bitmap is limited only by system RAM. Only one bitmap image may be contained in any single bitmap file, although .RES (resource) files may contain multiple bitmap images.

Cursor and icon files contain multiple bitmap images, each of which has been built for display on a different device. The differences lie in pixel dimensions and color capacity, which are stylized to meet the requirements of different display devices. Each cursor or icon is loaded into the application by name. The Windows environment selects the appropriate image for that cursor or icon. The criteria for this imaging process depends upon the pixel dimensions and the color capacity of the device driver.

Resolution information for device drivers is found in the WRT.DAT file. This information is essential for creating a new image for cursors or icons. Most devices require 32-x-32-pixel images, so one image must assume that dimension. A separate image for devices that don't use the 32-x-32-pixel format can then be created.

Each file record contains display information for a different device. The fields in the record are separated by commas and are made up of the following information:

Name: This is the name used in the file to reference a particular display device. The name may be any legal string with a maximum length of 10 characters.

Number of Colors: This is a numeric value that specifies the number of colors for the image.

Cursor Width: A numeric value stating the width, in pixel units, of the cursor .

Cursor Height: A numeric value stating the height, in pixel units, of the cursor.

Icon Width: Same as cursor width.

Icon Height: Same as cursor height.

To create a new image for an existing cursor or icon, the New option is chosen from the Image menu. A dialog box is opened and the user is asked to specify a resolution for the image. One image is created for each record in the WRT.DAT file. Default values are 32-x-32 pixels for both cursors and icons. Cursors default to 2 colors and icons to 16 colors.

In order to create a new cursor or icon, the New option is chosen from the File menu. The same information then (as was described in the operation above) needs to be entered.

The graphics editors are very similar in many ways to paint programs, which have been a part of the microcomputer graphics environment for a number of years. At the left side of the screen is a Color palette that allows the user to select colors to be utilized. The currently selected color is displayed in a color box above the Color palette. For the Cursor and Icon Editors, three color modes exist.

Color: This is used to select colors that will not change— regardless of the background screen color.

Screen: This mode selects colors that will always match the screen background and will change with screen background changes.

Inverse: This mode selects colors that reflect the true inverse color of the background screen color.

The Tools palette is located across the top of the editor screen. Tools are used to draw the bitmap, cursor, or icon proper. Colors may be toggled automatically, and a series of drawing tools is provided, along with a line-width option for choosing various thicknesses of all lines drawn with the drawing-tools complement.

Rulers are provided at the left and top sides of the editing area and show the location of the current drawing tool. The editing area is the screen location where the images are actually created. To the right of this area, a small view window is provided that displays the image as it will appear in the application. This window is constantly updated so that it reflects the contents of the editing area. This editing area displays a magnified view to facilitate image design.

At the bottom right corner of the editor is a Resource Statistics area. This constantly displays the number of colors allowed for the image, along with image height and width in pixel units.

Before any image is drawn, it is necessary to select the color desired. This is the color which the image lines will assume. For cursor and icon images, the user must decide whether to draw in color, screen, or inverse mode. The Color palette will display the available colors for the current resource.

In this usage, there are two types of colors available for manipulation. Pure colors are those that can be generated directly by the monitor and monitor adapter card. Pure colors are simply combinations of red, blue, and green—the three primary colors. All lines drawn by graphics tools use pure colors.

Dithered colors are those that the windowing environment synthesizes. Synthesis is necessary due to the fact that the monitor cannot generate them directly. Most users will be familiar with dithered colors, which are made up of pure colors combined in a pattern of dots to approximate another color. The percentage of one color to another within the dithering pattern determines the final dithered color. A good example of a dithered color is the various shades of gray that can be produced by dithering black and white. A higher percentage of white produces a lighter shade of gray. The screen or output device may not be capable of producing a true gray, but the pattern "simulates" gray through the dithering process—at least, the user's eye is convinced that the color is gray. Again, these are simulated colors and not true, or pure, colors.

Lines cannot be drawn in dithered colors. Should the user select a dithered color for line-drawing use, the editor will automatically choose the closest pure color instead. If the user is not sure whether a color is pure, the Pouring tool is available to fill a large area with the color in question. If the painted area appears to be solid, then the user is dealing with a pure color. A dithered color will result in a checkered pattern.

Twenty eight colors are available in the Color palette of the Bitmap Editor. When a 16-color bitmap is selected, the first 16 of these 28 colors are pure colors. The rest are dithered. Where a two-color bitmap is specified, the palette contains only black and white as pure colors, along with 26 shades of gray. Another feature of the editor includes customizing color palettes.

Graphics Drawing

Using the graphics tools is a simple procedure akin to using any of a number of simple paint programs that have been popular for years. Figure 9-2 shows the graphic-tools icon list, which includes the usual host of tools for drawing filled and unfilled rectangles, circles, and polygons. For freehand drawing, the Pencil tool may be utilized, along with others that will cut and paste images and fill them with user-selected patterns and colors.

Before any drawing tool is called up, the user should use the Line Width tool to select the width of the lines that will be used for a particular drawing or a particular portion of an image. All widths are measured in pixels, and three options are available. Lines may take on a width of 1, 3, or 5 pixels. The one-pixel width is the default.

After the line width has been selected, the Magnifying tool is usually called to select a scale for the editing area. Three options are available with this tool. The first provides no magnification, and the image is shown in actual size. Two other options allow a multiplication factor of x4 and x8. The default here is x4. When magnification is incorporated in producing an image, the entire image may not be visible within the editing area. However, the View window will give the user a full—if somewhat miniature—view.

From this point on, the user may select any drawing icon that is suitable to produce the desired image. Straight lines are drawn using the Line tool. Lines may be drawn in any direction. However, a line that is a multiple of 45 degrees should be drawn using the Constrained Line tool. This tool produces lines that are vertical or horizontal or at any multiple of 45 degrees. Free-form lines and shapes are drawn using the Pencil tool, which works like every other pencil tool ever included in any type of graphics drawing program. By moving the mouse cursor, a line is created at any point the cursor touches. To produce a single point, the user simply clicks the desired spot without dragging the mouse. Circles (ellipses) and rectangles can also be created using the appropriate tool, and the user may select hollow or filled images. Choosing a filled tool draws a solid image in the selected color. If the image is to be filled with a different color than that of its lines, then choose the hollow-image drawing tool and select the Pour icon to fill the image with the desired color after it is drawn.

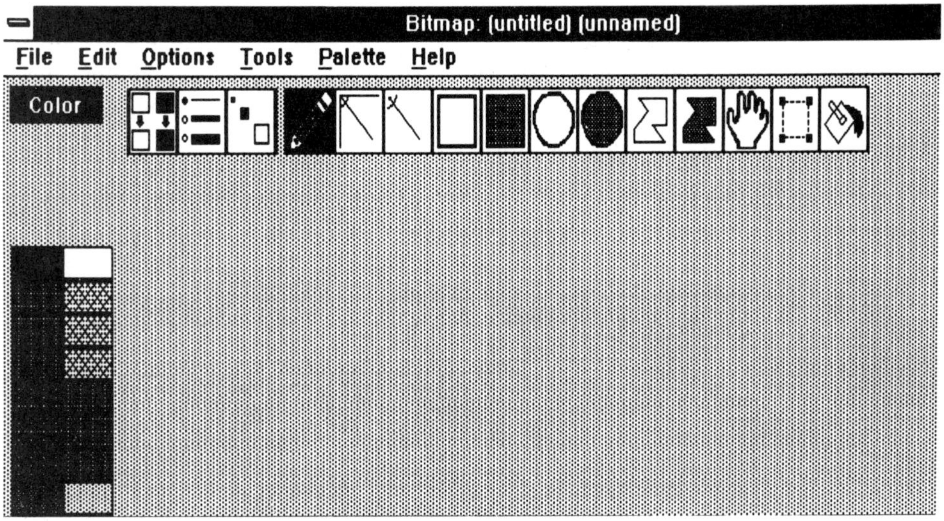

Figure 9-2. Screen showing the graphic-tools icon list.

One tool that is provided with the Cursor Editor that is not common to other paint programs is called the Hot Spot tool. Every Windows cursor has one pixel that identifies the one point at which cursor operations occur. Because cursors are almost always more than one pixel in height and width, this one unique pixel lies at the center of the cursor (usually) and defines the exact spot on the screen at which an operation is to occur. In popular terminology, the location of this single pixel is called the "hot spot." The Hot Spot tool is used to designate a "hot spot." The tool is simply selected and a click marks the location.

The Dialog Box Editor

The Dialog Box Editor is used to design dialog-box resources. The dialog box is a window that contains such items as list boxes, edit fields, and push buttons. This editor is used in the same manner as that of a drawing program. Dialog boxes are created and edited by selecting, positioning, and modifying their controls. The editor may be used with boxes contained in resource files, executable files, and dynamic link libraries. The editor will save a dialog box resource directly into an existing .RES file or to a dialog-box resource script file (.DLG).

Two palettes are contained in the Dialog Box Editor. The Tools palette allows the creation of dialog boxes and all of their controls. The Alignment palette is used to change the alignment of controls within a box. Figure 9-3 shows the Tools palette. After a tool is selected, the Pointer tool is activated automatically. This tool allows you to draw with the selected tool or to choose a dialog box or other existing controls so that you can move them or change their size.

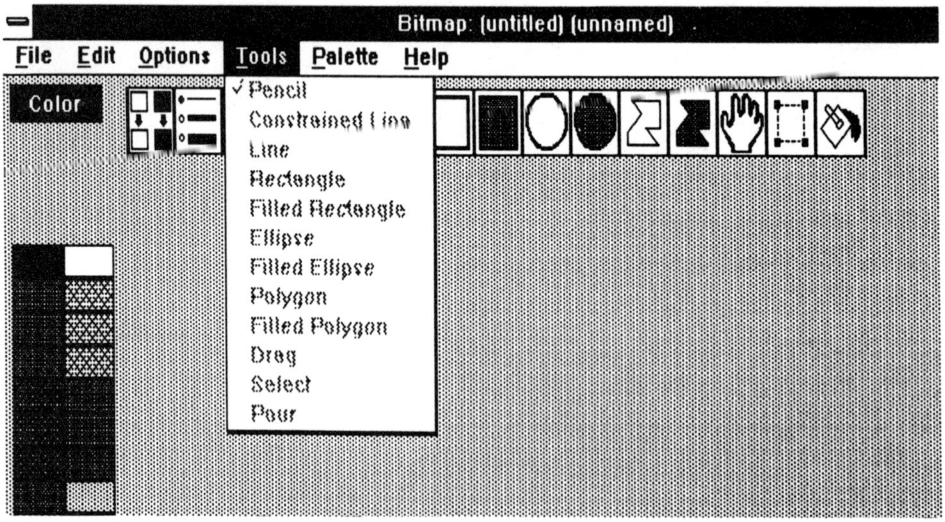

Figure 9-3. Example of the Tools palette.

The Dialog Box tool is used to create either a standard dialog box or a captioned dialog box. The default is a captioned dialog box, and it is drawn automatically when a new file is created using this editor. By double-clicking the Dialog Box tool, the box style is toggled between standard and captioned. A standard dialog box can be converted to a captioned dialog box by selecting the Caption button in the Dialog Attributes box.

It is necessary to actually create the dialog box before its controls can be added. Options are available that display the control-tab order, the ID number of each control, and that show logical groups among controls.

The Dialog Box menu provides numerous options. One allows you to define attributes for the box, while others allow the user to set the grid resolution that determines the actual positioning of controls. The Controls menu is used to open an attributes dialog box, which allows you to define specific attributes for the control. The Set Tab Stop item activates the tab stop bit for the selected control. Other items include Start Group, which defines dialog box controls as a logical group; Move Forward, which moves the control forward one tab stop; and Move Backward, which moves the control back one tab stop.

Overall, the usage of this editor is quite straightforward and allows for an efficient and yet simple method of creating highly elaborate dialog boxes. All the editors in the Whitewater Resource Toolkit seem to follow a central pattern, so when one is mastered, learning the others is a much simpler task.

The Menu Editor

The Menu Editor is used to create and edit menu resources. This allows the user to decide on the appearance and content of any menu utilized in a Windows application. Resource, executable, and dynamic link library files can be edited using this utility. This editor can also open a header file to correlate with the menu resource, symbolic constants from the file being edited. The menu editor screen is shown in Figure 9-4. Its features include a test window, a menu table, movement buttons, style fields, and attribute fields.

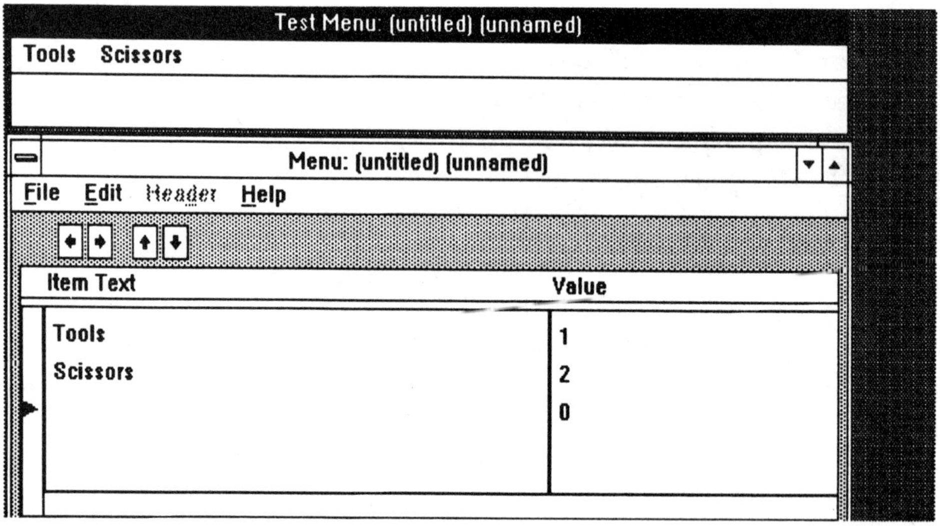

Figure 9-4. Example of the Menu Editor screen.

The test window is used interactively to test a menu. The menu table contains two columns of edit fields, one marked Text and the other marked Value. The Text area allows the user to edit menu text, while the Value column is where a value for the current item can be entered or edited. Whenever a header file has been opened, a third column will be displayed, showing the symbolic name for each menu item.

Movement buttons allow the user to change the hierarchy of a menu item or to change an item's row in the text field. These buttons are marked Up, Down, Left, and Right, with arrows. The Left/Right buttons perform a hierarchy change, while the Up/Down buttons are used for row changes.

The style and attribute fields located beneath the menu table are used for definition of menu styles and attributes, including adding separator lines to pop-up menus, aligning menu items in columns, and asigning help attributes.

The String Editor

The String Editor is used to create and edit string resources. These are strings used by an application for all text display, including window captions, status messages, and error messages. These strings are loaded as needed from an executable file. The editor stores strings in a string table that is arranged in the following order:

Column 1: String ID—an integer value

Column 2: The string proper

Column 3: The symbolic name of the ID

The third column appears only when a header file has been opened. The maximum size of a string table is 64K, and you can define only one string table for an executable file.

A field indicator is provided which will indicate which field in the table is active. An accompanying row indicator shows the row in which the active field is found. The row indicator uses an arrow on the far-left margin to indicate the row, while the field indicator simply frames the active field.

Figure 9-5 shows the string table. Note that the Value field is at the left and contains the ID number (an integer) for the string that is contained in the String Text column. This latter column shows the string itself. Note that these strings are not enclosed in quotation marks. If they are, then the quotation marks will become a part of the displayed string.

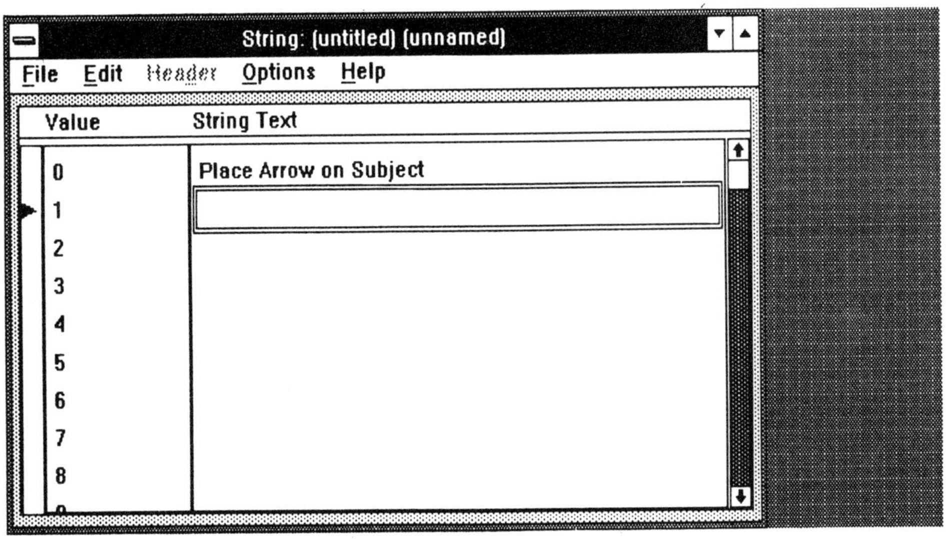

Figure 9-5. Screen showing the string table.

The Header Editor

The Header Editor is incorporated to allow the creation and editing of symbolic constants—better known as symbols. These can be substituted for the ID numbers that Windows uses to identify resources. When the symbols have been defined, resources may be loaded from source code by referencing defined symbols rather than numeric values. All symbolic constants saved by this editor are stored in header files.

The Header Editor is never invoked by itself as a stand-alone editor might be. This editor is designed for symbol definition during the creation or editing process of resources which will be represented by these symbols. A standard editing process here would begin with resource editing. The Header Editor is then invoked from within the Resource Editor. This makes the Header Editor a child window of the editor used to invoke it. Only a single header file can be opened at any one time within each Resource Editor.

Summary

The Whitewater Resource Toolkit performs a large number of highly complex operations in a simple manner. This speaks for the power of the Toolkit and the planning that went into its design. This chapter has provided the briefest of overviews of the WRT, however, the reader will have obtained sufficient knowledge to be aware of the power and flexibility that this complex utility offers. Certainly, Borland C++ could be successful without it, but the bundling of the Whitewater Resource Toolkit with Borland C++ results in a sophisticated Windows development system as opposed to a C++ compiler that merely supports Windows.

Index

N

O

P

R

S

T

U

V

W

Z

A Library of Technical References from M&T Books

The NetWare Manual Makers
Complete Kits for Creating Customized NetWare Manuals

Developed to meet the tremendous demand for customized manuals, The NetWare Manual Makers enable the NetWare supervisor and administrator to create network training manuals specific to their individual sites. Administrators simply fill in the blanks on the template provided on disk and print the file to create customized manuals and command cards. Included is general "how-to" information on using a network, as well as fill-in-the-blank sections that help administrators explain and document procedures unique to a particular site. The disk files are provided in WordPerfect and ASCII formats. The WordPerfect file creates a manual that looks exactly like the one in the book. The ASCII file can be imported into any desktop publishing or word processing software.

The NetWare 286 Manual Maker
The Complete Kit for Creating Customized NetWare 286 Manuals
by Christine Milligan

Book/Disk **Item #119-9** **$49.95 314 pp.**

The NetWare 386 Manual Maker
The Complete Kit for Creating Customized NetWare 386 Manuals
by Christine Milligan

Book/Disk **Item #120-2** **$49.95 314 pp.**

The NetWare for Macintosh Manual Maker
The Complete Kit for Creating Customized NetWare for Macintosh Manuals
by Kelley J. P. Lindberg

Book/Disk **Item #130-X** **$49.95 314 pp.**

1-800-533-4372 (in CA 1-800-356-2002)

A Library of Technical References from M&T Books

NetWare Programmer's Guide
by John T. McCann

Covered are all aspects of programming in the NetWare environment — from basic planning to complex application debugging. This book offers practical tips and tricks for creating and porting applications to NetWare. NetWare programmers developing simple applications for a single LAN or intricate programs for multi-site internetworked systems will find this book an invaluable reference to have on hand. All source code is available on disk in MS-PC/DOS format. 425 pp.

Book/Disk (MS-DOS)	**Item #154-7**	**$44.95**
Book only	**Item #152-0**	**$34.95**

Troubleshooting LAN Manager 2
by Michael Day

The ideal reference for network supervisors responsible for the maintenance of a LAN Manager 2 network. *Troubleshooting LAN Manager 2* builds a functional model of LAN Manager from the ground up, beginning with OS/2 and ending with fault tolerance and printer setup. Key components such as data structures, protocols, services, and applications are placed in a troubleshooting context, examining possible problems and providing hands-on solutions. More than basic hints and tips, this book lays a solid foundation upon which you can build a truly outstanding troubleshooting methodology. 337 pp.

Book only	**Item #161-X**	**$34.95**

Troubleshooting NetWare for the 286
by Cheryl Snapp

The ideal reference for network supervisors responsible for the installation and maintenance of a NetWare 286 network. Contains a thorough overview of the NetWare 286 operating system plus step-by-step instructions for troubleshooting common and not-so-common problems. Detailed chapters emphasize the information most helpful in maintaining a healthy NetWare 286 LAN, including installation, file server and workstation diagnostics, printing utilities, and network management services. Covers NetWare 286 version 2.2. 350 pp.

Book only	**Item #169-5**	**$34.95**

1-800-533-4372 (in CA 1-800-356-2002)

M&T BOOKS

A Library of Technical References from M&T Books

Fractal Programming in C
by Roger T. Stevens

If you are a programmer wanting to learn more about fractals, this book is for you. Learn how to create pictures that have both beauty and an underlying mathematical meaning. Included are over 50 black and white pictures and 32 full-color fractals. All source code to reproduce these pictures is provided on disk in MS-DOS format requiring an IBM PC or clone with an EGA or VGA card, a color monitor, and a Turbo C, Quick C, or Microsoft C compiler. 580 pp.

Book/Disk (MS-DOS)	**Item #038-9**	**$39.95**
Book only	**Item #037-0**	**$29.95**

Fractal Programming in Turbo Pascal
by Roger T. Stevens

This book equips Turbo Pascal programmers with the tools needed to program dynamic fractal curves. It is a reference that gives full attention to developing the reader's understanding of various fractal curves. More than 100 black and white and 32 full-color fractals are illustrated throughout the book. All source code to reproduce the fractals is available on disk in MS/PC-DOS format. Requires a PC or clone with EGA or VGA, color monitor, and Turbo Pascal 4.0 or later. 462 pp.

Book/Disk (MS-DOS)	**Item #107-5**	**$39.95**
Book	**Item #106-7**	**$29.95**

Graphics Programming in C
by Roger T. Stevens

All the information you need to program graphics in C, including source code, is presented. You'll find complete discussions of ROM BIOS, VGA, EGA, and CGA inherent capabilities; methods of displaying points on a screen; improved, faster algorithms for drawing and filling lines, rectangles, rounded polygons, ovals, circles, and arcs; graphic cursors; and much more! Both Turbo C and Microsoft C are supported. 639 pp.

Book/Disk (MS-DOS)	**Item #019-2**	**$36.95**
Book only	**Item #018-4**	**$26.95**

1-800-533-4372 (in CA 1-800-356-2002)

A Library of Technical References from M&T Books

Advanced Fractal Programming in C
by Roger T. Stevens

Programmers who enjoyed our best-selling *Fractal Programming in C* can move on to the next level of fractal programming with this book. Included are how-to instructions for creating many different types of fractal curves, including source code. Contains 16 pages of full-color fractals. All the source code to generate the fractals is available on an optional disk in MS/PC-DOS format. 305 pp.

Book/Disk (MS-DOS)	**Item #097-4**	**$39.95**
Book only	**Item #096-6**	**$29.95**

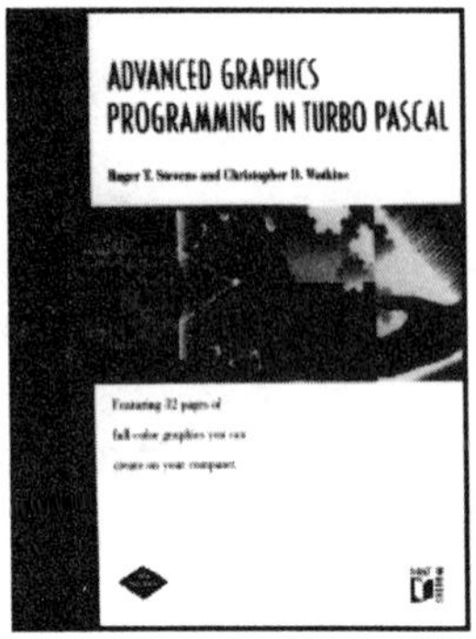

Advanced Graphics Programming in Turbo Pascal
by Roger T. Stevens and Christopher D. Watkins

This new book is must reading for Turbo Pascal programmers who want to create impressive graphic designs on IBM PCs and compatibles. There are 32 pages of full-color graphic displays along with the source code to create these dramatic pictures. Complete explanations are provided on how to tailor the graphics to suit the programmer's needs. Covered are algorithms for creating complex 2-D shapes, including lines, circles and squares; how to create advanced 3-D shapes, wire-frame graphics, and solid images; numerous tips and techniques for varying pixel intensities to give the appearance of roundness to an object; and more. 540 pp.

Book/Disk (MS-DOS)	**Item #132-6**	**$39.95**
Book only	**Item #131-8**	**$29.95**

1-800-533-4372 (in CA 1-800-356-2002)

ORDER FORM

To Order:

Return this form with your payment to M&T books, 501 Galveston Drive, Redwood City, CA 94063 or **call toll-free 1-800-533-4372 (in California, call 1-800-356-2002).**

ITEM #	DESCRIPTION	DISK	PRICE
		Subtotal	
		CA residents add sales tax ___%	
		Add $3.75 per item for shipping and handling	
		TOTAL	

NOTE: **FREE SHIPPING** ON ORDERS OF THREE OR MORE BOOKS.

Charge my:

- ❑ **Visa**
- ❑ **MasterCard**
- ❑ **AmExpress**

❑ **Check enclosed, payable to M&T Books.**

CARD NO. ____________________

SIGNATURE ____________________ EXP. DATE ____________

NAME ____________________

ADDRESS ____________________

CITY ____________________

STATE ____________________ ZIP ____________

M&T GUARANTEE: If your are not satisfied with your order for any reason, return it to us within 25 days of receipt for a full refund. Note: Refunds on disks apply only when returned with book within guarantee period. Disks damaged in transit or defective will be promptly replaced, but cannot be exchanged for a disk from a different title.

8032

1-800-533-4372 (in CA 1-800-356-2002)

NO POSTAGE
NECESSARY
IF MAILED
IN THE
UNITED STATES

BUSINESS REPLY MAIL

FIRST CLASS MAIL PERMIT 871 REDWOOD CITY, CA

POSTAGE WILL BE PAID BY ADDRESSEE

M&T BOOKS
501 Galveston Drive
Redwood City, CA 94063-9929

PLEASE FOLD ALONG LINE AND STAPLE OR TAPE CLOSED